EMPOWERING THE CHILDREN'S AND YOUNG PEOPLE'S WORKFORCE

While the provision in Children's and Young People's Services endures much change and turbulence, the calling for well qualified and critically reflective practitioners remains ever present. This innovative and accessible core textbook explores the key themes, ideas, concepts and topics that are central to practitioners working across the 0-19 sector. It aims to help students develop the professional knowledge, practical skills and core values they need to work effectively with children and young people.

Clearly divided into four sections, *The Practitioner*, *The Learner*, *The Workplace* and *The Community*, the book covers a broad range of issues including:

- the different roles and responsibilities of the workforce;
- multi-agency working and its challenges;
- working with parents, carers and the community;
- supporting children and young people with additional needs and meeting the needs of gifted learners;
- work-based reflective practice; and
- language learning and communication.

At each stage the book facilitates opportunities for personal and professional reflection, discussion, debate and action through case studies, activities, reflective tasks, areas for further consideration, and annotated further readings. The text also features a glossary of terms and links to practice standards.

The book is supported by a free companion website featuring instructor resources such as assignable case studies, reflective tasks and activities, tables and figures from the book available to download, and sample chapters from the book; and student resources including helpful links to further information, links to relevant video material, and an interactive flashcard glossary.

Empowering the Children's and Young People's Workforce seeks to empower the reader by supporting their initial and continuing professional development, enabling them to positively influence provision for children and young people. It is essential reading for anyone studying or working in this sector.

Simon Brownhill (editor) is a Senior Teaching Associate in the Faculty of Education at the University of Cambridge.

EMPOWERING THE CHILDREN'S AND YOUNG PEOPLE'S WORKFORCE

Practice based knowledge, skills and understanding

Edited by Simon Brownhill

 Routledge
Taylor & Francis Group

LONDON AND NEW YORK

First published 2014
by Routledge
2 Park Square, Milton Park, Abingdon, Oxon OX14 4RN

and by Routledge
711 Third Avenue, New York, NY 10017

Routledge is an imprint of the Taylor & Francis Group, an informa business

British Library Cataloguing in Publication Data
A catalogue record for this book is available from the British Library

Library of Congress Cataloging in Publication Data
A catalog record for this book has been requested

ISBN: 978-0-415-51739-3 (hbk)
ISBN: 978-0-415-51740-9 (pbk)
ISBN: 978-0-203-12370-6 (ebk)

Typeset in Interstate
by Saxon Graphics Ltd, Derby

Printed and bound by CPI Group (UK) Ltd, Croydon, CR0 4YY

For all students on professional work-based programmes.

CONTENTS

List of figures		ix
List of tables		x
About the authors		xi
Acknowledgements		xiv
Abbreviations		xv

1   **Looking at *Empowering the Children's and Young People's Workforce*: an introduction**   **1**
Simon Brownhill

SECTION 1: THE PRACTITIONER   **9**

2   **Skills for successful study**   **11**
Helen Wilson

3   **Work-based learning**   **29**
Lesley Faulconbridge

4   **'The Researcher and the Researched': ethical research in Children's and Young People's Services**   **45**
Simon Brownhill

SECTION 2: THE LEARNER   **63**

5   **Gifted and talented learners**   **65**
Lynn Senior

6   **Special educational needs and disabilities: supporting the needs of children and young people through inclusive practice**   **83**
Rosemary Shepherd

7   Children, young people and risk – *just about managing?*   100
Sarah McMullen

SECTION 3: THE WORKPLACE   119

8   Skills and knowledge for effective practice   121
Deborah Hussain

**9   Learning a language: how practitioners and those training to work with
young people could use language learning in their practice**   140
Mike Jackson

10   '*Reflecting on reflection*': work-based reflective practice   157
Simon Brownhill

SECTION 4: THE COMMUNITY   175

11   Parents, carers and the community: the collaborative relationship   177
Debrah Turner

12   Integrated working: from the theory to the practice   193
Deborah Hussain and Simon Brownhill

13   The learning community: international lessons   210
Mabel Ann Brown

Looking back, looking forward   228
Simon Brownhill

Glossary   230
Index   235

FIGURES

2.1   Stairway to critical thinking (Williams, 2009)   22
3.1   Assessment methods for work-based learning   41
5.1   The Personalised Learning (PL) framework   79
8.1   Examples of observational recording techniques   130
10.1 Greenaway's (2002) reflective cycle   162
10.2 Gibbs' (1988) reflective cycle   163
10.3 Reflective prompts to support reflective diary entries   167
11.1 Adapted from Bronfenbrenner's Ecological Model (1979)   187

TABLES

1.1   Readership that *Empowering the Children's and Young People's Workforce*
is designed for. An adaptation of *Figure 1.2: The Children's and Young People's
Workforce* (DCSF, 2008: 14)   3-4

2.1   Active and passive learning: questions for reflection   16

2.2   '12 Grid' method to essay writing (devised by Brownhill)   24

4.1   Thinking critically about 'doing good' and 'not doing harm' when engaged
in research activity   48

4.2   The practicalities of the right to withdraw   57

5.1   Select Initiatives 1997-2012   69

5.2   Six types of gifted children and young people and young people with
particular needs (Betts and Neihart, 1988)   72-74

6.1   Medical model thinking and Social model thinking: a comparison
(adapted from Reiser, 2010)   87

6.2   From integration to the inclusion of children and young people with a SEND:
Policy/Legislation 1970-2012   88

6.3   Categories of SEND (adapted from DfES, 2005 and Gibson and Blandford,
2005: 21)   92

7.1   Management and development of risk framework   109

7.2   Exposure, responses and outcomes of risk   113

8.1   The categories for safeguarding   132

11.1   Community support and the potential help they offer   188

13.1   A sample from the OECD PISA 2009 Database   211

13.2   Comparative practice in the early years (adapted from Brown, 2010)   213

13.3   Proposed structure of the new National Curriculum (DfE, 2013)   217

13.4   International comparisons of pre-school and school provision   218

13.5   European comparison of curriculum time allocation
(adapted from Brown, 2008)   222

ABOUT THE AUTHORS

Deborah Hussain is a Senior Lecturer at the University of Derby teaching on two undergraduate programmes – the BA (*Hons*) Child and Youth Studies and the FdA Children's and Young People's Services (*Pathway*). Deborah began her professional career working with children with special needs before moving into the early years sector as a nursery manager. Deborah has experience of working as a senior learning mentor within a multi-agency team supporting children, families and educational settings to remove barriers to children's learning (0–19). Her research interests include behaviour, equality and diversity, removing barriers to learning, and working with parents and carers. She is currently planning research into the role of the personal tutor in Higher Education.

Debrah Turner is the Programme Leader for the Early Years Initial Teacher Training (EYITT) Programme at the University of Derby. She has taught on a small range of undergraduate and postgraduate education-based programmes. With 15 years' practical experience of nursery management within the early years sector (0–5), Debrah actively gained experience of providing supportive play and learning environments in a variety of contexts. While being responsible for managing three settings simultaneously, Debrah achieved an 'Outstanding' grade from OFSTED for each setting. Her research interests include exploring the role of the parent as co-educators of their child (the focus of her MA dissertation). While lecturing in the FE sector she was involved in research which explored how to support adult learners.

Helen Wilson is the Programme Leader for the BA (*Hons*) Child and Youth Studies Degree at the University of Derby. Previously she lectured for three years on select Level 3 and PGCE courses in Further Education. Helen gained 24 years of experience of the 3–11 age range through working in various teaching roles. Her research interests include student transition into Higher Education and the role of induction and the use of personal tutors in the retention of students. She contributed to the professional book *A Quick Guide to Behaviour Management in the Early Years* (Bullock and Brownhill) which was published by Sage in 2011.

Lesley Faulconbridge is currently Acting Head of Subject for Social Studies at the University of Derby. She teaches on a range of undergraduate education-based programmes. Lesley has experience of teaching children and young people across the full 0–19 age range in a variety of contexts both in the maintained and voluntary sector. She has also worked in multi-agency teams supporting parents and carers as part of commissioned work for Social

Services. Her research interests include work-based learning, communities of practice, adult teaching and learning approaches, and flexible learning (the focus of her Masters dissertation).

Lynn Senior is currently acting Head of the School of Education and Social Sciences at the University of Derby with responsibility across a range of education and childcare programmes, along with health and social care and other related disciplines. A former teacher, trainer and lecturer in Education Studies, Lynn has taught across a range of PGCE programmes including secondary vocational and the post-16 sector. Her research interests include vocational education – her book *The Essential Guide to Teaching 14-19 Vocational Education* was published by Pearson in 2010. She has also contributed to a range of texts in lifelong learning and CPD for the lifelong learning sector.

Mabel Ann Brown is a Senior Lecturer at the University of Derby. She was previously a Key Stage One and Foundation Stage Co-ordinator in a large Primary School. Her research interests are comparative education with a particular focus on Finland and the enhancement of early years and primary provision. She has also researched and explored the role of Teaching Assistants and the use of Skype in education. Her book *Exploring Childhood in a Comparative Context: An introductory guide for students* (co-edited with Jon White) was published by Routledge in 2014.

Mike Jackson is a Senior Lecturer on the BA (*Hons*) Child and Youth Studies Degree at the University of Derby. He also teaches on the PGCE programme with a module with French specialism. He is the Secondary Co-ordinator for the GTP programme and is moving into School Direct in September 2013. He gained experience of the 5-18 age range through teaching languages for 22 years in local comprehensive schools. He has three children who have sparked an interest in how language develops. His research interests include the acquisition of languages, delivery of languages in all settings and the knowledge required to deliver a language.

Rosemary Shepherd is a Senior Lecturer at the University of Derby. She is currently the SEND Pathway Leader on the BA (*Hons*) Education Studies degree, teaching a range of modules in Special Educational Needs and Disability and Educational Psychology. Rosemary, who has an MA Ed in Special Educational Needs and Disability, has taught in Higher Education since 2004 and is currently undertaking a Doctorate in Education. Rosemary has experience of teaching children, young people and adults within the voluntary sector for the past 35 years. Her research interests include inclusion for all in higher education classrooms, engaging and motivating students, managing the needs of students with Asperger's Syndrome in educational settings (the focus of her current doctoral research), managing the well-being of students and supporting adult learners. Rosemary has co-authored a chapter for *Exploring Education Studies* (edited by Vivienne Walkup) which was published by Pearson in 2011.

Sarah McMullen is a Senior Lecturer in youth work and community development at the University of Derby, where one of her responsibilities is preparing students for work-based learning. Sarah has over 20 years of qualified youth and community work practice experience, which include faith-based youth work, centre-based work, music development and managing Student Support Services in Further Education. Sarah has particular interests in a variety of practices with young people including informal education, career education, group work, reflexivity, change management, working with risk and developing resilience. Her MA research explored the driving factors of young learners at risk in Further Education and her current doctoral research is based on a practical approach to developing a resilience perspective for trainee community and youth work practitioners.

Simon Brownhill is a Senior Teaching Associate at the University of Cambridge. He was previously a Senior Lecturer at the University of Derby where he taught on a range of undergraduate and postgraduate education-based programmes. A former assistant head teacher for the Early Years (3-6), Simon actively gained experience of teaching across the full 3-11 age range in a range of educational contexts. His research interests include behaviour management, international perspectives of reflective practice, creativity, children's story writing, cultural diversity, children's physical development, supporting adult learners, and the male role model in the early years (the focus of his doctoral thesis). His latest professional book - *Getting Children Writing: Story ideas for 3-11 year olds* - was published by Sage in 2013.

ACKNOWLEDGEMENTS

It is with the most heartfelt thanks that the following people are recognised:

- Annamarie Kino-Wylam, Commissioning Editor at David Fulton, for her wonderful support and encouragement during the writing of this book - thank you for giving us the extra time we needed to get it completed!
- Holly Davis for her amazing collation of reviewer feedback - we have never had this amount of feedback on anything that we have written before so thank you so much for helping us to clearly know what we were doing well and what we could do to improve!
- All of the anonymous reviewers who offered us an absolute wealth of constructive feedback on all of the chapters which make up this book; we hope that you all feel we have done justice to all the time and effort you put into helping us to make our work the very best it could be.
- JG and DHo for their efforts in helping to develop the initial proposal.
- Our families and our friends for their continued love and support during the writing of our respective chapters!

Thank you all *very* much indeed.

ABBREVIATIONS

The following terms/abbreviations are used throughout this book:

ADHD	Attention Deficit Hyperactivity Disorder
AIDS	Acquired Immune Deficiency Syndrome
AT	Attainment Target
BASES	British Association of Sport and Exercise Sciences
BCRP	Better Communication Research Programme
BDA	British Dyslexia Association
BERA	British Educational Research Association
BPS	British Psychological Society
BTEC	Business and Technology Education Council
CAMHS	Child and Adolescent Mental Health Services
CASRO	Council of American Survey Research Organizations
CCEA	Council of Curriculum, Examinations and Assessment
CfBP	Centre for British Practitioners Education Trust
CPD	Continuing Professional Development
CIAG	Children and Young People's Inter-Agency Group
CILT	The National Centre for Languages
CLIL	Content and Language Integrated Learning
CoP	Community of Practice
CRB	Criminal Records Bureau. Now known as Disclosure and Barring Service (DBS)
CSIE	Centre for Studies on Inclusive Education
CWDC	Children's Workforce Development Council
CYP	Children and Young People
CYPS	Children's and Young People's Services
DCSF	Department for Children, Schools and Families
DES	Department of Education and Science
DfE	Department for Education
DfEE	Department for Education and Employment
DfES	Department for Education and Skills
DoH	Department of Health
EAL	English as an Additional Language
EBD	Emotional and Behavioural Difficulties
ECM	Every Child Matters. Now known as *Helping Children Achieve More*

EEA	European Economic Area
EiC	Excellence in Cities
EPPE	Effective Provision of Preschool Education
ERA	Education Reform Act
EU	European Union
EWO	Education Welfare Officer
EYFS	Early Years Foundation Stage
EYITT	Early Years Initial Teacher Training
EYP	Early Years Professional
EYPS	Early Years Professional Status
EYTS	Early Years Teacher Status
FE	Further Education
FIP	Family Intervention Programme
GCSE	General Certificate of Secondary Education
GLF	Graduate Leader Fund
GP	General Practitioner
HCAM	Helping Children Achieve More – formally known as *Every Child Matters*
HE	Higher Education
HEI	Higher Education Institution
HIV	Human Immuno-deficiency Virus
HLP	Higher Learning Potential
HLTA	Higher Level Teaching Assistant
ICT	Information and Communications Technology
IEP	Individual Education Plan. Also see MEP
ILP	Individual Learning Plan
IPD	Initial Professional Development
INSET	IN-SErvice Training
IQ	Intelligence quotient
IU	Intercultural or Cultural Understanding
JUCSWEC	Joint University Council Social Work Education Committee
KS	Key Stage
LA	Local authority
MA	Master of Arts (degree)
MENSA	An organization that claims to have the most intelligent (IQ) people in the world in it
MEP	Multi-Element Plan
MFL	Modern Foreign Languages
NAGC	National Association of Gifted Child and Young Person. Now known as Potential Plus UK
NAS	National Autistic Society
NC	National Curriculum
NCB	National Children's Bureau
NHS	National Health Service
NLS	National Literacy Strategy

NOS	National Occupational Standards
NQT	Newly Qualified Teacher
NSPCC	National Society for the Prevention of Cruelty to Children
NVQ	National Vocational Qualifications
NYA	National Youth Agency
OECD	Organisation for Economic Cooperation and Development
OFSTED	Office for Standards in Education – now known as the Office for Standards in Education, Children's Services and Skills
PDP	Personal/Professional Development Portfolio
PECS	Picture Exchange Communication System
PEET	Point, Explain, Example, Theory
PGCE	Post Graduate Certificate in Education
PHSE+C	Personal, Health and Social Education and Citizenship
PISA	Programme for International Student Assessment
PL	Personalised Learning
PPA	Planning, Preparation and Assessment
QAA	Quality Assurance Agency for Higher Education
QCA	Qualifications and Curriculum Authority
QIA	Quality Improvement Agency
SCoTENS	Standing Conference on Teacher Education North and South
SEAL	Social and Emotional Aspects of Learning
SEN(D)	Special Educational Needs (and Disabilities)
SERA	Scottish Educational Research Association
SMARTCE	Specific, Measurable, Achievable, Realistic, Timely, Challenging, Enjoyable
SMT	Senior Management Team. Also known as Senior Leadership Team (SLT)
SQ3R	Survey, Question, Read, Review and Recall
SRA	Social Research Association
SWOT	Strengths, Weaknesses, Opportunities, Threats
TASC	Thinking Actively in a Social Context
TDA(S)	Training and Development Agency for Schools
UK	United Kingdom
UKCES	UK Commission for Employment and Skills
UKRIO	UK Research Integrity Office
UNCRC	United Nations Convention on the Rights of the Child
UNESCO	United Nations Educational, Scientific and Cultural Organization
UNICEF	United Nations Children's Fund (formerly known as United Nations International Children's Emergency Fund)
WMA	World Medical Association
WO	Welsh Office
YISP	Youth Inclusion and Support Panel
YOT	Youth Offending Team

1 Looking at *Empowering the Children's and Young People's Workforce*: An introduction

Simon Brownhill

Take a moment to consider the following:

- Imagine if there were no drugs and alcohol workers who could support children and young people who had become dependent on solvents...
- Imagine if there were no play workers to support and enrich the learning experiences of young children...
- Imagine if there were no sports coaches to support children and young people with a passion and skill for netball or tennis...
- Imagine if there were no learning mentors to deal with the challenging behaviours of children and young people with low self-esteem in various learning environments...

It is hard to imagine the above. The existence of Children's and Young People's Services (CYPS) and its powerful ability to transform the lives of children and young people cannot be underestimated; it is recognised that '[s]ince the publication of the *Every Child Matters* (ECM) Green Paper in 2003 there ha[s] been a preoccupation in England with the better [presence, quality and] integration of children's services' (CfBT, 2010: 2) to help improve outcomes for children, young people and families. Laming (2009) acknowledges how the underlying philosophy which underpins the way in which CYPS operates continues to receive 'overwhelming support' across political parties and **professionals**, and there is evidence to suggest that *most* children and young people are doing well from the huge investment in ECM (CIAG, 2009). We recognise that this improvement could only have been made as a result of important strategic decision making at a national level, industrious co-ordination and management at a local authority/regional level, and the hard work, dedication and commitment from those individuals who work at a 'shop floor' service level. But how do we sustain what has already been achieved, supporting those who are new to the 0-19 **workforce** (DfES, 2003) while continuing to make improvements in CYPS, particularly as evidence suggests that there are still many children and young people whose life chances remain poor - CIAG (2009) cite the figure of 20 per cent - and who are not benefiting from what might be regarded as the 'presence and power' of CYPS (see NCB, 2011; Brandon *et al.*, 2012). Indeed, with an increasing number of high profile child protection cases - Victoria Climbié (2003), 'Baby P' (2009), the Oxford grooming sex gang (2013) - it is imperative for us all to take a shared responsibility to ensure *all* children and young people are well protected, cared for and supported to the very best of our abilities. It is our firm belief that '**targeted support**' is the best way to continuously develop, enrich and strengthen provision and practice in the 0-19 sector. This book serves as a way of targeting support by empowering those who work/wish to work on the 0-19 front-line.

Looking at this book and why it has been written

For a number of years now **practitioners** and those training in the 0-19 workforce have had limited access to relevant professional/academic literature to support their studies and practice. Much of the available literature about the 0-19 workforce tends to focus its attention on *teachers*, *children* and *schools*, which alienates those readers who regard themselves as *practitioners* or *professionals*, who work with *service users*, *young people* or *learners* and who are employed/training in *settings*. This book sets out to utilise and promote key and transferable terminology, themes, concepts and ideas which are applicable to specific and various sectors which make up the 0-19 workforce (see pages 3-4).

> For the purposes of this book we have decided to use the generic terms ***practitioner/professional*** and ***setting*** to describe those who work/train in the 0-19 sector, the service that they provide for children, young people and families and the location where this service is offered.

This book aims to respond to a real need for up-to-date and relevant literature to support practitioners and those training in embracing the core values and principles which are an integral feature of quality practice and are applicable to all who work/train in the 0-19 sector. This book sets out to empower the reader by critically examining professional knowledge, practical skills and personal values which will lead to an enriched understanding of policy and practice to support the workforce; in turn this will develop the reader's capabilities in critical reflection, analysis, responding positively to change, embracing innovation, and utilising professional standards and ideas to offer a 'world class' service for the benefit of future generations.

This book locates itself within the heart of a national time of change and turbulence in the 0-19 sector. A change in UK government in 2010 resulted in radical changes and concerning cutbacks being made to service provision for children and young people; an exploration of these changes is highlighted in many of the chapters offered in this book. The 'scaling down' or abolition of local authority (LA) departments, reductions in the number of workforce employees and budgetary constraints have all impacted, and continue to impact, on the availability, quality and consistency of provision which service users have access to (see Action for Children, 2010). This book considers the implications of the above in relation to key themes and ideas that are integral to working in CYPS, e.g. roles and responsibilities, parents, carers and the community, and different types of learners/service users. The calling for more qualified and competent people to work in the 0-19 sector is positively embraced by this book as it supports initial and continuing professional development (IPD/CPD) in select areas and aspects of CYPS working which are paramount for effective provision, e.g.

communication, communities of practice on a local, national and international level, and work-based learning.

Look at who this book is for

Empowering the Children's and Young People's Workforce has been written for those individuals who work/wish to work with children, young people and their families in CYPS. It is principally written to empower those individuals who are initiating their professional studies in CYPS at a Higher Education (HE) level and those who are undertaking practice-based courses to complement their academic understanding and enrich their established practice in the sector. Table 1.1 is an adaptation of *Figure 1.2: The Children's and Young People's Workforce* (DCSF, 2008: 14) and is presented by way of acknowledging many of the readers that this book aims to serve.

Table 1.1 Readership that *Empowering the Children's and Young People's Workforce* is designed for. An adaptation of *Figure 1.2: The Children's and Young People's Workforce* (DCSF, 2008: 14)

	Core Children's Workforce: *People who work or volunteer with children, young people and their families, or are responsible for their outcomes all the time.*		**Wider Children's Workforce:** *People who work or volunteer with children, young people, and/or their families part of the time, or are responsible for their outcomes as part of their jobs.*
Managers and leaders	• Strategic, senior and middle managers in all Children's Trust partner organisations • All commissioners of services for children and/or young people		• Planners, Housing and Transport providers/ commissioners • HR in organisations that provide services to children/ young people
Education	• Head teachers • Teachers • School support staff • Providers of extended schools activities • Learning mentors • 14-19 providers	• Behaviour and Educational Support Teams • Educational Psychologists • Educational Welfare Officers • School meal staff	• Staff and leaders of FE colleges • Adult and Community education providers
Health	• Health visiting teams • School nurses • Community children's nurses • Children's nurses • Child psychologists • CAMHS	• Paediatricians and sub-specialists • Community paediatricians • Children's allied health professionals • Teenage pregnancy workers	• GPs • Dentists • Primary and community health practitioners • Clinical practitioners • Hospitals • Community health services • Sexual health services • Drugs and alcohol services • Adult mental health services

Social, family and community support	• Children and families social workers • CAFCASS advisers • Foster carers • Private foster carers • Outreach and family support workers	• Managers and staff in: family centres, day centres, residential children's homes • Portage workers • Play workers	• Parenting practitioners • Adult social care workers • Supporting People teams • Drug and alcohol workers • Housing Officers and Accommodation Support workers • Job Centre Plus Advisers • Child Support Agency workers
Youth	• Connexions personal advisers • Youth workers in voluntary, community or faith sector	• Youth workers • Youth support workers • Young people's housing and accommodation support workers	
Justice and crime prevention	• Youth offending teams • Staff and managers of: Youth Offending Institutions, Secure Training Centres, Secure Children's Homes • Police in school liaison/child protection roles		• Probation officers • Multi-agency public protection teams • Policing and law enforcement • Prosecution services • Custodial care
Sport and culture	• Sports Coaches and Officials • School and FE Sport Co-ordinators	• County sports development officers • Sport competition managers • School library service	• Health and fitness providers • Outdoor education/recreation providers • Workers in cultural heritage, museums and galleries • Performers in visual and literary arts • Teachers of music and performing arts • Library staff
Early years and childcare	• Managers, deputies, assistants and workers in: Playgroups, children's centres, day nurseries, nursery schools • Nursery classes in primary schools • Registered child minders and nannies • Play workers		

You may be able to easily identify your role in the table above whereas others may find that their role is not listed; others may note roles whose job title has either changed, been merged into another role title, or now no longer exists. It is recognised that because of the breadth of the 0–19 workforce it is not possible to list the current job titles of every single professional who works in CYPS due to wordage limitations (consider visiting www.cypnowjobs.co.uk/); however, it is hoped you will feel that this book is written with you in mind when reference is made to particular areas of the 0–19 workforce, e.g. youth, health and sport and culture, and CYPS as an entire entity. You will note that certain chapters have a relevance right across the 0–19 age range whereas particular chapters have a specific area of focus (education, for example) – this is in response to the chapter focus and the knowledge and expertise of the author(s). We make no apology in offering chapters that are pertinent for readers who work in particular areas of the 0-19 workforce as we are responding to the needs and requests of practitioners and **trainees** who have helped us to formulate the content of this book during its development, along with the interests of the individual authors. It is hoped that all readers will actively engage with all of the chapters in this book so that you build up a breadth of knowledge and understanding, not only in your own sector but in the working practices of others. We recognise that a book of this nature is never 'complete' and we would be making a false claim if we said that we are able to address every single aspect of provision and practice in CYPS in a book of this size. While there are exciting topics that are interesting and valuable 'foci' for discussion, such as using expressive arts with children and young people with emotional difficulties, outdoor/adventure settings and children and young people 'at risk', and working with diverse and 'troubled' identities, we feel that we have offered the most prominent topics for discussion (see Contents page) which relate to the notion of empowering the workforce across the 0-19 age range.

Looking at the 'theory' of this book

To complement the wealth of practice which is explored in this book, you will find an abundance of theory in each chapter to support your knowledge and understanding. The authors of this book have strived to offer you a range of theoretical perspectives, thought-provoking research findings, critiques of policy making and links to fascinating professional literature/online materials* to inform, educate and enrich the content of their respective chapters. We recognise that much of the literature relates to the UK context (apart from Chapter 13) and this is purposeful as this is primarily the audience this book has been written for. International readers are encouraged to compare the literature explored in the chapters with that which has been written by academics and policy makers in their own countries, drawing similarities and differences with regard to thinking and practice. Readers will also note that authors in this book give reference to literature which has been published in the last 40 years; you are encouraged to reflect on the thinking being shared, taking into account its applicability (continued or not) in CYPS today.

---

* Note!

At the time of writing all of the *tinyurl.com* [web] links offered in this book were active. As information on the web is regularly changed, updated or removed, it is anticipated that some links may not work for the reader. The author[s] apologise for this, but it is hoped that readers will recognise that this is out of the author[s'] control.

(Brownhill, 2013: 28)

Looking at how this book works

This book sets out to empower the CYPS workforce by exploring themes and foci which are 'key' in supporting the initial and continuing professional development of those training and those rooted in practice. The book aims to address concepts, ideas and thinking which inform practice, shape personal thinking, and positively influence provision for children and young people. The book is organised in four distinct yet interrelated themes – *The Practitioner*, *The Learner*, *The Workplace* and *The Community*. Each theme is written with the reader in mind, considering essential and current knowledge, skills, understanding and attitudes that support, challenge and extend workforce provision in the short, medium and long term.

Section 1 (*The Practitioner*) focuses specifically on the reader and explores pertinent concepts that relate to the notion of studying. Chapter 2 sees Helen Wilson consider the *successful study skills* that are necessary for readers who are initiating their studies of CYPS or who are returning to their studies. Lesley Faulconbridge, in Chapter 3, critically 'unpicks' the concept of *work-based learning*, helping readers to appreciate its relevance and importance as they engage with their professional studies. With Goldacre (2013) advocating the importance of research and evidence-based practice, Simon Brownhill in Chapter 4 explores the *ethical implications of practice based research* which involves children, young people and their families that is undertaken by practitioners and those training as part of their professional studies.

Section 2 (*The Learner*) focuses its attention on select groups of children and young people who practitioners and those training work with in the 0–19 sector. Chapter 5 sees Lynn Senior reflect on the needs of those who are regarded as *gifted and talented*, exploring approaches and strategies to support these learners in educational contexts. In response to the publication *Support and aspiration: A new approach to special educational needs and disability* [SEND] – *Progress and next steps* (DfE, 2012b), Rosemary Shepherd in Chapter 6 focuses her chapter on exploring the needs of those children and young people who have a *SEND* within educational contexts, highlighting best practice in terms of supporting these individuals to reach their full potential in school and in day-to-day/later life. There are unfortunately many children and young people in our society who may be a victim of neglect, abuse or cruelty. Sarah McMullen in Chapter 7 considers the needs of those *children and young people who are 'at risk'*, offering support, guidance and advice to support practitioners and those training in responding positively and effectively to issues surrounding the maltreatment of children and young people.

Section 3 (*The Workplace*) focuses its attention on the settings where professionals and those trainees practice. Chapter 8 sees Deborah Hussain explore the numerous *knowledge and skills* required of practitioners and those training, emphasising those which are transferable across the full 0–19 workforce and those which can be utilised to support best practice. With recent research from the Better Communication Research programme (BCRP) (DfE, 2012a) emphasising 'the importance of appropriate support for the language skills of all children in classrooms to minimise disadvantage and to raise attainments' (Lindsay, 2012), Mike Jackson in Chapter 9 highlights the importance of *learning a language*, exploring the historical development of modern foreign languages in education and practical ways to develop this lifelong skill. Chapter 10 by Simon Brownhill serves to draw attention to the workplace as a salient location in which *work-based reflective practice* can take place, discussing the importance of reflective practice to the service that readers provide/train in and the value/use of reflective tools to support readers' reflective endeavours.

The final section of *Empowering the Children's and Young People's Workforce* focuses its attention on *The Community*, considering those that represent 'the community' and the contribution that they make to the lives of children and young people. Chapter 11 by Debrah Turner focuses its attention on the role of *parents, carers and the community*, highlighting the importance of 'partnership' to allow effective collaborative working to support the needs of children, young people and families. Deborah Hussain and Simon Brownhill continue to discuss this notion of collaborative working in Chapter 12 by exploring how *integrated working* helps all children's and young people's service providers work together towards the five outcomes of the ECM agenda (DfES, 2004) as a strong community. Chapter 13 by Mabel Ann Brown considers the lessons that can be learned from *international communities*, highlighting comparative educational practice across the globe for children aged 0–11.

Looking at the features of this book

This book follows a consistent format to support your engagement with the text, irrespective of which chapter you choose to read. Select pedagogical features are utilised to enhance the reading experience:

- Each chapter offers *three or four objectives* which you as the reader will achieve once you have engaged with the chapter.
- Each chapter offers a concise *introduction* at the start which sets out what the chapter will explore.
- Each chapter contains *terms* which are relevant to the content of the chapter – these are **emboldened** in the text and are defined either by the author in the chapter or in the glossary (pages 230–234).
- Each chapter contains *reflective tasks* which are designed to make you reflect on what you have read, your personal and professional thinking or your practice with children and/or young people.
- Each chapter offers you *activities* which you can engage in on your own or with colleagues/peers. They serve as a strategy to make your reading experience more active and engaging.
- Each chapter includes *case studies* which contextualise key concepts and ideas being discussed within the chapter. Reflective questions are sometimes offered to stimulate thought and discussion.
- Each chapter offers you a *conclusion*, summing up what the chapter has covered and what you should 'come away with' in relation to improved knowledge, acquired skills, a deeper understanding or a change in attitude.
- Each chapter presents a select number of *areas for further consideration* for you to engage with in your own time. As wordage limitations for each chapter prevent authors from exploring *everything* linked to the main focus, areas for further consideration highlight ideas that you can research depending on your own personal/professional interests.
- At the end of each chapter the reader is offered a selection of annotated *further readings*, informing the reader what these particular readings cover and how relevant they are to the main focus of the chapter. These readings are made up of varied sources of information, e.g. books, academic journal articles and websites.

We hope that you will enjoy using this book to support your professional studies and to complement/enrich your practice. As has already been suggested, improvements in the workforce can only take place with hard work, dedication and commitment on the part of those individuals who work at a 'shop floor' service level; we hope that you will go forth and feel *empowered* in your studies and practice as a result of engaging with this book.

References

Action for Children (2010) *The Red Book. Impact of UK Government spending decisions on children, young people and families 2010-2011.* [Online]. Available at: www.actionforchildren.org.uk/media/1417792/the_red_book_final.pdf (Accessed: 22 May 2013).

Brandon, M., Sidebotham, P., Bailey, S., Belderson, P., Hawley, C., Ellis, C. and Megson, M. (2012) *New learning from serious case reviews: a two year report for 2009-2011.* Research Brief DFE-RB226. [Online]. Available at: www.gov.uk/government/uploads/system/uploads/attachment_data/file/181900/DFE-RB226_Research_Brief.pdf (Accessed: 22 May 2013).

Brownhill, S. (2013) *Getting Children Writing: Story Ideas for Children Aged 3-11.* London: Sage.

CfBT (2010) *An international perspective on integrated children's services. A report commissioned by CfBT Education Trust.* Berkshire: CfBT Education Trust. [Online]. Available at: www.cfbt.com/evidenceforeducation/pdf/2646_childrens_services_web.pdf (Accessed: 21 May 2013).

CIAG (2009) *Serving children and young people better.* [Online]. Available at: www.ncvys.org.uk/UserFiles/Policy/CIAG_ServingChildrenAndYoungPeopleBetter_Oct09.pdf (Accessed: 22 May 2013).

Department for Children, Families and School (DCSF) (2008) *2020 Children and Young People's Workforce Strategy.* Nottingham: DCSF Publications. [Online]. Available at: http://webarchive.nationalarchives.gov.uk/20130401151715/https://www.education.gov.uk/publications/eOrderingDownload/CYP_Workforce-Strategy.pdf (Accessed: 20 May 2013).

Department for Education (DfE) (2012a) *Better Communication Research programme.* [Online]. Available at: www.gov.uk/government/organisations/department-for-education/series/better-communication-research-programme (Accessed: 20 May 2013).

——(2012b) *Support and aspiration: A new approach to special educational needs and disability – Progress and next steps.* [Online]. Available at: www.gov.uk/government/uploads/system/uploads/attachment_data/file/180836/DFE-00046-2012.pdf (Accessed: 20 May 2013).

Department for Education and Schools (DfES) (2003) *Every Child Matters.* Cm 5860. Norwich: TSO. [Online]. Available at: http://webarchive.nationalarchives.gov.uk/20130401151715/https://www.education.gov.uk/publications/eOrderingDownload/CM5860.pdf (Accessed: 22 May 2013).

——(2004) *Every Child Matters Change for Children.* [Online]. Available at: http://tinyurl.com/bcnpwv5 (Accessed: 23 January 2013).

Goldacre, B. (2013) *Building evidence into education.* [Online]. Available at: http://media.education.gov.uk/assets/files/pdf/b/ben%20goldacre%20paper.pdf (Accessed: 20 May 2013).

Lindsay, G. (2012) *News and Events. Press Release: New Research on Speech, Language and Communications Needs for Children.* 27 December. University of Warwick. [Online]. Available at: www2.warwick.ac.uk/newsandevents/pressreleases/new_research_on/ (Accessed: 20 May 2013).

NCB (2011) *Childstats: Statistics on children and young people 2011.* London: NCB. [Online]. Available at: http://resources.ncb.org.uk/media/72550/childstatssummer2011.pdf (Accessed: 22 May 2013).

The Lord Laming Report (2009) *The Protection of Children in England: A progress report.* HC 330. London: The Stationery Office.

Section 1
The Practitioner

2 Skills for successful study

Helen Wilson

LEARNING OBJECTIVES

After studying this chapter, you will be able to:

✔ Identify your current strengths in terms of successful study skills.
✔ Define key concepts such as deep learning, academic reading and critical thinking.
✔ Evaluate the applicability of strategies in relation to personal study skills.
✔ Identify key areas for development and the relevant strategies to support your future study skills.

Introduction

In this chapter we seek to help you develop a better understanding of the skills required for successful study in Higher Education (HE) for all entrants. Successful study at this level is dependent on you acquiring a 'skills set' around academic study. A **skill** by its very definition is the ability to do something well (in this case academic study) and these study skills are determined by initial input, training and practice. It is not assumed that entrants to HE arrive fully equipped with the skills needed to succeed in their studies. The content of this chapter thus aims to introduce you to a range of approaches that introduce, guide and encourage the development of skills that will enable you to get the optimum from your studies in HE. The chapter aims to facilitate a reflective, active, self-evaluative approach to understanding your individual role by actively participating in the development of successful study skills, thus enabling you to maximise your potential for successful study in HE, particularly as effective and efficient study skills are seen to have a direct correlation with academic success (Gurcu, 2011; Jansen and Suhre, 2010).

Activity: Skills audit

It is important to note that in order to develop your study skills it is vital to know where you are starting from.

Consider your study skills at present. Visit http://tinyurl.com/al6wfbs and complete the skills audit; the sample is seen below:

COMMUNICATION: READING	1	2	3	4
1 I feel confident about my reading for study				
2 I know how to find information from a wide range of sources				

Answer all the questions and tick the numerical value that you feel is most appropriate to you:

1   Strongly disagree
2   Tend to disagree
3   Tend to agree
4   Strongly agree

Review your responses once you have completed this chapter, identifying areas of strength and areas for development.

Preparing for study

It is very important to realise that when you are studying or learning anything new the process will probably not be 'pain free'; do you remember finding something really hard to learn when you were at school? Did an exam or test leave your mind *whirling*? Do you feel you will never understand something? This is known as the '**learning pain barrier**' and is a normal part of the learning process so please do not let this initial feeling leave you demoralised. You just need to persevere; use appropriate strategies to support the new learning and the pain will ultimately lead to gain. This 'painful learning' process is known as the four stages of learning (Maslow, 1940):

- *Stage 1*: *Unconscious incompetence.* This is when you do not know or understand the relevance of a skill area or that you are unaware that there is an area in need of development, for example reading academically. This is why the Skills Audit (above) is vital as it highlights which areas are in need of development.
- *Stage 2*: *Conscious incompetence.* This is when you become aware of the areas or skills that will support you in your academic studies.
- *Stage 3*: *Conscious competence.* This is when you can now perform the new skill but you need to practice, e.g. academic referencing.
- *Stage 4*: *Unconscious competence.* This is when the skill becomes automatic.

Activity: Taking stock

Review the three areas of development that you have identified from your Skills Audit (page 12). Using the four stages of learning (as described on page 12) consider at which point you are in each of the three areas of development. Devise a strategy for each skill identified to move it onto the next stage and what actions you can take to ensure it becomes a conscious competent study skill. Share your thoughts with colleagues/peers.

When you are preparing yourself for any type of new learning experience you need to be aware of yourself as a learner. Every learner is different and different learning strategies will work better for different learners. There is extensive research into how people learn and what suits different people in terms of creating effective learning environments, so it is very important that you take time to reflect on what strategies and environment best suits *you* as an individual regardless of what anyone else does; this is about *you* becoming an effective learner and knowing what works best for *you*. Take time to reflect on your past learning experiences by engaging in the activity below.

Activity: Exploring positive and negative learning experiences

- Think back to a successful learning experience (this does not have to be one that you had at school or college). Try to work out why it was successful – *why did you learn*?
- Now think of an unsuccessful learning experience. *What was this? Why did little/no learning take place?*

From these two experiences make two lists:

1   Things that have helped you learn.
2   Things that prevent you from learning.

Compare your lists with those of your colleagues/peers.

With this information you can begin to devise useful personal tips and strategies in creating effective learning experiences. If learning is to be effective then it needs to be 'deep' rather than 'surface' learning. **Surface learning** describes the ability to recall significant pieces of information, e.g. key dates or theories. **Deep learning** is learning that connects with other skills or knowledge that you have learned previously; this is when the learning *makes sense* to you. What is happening and what you must strive for is making connections effectively between existing and new learning experiences (Petty, 2004). Deep learning starts from prior learning experiences which then layer in, make sense, or connect with new learning experiences.

Examples of this are when you have that 'eureka' moment: *can you think of any examples?* Again think: what helped this '**synaptic connection**' (the information being passed between nerve cells in the brain) to occur and made the learning easier to understand? It is useful to remember that in order for learning to be truly internalised, you must ensure that you do the following:

- create intrinsic motivation;
- be active in the learning situation;
- interact with others; and
- have a well-structured knowledge base.

Let's look at these in turn.

Get motivated

If you are going to be successful when learning you must *want* to learn; you have to be interested and motivated in whatever the topic/concept is about. Feelings and emotions do matter when it comes to learning effectively; how you feel impacts on how effectively you learn (Moore *et al.*, 2010). Learning does not take place in isolation; it is explicitly linked to your emotions. Think of a time when you were stressed or unhappy – *how effectively could you concentrate and absorb the material you were meant to be studying?* Very little, I would suspect? It is vitally important that you are aware of and take care of your **emotional health**. Emotions motivate action, both positively and negatively, towards learning effectively. Refer back to the activity in identifying positive and negative learning experiences (page 13) – *can you attach any specific emotions to both situations?* Negative emotions often are attributed to causing stress and it is very easy to let this negative, fearful feeling spiral and escalate, making it very difficult to keep things in perspective. The reasons behind the feeling of pressure and stress may not be irrational; you may have more than one piece of coursework due in at the same time or an exam looming. The important thing is to manage these fearful and stressful feelings. **Physical health** is closely linked to emotional health. Exercise is very important to help reduce this level of negative arousal so it is very important to build some regular exercise into your schedule to act as an outlet for the adrenalin that is naturally generated by the feelings of anxiety or stress. Another useful strategy is to 'reframe' the stress or fear and recognise that stress and fear is a natural reaction when embarking on something new:

- *See fear/stress as a positive attribute.* When embarking on something new celebrate the fear/stress feeling as it means you are growing, changing, taking risks and embarking on new challenges.
- *You are not alone.* Sometimes we feel that we are the only person that feels stressed or afraid in new learning situations. Cohen (1997), however, believes that everyone feels fearful and stressed in unfamiliar situations.
- *Have a go.* The only way to get rid of the fear/stress of something is to try it; often it is not as bad as we first thought it was going to be.
- *Embrace the fear/stress rather than keep living with it.* The more we give in to fear and stress the more it takes hold – break the cycle, face the fear and remember it will become easier.
- *Create a belief system.* From being open to doubt be open to the belief that you can and will succeed.

- *Use questions to remove distortions.* When you question whether you can achieve something, use a question to change the negative belief, e.g. negative belief = *I can't write academically!* Reframe the question: *What stops you? What would happen if you could?*
- *Reframing takes time.* Remember this change in attitude and behaviour will not happen overnight; like any behaviour it is learned and needs time to be unlearned. Practice will make perfect.

Motivation linked to the desire to learn is regarded as the pre-requisite to effective learning and the key to all successful learning (Gorard *et al.*, 2007; Meneghetti, Benitti and Cornoldi, 2007; Erdarmer, 2011). There are two types of motivation: **intrinsic** and **extrinsic motivation**. Intrinsic motivation is when we want to do something for its own sake, for our own interest and enjoyment, and when we get a feeling of satisfaction *during* rather than *after* an activity. Participation in the experience is its own reward and we do not depend on incentives or disincentives. Extrinsic motivation is the desire to act or experience something that is stimulated by a reward. Equally, the desire may be stimulated by avoidance of undesirable consequences. You may be embarking on a degree or a college course for the love of learning and increasing your knowledge around a subject area; this is intrinsic motivation. On the other hand, you may be motivated to get a degree in order to increase your earning potential and secure a better job; this is extrinsic motivation. However, whether you are intrinsically or extrinsically motivated, in order to succeed in your studies you must be motivated and want to be involved in the learning experience, whatever it may be, to make your learning effective.

Style matters: match your type to effective learning

If you are to become an effective learner then you need to know how you function optimally as a learner. Knowing how you learn most effectively will be an important key in unlocking your true learning potential. Your **learning style** refers to the way that you process information presented to you most effectively and how you interact and respond to the way in which information is presented. It is important to note that no one style is any better than any other and at the moment your learning style has developed with time and your unique exposure to many learning situations. These learning styles are not set in stone; exploring new ways of learning can introduce alternative learning approaches that once experienced may become a preferred method. You may gravitate to one particular method depending on the learning situation and what information needs to be learned. Learning in HE involves handling significant amounts of information in various guises. If you know how best to re-present particular types of information to yourself in a way that matches your preferred learning style this will create a more stress free, deep learning situation. There are four main types:

- *visual* learners learn best by using visual prompts such as spider diagrams, flow charts and labelled diagrams;
- *auditory* learners learn best by listening and discussing;
- *read/writers* learn best using words and typed font; and
- **kinaesthetic** learners learn best from experience and practice. (Vark-learn, 2013)

This list is extended by Gardner (1983), a Professor of Education at Harvard University, who has suggested that different 'intelligences' exist; depending on the preferred or the type that you are most inclined to will have a direct impact on how you process and engage in learning effectively. It should be noted that there is an ongoing debate (as in any theoretical field) around the concept of learning styles and this is useful to explore to form and evaluate your own opinions on the concept - the beginnings of critical thinking!

Activity: Find your learning style/intelligence type

Visit the web links offered below to ascertain which category of learner you are and how to re-configure information to best suit your learning style:

- For VAK access: http://tinyurl.com/asnmh87
- For Gardner's intelligences access: http://tinyurl.com/84Irl9q

As a student on a formal HE course of study there may be little choice about how the information is presented to you, e.g. formal lectures or seminars. However, you can adopt different learning styles in the way you study; to make learning really effective we should use a variety of learning styles and techniques (Burns and Sinfield, 2012).

Active or passive learner

Take time to review Table 2.1 and determine which type of learner you are at present, shading the statement that most reflects your approach to learning in relation to the situations listed:

Table 2.1 Active and passive learning: questions for reflection

Active approach to learning	Passive approach to learning
Do you actively ask questions to clarify key concepts and check understanding?	Do you accept what is said without question, making notes, not checking your understanding?
Do you think, reflect, explore and challenge information to enhance your own knowledge of a subject?	Do you just learn and reproduce what you think are the key facts around a topic?
Do you regularly read, make notes and generally engage with the learning material?	Do you leave reviewing any notes or information and 'cram' learning before an assignment?
Do you engage readily and interact in sessions?	Are you reluctant to engage and involve yourself in sessions?
Do you generate your own learning options and strategies?	Do you wait for instructions on how to approach tasks?
Do you go beyond the recommended reading lists and explore aspects of the subject that particularly interest you?	Do you read the bare minimum?
Do you seek feedback and learn from it?	Do you avoid or ignore feedback?
Do you see your success or failure as dependent on you?	Do you see success or failure as beyond your control?
Do you have full control and responsibility for your learning?	Do you blame external factors for your inability to succeed?

Which column did you mainly identify with: *active* or *passive*? There will be occasions when you are under pressure and do lapse into passive behaviours but try to embrace the behaviours described in the 'active' column as it contains key potential strategies for effective learning and study. If you can strive to utilise the active learning strategies identified then you are committed to being active and engaged in your learning and the quality of your learning objectives are likely to be immensely more rewarding and effective (Moore *et al.*, 2010).

Time management

Time management is one of the biggest challenges you will face as a student as only part of your week will be formally timetabled. According to Jansen and Suhre (2010) time management is an essential skill that students need to develop in order to succeed in their first year of study. For some of you it will be the first time living independently, for others it will be trying to get the balance between home and university life with all that it has on offer. Your time in HE should not be purely focused on study; you should aim to immerse yourself in some of the wider experiences that your university or college offers in order to maximise your experience. However, the majority of us know we should plan and manage time effectively but we do not manage to stick to the plan! You need to reflect on your attitude to planning and time management as it is your attitude that drives your behaviour. Most time management issues are caused by students making unrealistic or vague plans and this results in the feeling of stress and anxiety as tasks build up. The best way to start is to complete a 'time audit'; this can be created by making a timetable of an average week with all of the activities you engage in including sleep, exercise and family commitments. Now evaluate and analyse the schedule – are there times when you can use your time more effectively?

 Activity: The time sponge (Reid, 2010)

Try this with your colleagues or your study group:

1   Take a 'sticky label' note and write on it your biggest *time sponge* (it could be time spent on social media, your family, your hobbies).
2   Everybody passes their 'sticky label' to the person on their left. You then write a possible solution (realistic!) to the time sponge problem.
3   Keep passing it to the left with everyone writing a possible solution until it gets back to the originator.
4   Everybody takes turns in reading out a time sponge problem and a possible solution.
5   Everybody says one thing that they will change after listening to the time sponges and solutions.

The most important thing when dealing with managing your time is to be realistic; there is no point scheduling yourself to work at times as you do not function well so decide whether you work best in the afternoon or evening. Also, prioritise tasks you have to complete, being aware that many aspects of study take longer than expected, e.g. locating relevant source material. When planning your time remember to set yourself SMARTCE targets:

- S = Specific; break larger tasks into smaller specific ones such as reading for an assignment into finding five sources related to the topic.
- M = Measureable; such as a set number of words e.g. 500 towards an assignment.
- A = Achievable; set yourself mini goals or targets around your study so that you have a key focus to achieve as this will result in you having a sense of achievement when the task is completed.
- R = Realistic; do not set unrealistic goals, for example spending five hours in the library.
- T = Timely; give yourself a start time and a target end time but if you have not completed the task within the allocated time then carry on until it is completed. The important thing is not how long you have spent studying but that you have completed your mini goal.
- C = Challenging; do not opt for an easy option! Make sure you are 'stretching' yourself; do not just accept what you first read, look for opposing viewpoints and debates.
- E = Enjoyable; make the experience enjoyable by treating yourself when you have completed the task (a snack, a nice walk, catching up with friends on the phone).

Time patterns

Always look for time patterns that suit your needs. You may work better by using the '**shower mapping**' (thought shower) technique to plan your assignment in the morning when you are more alert, or spending time in the library straight after lectures when the information is still fresh in your mind. You may prefer to study in short spells of 20 minutes. It is important to start with short study spells then gradually build up your study time (especially if you get engrossed in a subject) but never study for more than an hour without taking a break; it is very difficult to maintain high levels of sustained concentration for longer than that. Remember to include time for relaxation and exercise and to always allow for unexpected events such as illness or family circumstances. The most important thing is *not* the amount of time you have spent; you could have spent three hours in the library daydreaming! It is the *effectiveness* and *efficiency* of the time you have spent that is the key.

Study space

It is very important to find a study place that suits you and make that place work for you. Creating a designated study space helps everyone realise just how important your private study times are. Make this a positive space by saying positive statements (remember the importance of re-framing mentioned earlier) to yourself as you sit: 'Now I am ready to study.' Make sure your study space is well lit and comfortable; sitting with a window behind you or to one side will cut out distractions. Have your timetables, deadlines and study planner visible. Have your textbooks, notes, files organised and to hand. Remember that a chaotic working space will slow you down as it is more difficult to locate key items. Leave your work out if you possibly can; do not tidy it all away as keeping the work visible keeps it in your mind and you will not waste time tidying up and getting everything back out again (Cottrell, 2008; Burns and Sinfield, 2012). Remember too as you study to eat healthily (slow release, energy foods) to 'feed' your brain and keep hydrated as you work (not with high energy sugary drinks as they give you a 'rush' and then you dip as sugar levels fall) and ensure you have a healthy sleep pattern as when you relax and sleep your brain is in repair and is processing vital information.

Academic reading and critical thinking

Academic reading

If you have ever watched the BBC television programme *University Challenge* you may have noticed that the teams introduce themselves and then inform you what subject they are 'reading' not 'studying'. This is because in HE in the UK you are not 'taught' your degree; the most important task that you have as a student, which is meant to fill the rest of the timetabled week outside lectures, is to read and research around your chosen subject or particular module. This is what is known as *academic reading* but it is vital to note that (in the words of Mortimer Adler) it is not how many books you get out but what you get out of them that is the key! Academic reading is a 'complex set of different activities requiring a range of skills' (Fairbairn and Fairbairn, 2001: 16). Remember, the key word here is *skills* – something that is learned and develops with time, patience and practice; this is exactly the same when learning to read academically.

Reflective task: What do you know about reading?

You probably haven't given the reading process much thought, but engaging with this activity will bring the process into conscious awareness.

- Write down your definition of reading and what specific skills you can identify in the process.
- Note down what aspects of the reading process you enjoy/do not enjoy.

Ask yourself the following:

- What are your strengths as a reader?
- What are your 'areas for consideration' (weaknesses) as a reader?
- What do you find easy to read?
- What do you find hard to read?
- What are the differences between the two?

Compare your thoughts with your colleagues/peers.

Obviously when you start the reading process on a new topic/subject the vast majority of information and some of the key terminology and vocabulary used will be new to you and as a result it may be difficult for you to understand. As you read more texts on the subject you will start to recognise key features and discover different perspectives on the same subject; this is the basic principle of reading academically – you start reading to gain an understanding of key concepts and then as you read more you begin to analyse and begin to critique the information you are reading, recognising similarities and differences in academic opinion. If you develop the habit of reading a portion of academic text every day, like any skill, you will improve. Remember you never have to read the whole textbook; it is about selecting the sections that are most appropriate to your needs. To read more effectively read for short, concentrated periods and follow the tips below to effective reading (adapted from Moore *et al.*, 2010 and Burns and Sinfield, 2012):

- Read at your best time of day with all electronic distractions switched off so you are alert.
- Set clear goals for each reading session, e.g. read one chapter, engage with one journal article.
- Have everything to hand, i.e. a dictionary for difficult vocabulary, a notebook, and highlighters.
- Read for no more than 45–60 minutes at a time.
- 'Test the text' by looking at the contents page – *do the chapter headings appear relevant?* Look at the index pages – *do some of the entries look relevant/useful?* Check the date of publication – *depending upon your subject, is the material sufficiently recent?*
- Check the tone – *is the book written in a way that you can follow?* If it is too difficult at first then choose another text. It is likely that if you are comfortable with the way this material is presented, then you will be so with information about areas you are not familiar with.
- Engage with the text by reading through the material, asking questions and finding answers. There should be a dialogue going on in your mind when engaging with a text. Engagement develops your ability to recall information because it is about deep learning.
- Use the *Survey, Question, Read, Review* and *Recall* (SQ3R) method: survey the passage, skim and scan paragraphs quickly for key vocabulary, question whether it is worth reading.
- Ask yourself questions about the text, e.g. *do you understand it? What argument is being made? What evidence is this based on? How current is the information? How reliable is the source? How can you use the information in an assignment?*
- Make notes and sum up what you have read in about three sentences, noting key references.
- Stop and take a short break. Have a drink and snack to keep you hydrated and energised.
- Start the whole process again.
- Read *beyond* texts that you agree with; stretch and challenge your beliefs as this will help to develop your critical thinking.
- Read a range of opinions and sources as this balance in your reading will then be reflected in your writing.

The advantage of reading is that you can decide on the pace and amount that you undertake at one time (Moore *et al.*, 2010) but it is vital that this habit is performed and practised daily. The best way to develop an effective habit is to read with your study group. You can share out reading tasks then meet and discuss key findings, discussing and summarising what each member has read. As everyone will bring their own interpretation of the reading this will aid your critical thinking skills as you begin to debate and analyse other's opinions and thinking against your own, and be able to justify your reasoning more skilfully (Judge, Jones and McCreery, 2009). Always remember that the reading list supplied by a tutor is a *guide* to the sorts of texts that you should engage with; if you just read the set texts then you are not extending and expanding your knowledge around the subject and this will be reflected in your assignment grade/score. Find new information and research that *supports*, *challenges* or *extends* (as advocated by Brownhill) the information/understanding that you started with as this demonstrates that you have read widely. Here are two top tips linked to references:

- Open an electronic file or note pad for every subject or module you are studying over the year as you will find that information in certain texts will be relevant to more than one module. This 'bank of references' can be utilised to support the writing of different assignments.
- When you find a relevant text keep a record of key information needed for referencing, i.e. author's surname, initials, date of publication, title of publication, where it was published and by whom for use in your assignment and **reference list** or **bibliography**. It is vital to reference information used as it is crediting the author for their intellectual property. If you do not reference material used in your work properly you may be accused of plagiarism which is an academic offence. Follow and use the referencing conventions from your institution to avoid plagiarising work.

Critical thinking

Critical thinking is an essential part of the academic reading and writing process. The ability to use critical thinking moves you from description to analysis and evaluation. It is about you as a student developing an enquiring and questioning mind. It relies on you as the reader being able to evaluate or critically assess what you have read - it is more than just showing you understand what you have read. Do remember that academic authors have their own points of view and these influence their writing; this is known as bias. Remember you are *not* a 'student sponge', soaking up information that is then squeezed out into your assignments to prove you know the subject. You need to be thoughtful and questioning about the information you read and the evidence and methods used to gain it. Critical thinking involves *interrogation* of the material; you need to examine the coherence and clarity of the text - *does it hold together well?* Look for strength in arguments and for relevance and strength in illustrations and examples used.

Activity: Critical thinking scenario

Consider the scenario below:

You have just had your hair cut and are about to get on your bike. Do you wear your cycle helmet or not? What evidence do you consider before making your decision?

You have at your disposal evidence from the media and evidence from systematic research undertaken by people who have:

- treated head injuries;
- media information;
- studied accident statistics;
- Done research in several settings, by methods set out clearly.

The 'critical thinking' part in answering the questions is facilitated by interrogating the studies and thinking about the quality of the evidence, the way the studies were carried out, who carried the studies out; was there any bias – then you make an *informed decision*!

Engaging in critical thinking gets you thinking in depth about a subject which in turn extends your understanding and also acts as a prompt to find more evidence or an alternative point of view on the subject. Review the 'Stairway to critical thinking' (Figure 2.1).

Use critical thinking to develop arguments, draw conclusions, make inferences and identify implications.						**JUSTIFY**
Transfer the understanding you have gained from your critical evaluation and use in response to questions, assignments and projects.					**APPLY**	
Assess the worth of an idea in terms of its relevance to your needs, the evidence on which it is based and how it relates to other pertinent ideas.				**EVALUATE**		
Bring together different sources to serve an argument or idea you are constructing. Make logical connections between the different sources that help you shape and support your ideas.			**SYNTHESISE**			
		COMPARE	Explore the similarities and differences between the ideas you are reading about.			
	ANALYSE	Examine how these key points fit together and relate to each other.				
	UNDERSTAND	Comprehend the key points, assumptions, arguments and evidence presented.				
PROCESS	Take in the information, i.e. what you have read, heard, seen or done.					

Figure 2.1 Stairway to critical thinking (Williams, 2009)

If you actively engage in regular academic reading you will move from the bottom stair from merely *processing* and *understanding* information, which results in work being descriptive to the higher order cognitive and academic skills of *synthesis, evaluation, application and justification* of the information you have read which can be transferred into your written submissions.

Academic writing

The culmination of all of your reading, note making and critical thinking is not only about extending your knowledge around a particular topic or subject; it is usually focused towards an assessment (an assignment). Writing a good assignment is one of the most daunting challenges you will face initially as a student (Cottrell, 2003). Academic writing involves a broad range of interconnected skills that need mastering and in order to be successful you have to know very clearly what is expected of you. The most important point to note is that you must fully understand the assessment brief and the following suggestions will support you in doing this (Judge, Jones and McCreery, 2010):

- Read your course handbook.
- Read your module handbook. These contain detailed information about what is expected of you in terms of the assignment criteria and the writing practices in terms of font size and type, formatting, consistency and referencing conventions (Craswell and Poore, 2012).
- Analyse the demands of the assignment title; assignment briefs contain specific verbs, for example 'critically reflect', that are crucial to you meeting the assessment criteria. Take the assignment title/question and underline/highlight key vocabulary, for example: 'demonstrate an understanding' or 'critically examine'.
- Print out the assignment title and stick it to the top of your computer monitor so as you work you are constantly reminded of the assignment focus.
- Highlight other key words, e.g. 'multi-professional'.

This task of breaking down the assessment criteria is best done in your study groups as everyone can bring their understanding of the task and if there is any uncertainty you can check with your tutor that you are on the right track. The next crucial stage is the planning of the assignment. Planning should follow this sequence:

- Break down the question.
- Thought shower your ideas of what to include.
- Devise a planning mind map or grid of what you are going to include in each section.
- Read your lecture notes.
- Collate your wider reading notes and references.
- Assign references to specific paragraphs.
- Allocate words to each section.
- Write your first draft. Remember this is your first attempt so write freely; the emphasis should be on allowing your thoughts to flow (Greetham, 2008). Once you have done this, then leave your assignment.
- Review, revise, re-draft and edit your assignment. Remember your target audience; you should be writing for a fellow student who has no understanding of your subject.

- Take great care with grammar, spelling and punctuation and ensure *no* informal/slang language is used, for example 'it was really hard', or contractions, for example, 'don't'. Beware of the spell checker: do not just select the top word on the spell checklist – ensure it is the correct word in the context you are using it in.
- After two days proofread by reading the assignment out loud as hearing what you have written will highlight areas that require review.
- Submit your work.
- Relax!

You may prefer the mind mapping method (visit www.mindmapping.com/) where you use the assignment title as the central focus and then use colour and key themes coming off the central point, acting as the content for paragraphs. Alternatively you can use the more linear '12 Grid' method for essay writing, devised by Brownhill (Table 2.2).

Table 2.2 '12 Grid' method to essay writing (devised by Brownhill)

Introduction to the essay – the topic, the structure of the essay and pertinent themes which will be explored	*Paragraph 1* Key theme 1 1 direct quote	*Paragraph 2* Key theme 1 continued 2 citations	*Paragraph 3* Key theme 2 1 direct quote 2 paraphrases
150 words	**100 words**	**150 words**	**200 words**
Paragraph 4 Key theme 2 continued Reference	*Paragraph 5* Key theme 3 1 direct quote 1 citation	*Paragraph 6* Key theme 3 continued 1 paraphrase	*Paragraph 7* Key theme 4 2 citations
200 words	**200 words**	**200 words**	**200 words**
Paragraph 8 Key theme 5 1 direct quote 2 citations	*Paragraph 9* Key theme 6 1 paraphrase	*Paragraph 10* Key theme 6 continued 2 citations	*Conclusion* – draw together key issues and themes and present conclusive statement 1 direct quote
200 words	**150 words**	**150 words**	**150 words**

Whichever method you choose to use ensure that you are taking into consideration how many and the type of references being used to support your discussion to ensure you have a *variety* of sources and types of reference. You must calculate your wordage so that you do not fall below or exceed the word limit for the assessment. However you plan, planning is a key element as it gives you a clear indication of what areas you are going to cover in your assignment and which references you are going to use to support which parts of your discussion. This should erase '**writer's block**' where you as the writer stare at the blank screen or page not knowing what to write.

Knowing the rules

There are clear rules about what makes writing academic; you must be clear and explicit about what you are writing. Remember the critical thinker in you: you must be objective and detached about the arguments and discussions you make and always refer to academic sources to support points that you raise. An important rule to follow is the 'PEET' rule:

- P = Point; make the key point related to your discussion;
- E = Explain; explain the point clearly and concisely;
- E = Example; try to link the point to a particular example from practice; and
- T = Theory; use a reference to academic reading to support the point made.

The points in the 'PEET' rule can be used in any order but following the pattern presented above ensures your work is academic and not merely descriptive or subjective. Academic writing uses a paragraph format. There is no set length for a paragraph but they must follow a pattern of announcing of the topic, development of the topic, with a concluding sentence which reflects back on the key structural elements of the paragraph. The next paragraph needs to link to the previous paragraph in order for the essay to 'flow'.

Essay structure

The whole of the essay must focus on the assignment title and contain:

- The introduction: this explains the journey the writing takes, identifying the issues you are going to explore and gives a brief outline of each area under discussion. It is often easier to write the introduction *last* as you know what your essay contains (Greasley, 2011).
- The main body: this is offered in paragraph format where you develop your argument. Everything in the essay should contribute in some way to the argument; if it does not, however interesting you feel the information is, leave it out!
- The conclusion: this is where you summarise your main argument and the key themes, stating your general conclusions and why these are important or significant. No new material should appear in the conclusion.
- A reference list and bibliography using the referencing conventions of your particular institution.

Important key points in essay writing to note!

- Logical structure – an essay should have an argument running through it from the title to the conclusion with punchy openings and crisp conclusions.
- Debate – an essay should respond to arguments, evidence and points of view that you have read by offering arguments of your own.
- Scholarship – an essay should show your arguments being linked to literature by using citations, references and paraphrasing (where you put the author's words into your own demonstrating higher order thinking skills).

- Critical analysis – an essay should not just 'present' an author's point of view; focus in on the strengths and weaknesses of their evidence.
- Evidence – an essay should present evidence to back up your arguments.
- Objectivity – an essay should be written in a detached, unemotional way, leaving the points to stand on their own merits.
- Precision – an essay should try to say exactly what you mean concisely; pay attention to detail!
- Audience – an essay should be written for another student even though it is for your tutor. *Think!* Imagine you are writing for someone who needs the subject explained in a well-argued and documented manner.

The importance of feedback

Remember that studying and writing at HE is a learning process; you are developing a whole new set of skills and you will not get everything right first time. Although the grade/percentage/score awarded to you is important, the most important aspect of feedback is the comments (written) made throughout your work and the final summative comment your tutor makes. The key to improving these skills is to act on the feedback given by your tutor so you can develop these key academic skills in future submissions; these comments are your ticket to a higher grade! Read through the comments, ensuring you understand what the tutor is referring to and re-frame any negative reactions into positive ones; keep asking yourself: *How will this help me improve?* In order to improve you need to use the feedback to 'feed-forward' into your next submission. Devise an action plan by selecting up to three areas for development, e.g. referencing or avoiding the use of informal language, and what strategies you are going to use to improve on these specific skills. Note the impact this development will have on your next assignment and if you need support in doing this arrange a tutorial with your tutor to discuss how to improve on these key areas. In this way your skills will improve and so will your grades/percentages!

Conclusion

This chapter set out to highlight the fact that you as a student entering into a HE institution are not initially equipped with all of the necessary skills to succeed at this level of study. Academic study is comprised of an interrelated, complex set of skills that need to be introduced and practiced in order for you to become increasingly competent in using the whole range necessary to maximise your potential success. It is important that you recognise that you are an individual and that there is no magic wand that will magically empower you with these skills; you need to transform yourself into a strategic student, one that can learn independently and guide your own learning. You need to identify and *practise* those skills that you reflected on in the initial Skills Audit (page 12) and try out different learning strategies until you select the ones that work for you. Using these learning strategies consistently could be the critical factor that determines your success as a student (Meneghetti, De Beni and Cornoldi, 2007).

Areas for further consideration

After reading this chapter you should now be aware of your own areas of strength and areas for development in terms of your study skills. There are a number of areas for consideration which you need to explore as part of your acquisition of effective study skills. The suggestions below merely offer other aspects of study skills which will help further your effective and strategic study skills set:

Note making	Referencing	Reflective writing
Report writing	Group work	Exam preparation

Further reading

Books

Bonnett, A. (2011) *How to Argue*. 3rd edn. Harlow: Pearson.
This is an essential read in supporting how to develop an academic argument, identifying key areas where most students need assistance and giving practical tips and solutions that enable you to improve developing an academic argument.

Cottrell, S. (2012) *The Exam Skills Handbook: Achieving peak performance*. Basingstoke: Palgrave.
This is a wonderful book as it offers practical tips and techniques in ensuring peak performance in exams.

Godfrey, J. (2010) *Reading and Making Notes*. Basingstoke: Palgrave.
This is a comprehensive guide in how to read and make effective notes to support your learning.

McMillan, K. and Weyers, J. D. B. (2011) *How to Write Dissertations And Project Reports*. Harlow: Pearson.
This comprehensive book guides the reader in the specialist skill of writing dissertations and the format and content necessary for producing reports.

References

Burns, T. and Sinfield, S. (2012) *Essential Study Skills*. 3rd edn. London: Sage.
Cohen, S. B. (1997) *The Maladapted Mind*. Hove: Psychology Press.
Cottrell, S. (2003) *Skills for Success*. 3rd edn. Hampshire: Palgrave Macmillan.
Craswell, G. and Poore, M. (2012) *Writing for Academic Success*. 2nd edn. London: Sage.
Erdamar, G. (2011) An investigation of student teachers' study strategies with respect to certain variables. *Educational Research and Evaluation: An International Journal on Theory and practice*, 17 (2), 69-83.
Fairbairn, G. J. and Fairbairn, S. A. (2001) *Reading at University*. Buckingham: Open University Press.
Gardner, H. (1983) *Frames of Mind*. New York: Basic Books Inc.
Gorard, S., Beng Huat, S., Smith, E. and White, P. (2007) What can we do to strengthen the teacher workforce? *International Journal of Lifelong Education*, 26 (4), 419-437.
Greasley, P. (2011) *Doing Essays and Assignments*. London: Sage.
Greetham, B. (2008) *How to Write Better Essays*. 2nd edn. Hampshire: Palgrave Macmillan.
Gurcu, E. (2011) An investigation of student teachers' study strategies with respect to certain variables. *Educational Research and Evaluations*, 17 (2), 69-83.
Jansen, E. P. W. A. and Suhre, C. J. M. (2010) The effect of secondary school study skills preparation on first-year university achievement. *Educational Studies*, 36 (5), 569-580.
Judge, B., Jones, P. and McCreery, E. (2010) *Critical Thinking Skills for Education Students*. Exeter: Learning Matters.

Learning styles questionnaire (2013) [Online]. Available at: http://psychology.about.com/library/quiz/bl-mi-quiz.htm (Accessed: 25 February 2013).

Maslow's hierarchy of needs (2013) [Online]. Available at: www.learning-theories.com/maslows-hierarchy-of-needs.html (Accessed: 23 August 2013).

Meneghetti, C., De Benitti, R. and Cornoldi, C. (2007) Strategic knowledge and consistency in students with good and poor study skills. *European Journal of Cognitive Psychology*, 19 (4-5), 628-649.

Moore, S., Neville, C., Murphy, M. and Conolly, C. (2010) *The Ultimate Study Skills Handbook*. Berks: Open University Press.

Northedge, A. (2005) *The Good Study Guide*. Oxford: The Open University.

Petty, G. (2004) *Teaching Today*. 3rd edn. Cheltenham: Nelson Thornes.

Reid, M. (2013) Time sponge. [Online]. Available at: www.reading.ac.uk/study (Accessed: 23 August 2013).

Study Skills Audit. (2013) [Online]. Available at: www3.surrey.ac.uk/Skills/pack/audit.doc (Accessed: 25 February 2013).

VARK-Learn (2013) [Online]. Available at: www.vark-learn.com/english/index.asp (Accessed: 23 August 2013).

Williams, K. (2009) *Being Critical*. Hampshire: Palgrave Macmillan.

3 Work-based learning

Lesley Faulconbridge

LEARNING OBJECTIVES

After studying this chapter, you will be able to:

✔ Identify legislation, policy and standards that have influenced workforce development in Children's and Young People's Services.
✔ Identify the benefits and disadvantages of flexible learning approaches.
✔ Evaluate a range of learning and teaching methods in providing a quality learning experience for the individual.
✔ Define the differences between a pedagogical and an andragogical approach to learning and teaching and how these are used in work-based learning.

Introduction

The Children's and Young People's workforce has undergone a dramatic transformation in the last decade. Workforce reform in CYPS has been driven by government policy, and increasingly staff in the maintained, private, voluntary and independent sectors are expected to take on demanding roles that include business management, supporting learning and teaching, health care, pastoral care and advisory/guidance roles (Edmond and Price, 2009). Work-based programmes in HE such as Foundation Degrees and Higher Apprenticeships have been designed to 'up skill' those working/training in the sector and develop the higher level skills, knowledge and understanding necessary for these professional roles.

This chapter examines ways in which practitioners and those training in CYPS can learn, with an emphasis on **work-based learning**. The chapter will explore a range of modes of delivery, considering the dilemma of meeting the demands of market forces to provide flexible study opportunities and ensuring a quality learning experience for students. The social learning model (Lave and Wenger, 1990), which views learning as a collective process that takes place in a 'community of practice' (CoP), and the andragogical approach (Knowles, 1980) that expects students to take control of their own learning, are also considered.

Legislation, policy and research

In all sectors across CYPS the last decade has seen a great deal of change for the workforce influenced by government **legislation** and **policy**. It could be argued that the most influential of these was the *Every Child Matters* policy initiative (DfES, 2004) (re-named in 2010 by the coalition government as *Helping Children Achieve More*) that highlighted the need to strengthen **inter-professional working**, the Children Act 2004 (c31) that provided the underpinning legislation for the implementation of the initiative, and the Children's Workforce Strategy (DfES, 2005) that identified the expertise that the workforce would need to deliver the outcomes set out in *Every Child Matters* across CYPS.

Research studies that suggest well qualified and trained staff can make a significant difference to outcomes for children and young people have also provided the catalyst for change and the professionalisation of the 0–19 workforce (Sylva *et al.*, 2004; TDA, 2009; Blatchford, Webster and Russell, 2012; DfE, 2012a, 2013). For example, the research findings from the Effective Provision of Pre-school Education (EPPE) Project (Sylva *et al.*, 2004) led to the government committing to developing a professional, graduate led workforce in the non-maintained sector. Through the Graduate Leader Fund (GLF) the Labour government invested £305 million with the long-term aim of ensuring that a practitioner in every children's centre and full day care setting achieved the Early Years Professional Status (EYPS) by 2015 (DCSF, 2008); however, due to a change in government this target was not adhered to. More recently the Nutbrown Review of early education and childcare qualifications, *Foundations for Quality* (DfE, 2012a), and the government's response to this review, *More Great Childcare* (DfE, 2013), has led to the discontinuation of the EYPS programme. The final recruitment to the EYPS programme was January 2013, replaced from September 2013 by Early Years Initial Teacher Training. The vision of the government is to increase the status of the profession so that in the future more graduates consider a career in the Early Years. When training or working in the sector you will find that in many settings Early Years Professionals lead practice and are considered experts in their profession. Although the EYPS programme of study was superseded by Early Years Initial Teacher Training, the government emphasises that both statuses have parity in the sector.

In the education sector (5–16), the government report *Time for Standards: Reforming the school workforce* (DfES, 2002) had a considerable impact upon training for **support staff**, suggesting that some teaching assistants might be trained to take on tasks traditionally associated with the role of the teacher (Butt and Lance, 2009). The government emphasised the need for a professional workforce with the skills and knowledge to work in conjunction with teachers in delivering high quality personalised learning. Following this, in 2004 the Higher Level Teaching Assistant (HLTA) qualification was launched (TDA, 2006). You will find that in the maintained sector HLTAs are employed in many schools to cover planning, preparation and assessment (PPA) time for qualified teachers and are expected to act as specialist assistants across the curriculum.

The Positive for Youth policy (DfE, 2011) set out a shared vision to improve outcomes for young people and clearly identified the role of youth professionals in shaping provision. In some local authorities youth support work and family crisis work has now been amalgamated to become Family Intervention Programmes (FIPs). These **multiagency teams** work with families through an integrated approach, offering a **holistic** service for young people who are showing the signs of being at risk (see Chapter 7 for further information).

Activity: Engaging with policy and legislation

Select any two of the legislation/policy listed below that are pertinent to the service you work/train in. Identify how these have influenced workforce development. Make personal notes to support your understanding.

Policy/Legislation	Web Link
Every Child Matters: Change for children (DfES, 2003)	http://tinyurl.com/6dnfz93
Children's Workforce Strategy: A strategy to build a world-class workforce for children and young people (DfES, 2005)	http://tinyurl.com/8dv89gw
2020 Children and Young People's Workforce Strategy (DCSF, 2008)	http://tinyurl.com/cu97k7u
Positive for Youth (DfE, 2011)	http://tinyurl.com/aeouewn
Review of Vocational Education: The Wolf Report (DfE, 2011)	http://tinyurl.com/6hzhzwq
Foundations for Quality: The independent review of early education and childcare qualifications (Nutbrown Review) (DfE, 2012a)	http://tinyurl.com/ax7jby3
More Great Childcare Raising quality and giving parents more choice (DfE, 2013)	http://tinyurl.com/cyz4ny4

A professional workforce - standards to achieve higher level skills

In all roles across CYPS there has been an increased emphasis on benchmarks of good practice that specify the standard an individual must achieve when carrying out their job in the workplace, in conjunction with the relevant underpinning knowledge and understanding necessary to be effective.

The Early Years Professional Status, an award (not a qualification) for graduates who lead practice from birth to the end of the Early Years Foundation Stage (EYFS) (0-5), requires that practitioners meet standards that cover essential aspects of high quality practice and leadership. These standards promote reflection and partnership working with both professionals and parents/carers to ensure effective early education and care of all children (DfE, 2012b). The eight standards are:

1   Support the healthy growth and development of children from birth to the age of five.
2   Work directly with children and in partnership with their families to facilitate learning and support development.
3   Safeguard and promote the welfare of children.
4   Set high expectations which inspire, motivate and challenge every child.
5   Make use of observation and assessment to meet the individual needs of every child.
6   Plan provision taking account of the individual needs of every child.
7   Fulfil wider professional responsibilities by promoting positive partnership working to support the child.
8   Lead practice and foster a culture of continuous improvement (DfE, 2012b).

Visit http://tinyurl.com/98dw43g for further information with regards to the above.

The Teachers' Standards (Early Years) introduced in September 2013 are designed for those who will lead education and care from birth to the end of the EYFS. Early Years Teacher Status is awarded to graduates who have been judged to have met all of the standards. The eight standards are:

1   Set high expectations which inspire, motivate and challenge all children.
2   Promote good progress and outcomes by children.
3   Demonstrate good knowledge of early learning and the EYFS.
4   Plan education and care taking account of the needs of all children.
5   Adapt education and care to respond to the strengths and needs of all children.
6   Make accurate and productive use of assessment.
7   Safeguard and promote the welfare of children, and provide a safe learning environment.
8   Fulfil wider professional responsibilities.

Visit http://tinyurl.com/knuu3m8 for further details with regards to the above.

Similarly, the professional standards for HLTAs in the 5–19 sector help to ensure that all HLTAs have the necessary skills and expertise to make an active contribution to pupils' learning (TDA, 2006). These standards are organised into three interrelated sections:

1   professional values and practice;
2   knowledge and understanding; and
3   teaching and learning activities.

Visit http://tinyurl.com/d86wmcm for further details.

While these sets of standards are pertinent to different roles in CYPS, National Occupational Standards (NOS) are often used across the sector to benchmark good practice and may be used for reflective practice and continuing professional development (CPD). These standards are also often used to inform the content of work-based qualifications and training such as Foundation Degrees and Higher Apprenticeships.

Reflective task: Gaining an awareness

Search the National Occupational Standards database which is available at http://tinyurl.com/aohf3ew

- Download a free copy of the professional standards that are relevant to the context that you are working/training in.
- Reflect on the content of the document. Use the standards as a basis of a personal training needs analysis. Identify two areas for further professional development.

In 2010 the Children's Workforce Development Council (CWDC), supported by the DCSF, developed the *Common Core of Skills and Knowledge* for those working in CYPS. You will find when training/working in the sector that this single framework underpins multi-agency and integrated working across the workforce, including paid staff and volunteers. This set of common values for practitioners and those training in CYPS were designed to reflect the skills and knowledge that all who work with children and young people are expected to have but are flexible enough to be relevant for a range of roles in a wide range of contexts.

Reflective task: Engaging with professional standards

Download a free copy of the *Common Core of Skills and Knowledge* (CWDC, 2010) – available at http://tinyurl.com/byafaaq.

Select *one* of the Common Core of Skills and Knowledge from *each* of the six areas of expertise listed below:

1 Effective communication and engagement with children, young people and families.
2 Child and young person development.
3 Safeguarding and promoting the welfare of the child or young person.
4 Supporting transitions.
5 Multi-agency and integrated working.
6 Information sharing.

Critically reflect upon how you can meet these standards as a practitioner/trainee in the workplace.

Flexible work-based learning

Foundation Degrees

The development of work-based Foundation Degrees that offer flexible learning opportunities were designed to meet the needs of employers and those working in CYPS who wanted to update their qualifications/training to meet the changing needs of the sector (Beaney, 2006). These types of programme aim to be flexible and responsive to the individual study needs of learners with regard to the demands of family and work commitments, factors that Snape, Parfrement and Finch (2007) argue may be a barrier to engagement and subsequently achievement. The characteristics of Foundation Degrees (QAA, 2010) are demonstrated through:

- employer involvement;
- partnership;
- accessibility;
- flexibility; and
- articulation and progression.

Visit http://tinyurl.com/cpyr6wc for further information.

These are key attributes for maximising accessibility for those in work/training and for meeting the operational needs of employers underpinned by work-based learning (Thurgate,

MacGregor and Brett, 2007). Furthermore, on completing a Foundation Degree, progression opportunities exist to allow students to 'top up' their degree on a range of honours degree programmes such as Early Childhood Studies, Child and Youth Studies, Health and Social Care and Education Studies degree courses. Some students may also decide to study to become an Early Years Teacher.

Higher Apprenticeships

More recently, Higher Apprenticeships are increasingly being recognised as the 'gold standard' for work-based learning and training (visit http://tinyurl.com/3ph4c8k). Through these programmes you can gain qualifications and workplace experience and earn as you learn. Study patterns are usually on a day-release basis and the flexibility of the qualification means that you can take between one and four years to complete. As with foundation degrees these programmes are designed with employers and you would be expected to demonstrate high levels of commitment, responsibility and the ability to use your initiative. On a Higher Apprenticeship programme you would work towards a Level 4 work-based qualification and demonstrate elements such as:

- competence in performing the skill, or occupation to which the competencies framework relates;
- technical skills and the knowledge and understanding of theoretical concepts relevant to the occupation to which the framework relates; and
- either Key Skills (e.g. working in teams, problem-solving, communication and using new technology) or Functional Skills (e.g. Maths and English) qualifications or a GCSE with enhanced content (e.g. Maths and English).

Visit http://tinyurl.com/3ph4c8k for further information.

Flexible learning

All of the programmes discussed are designed to be flexible to give you the opportunity to develop while you are training or working. The notion of work-based **flexible learning** in terms of delivery mode is a difficult concept to define and can include a flexible choice of programmes, the opportunity for you as a student to determine the programme of study within your course and the timeframe for completion. There may also be the opportunity for you to select from alternative modes of study, thus allowing you to determine when and where you will study. Opportunities to study may be offered in the daytime, evening, at weekends and through distance learning and e-learning.

All of these approaches are designed to allow you to have greater control of your learning and promote student-centredness. Hence it could be argued that you as the student are perceived as a consumer in the market place and flexible delivery is provided according to demand and your personal and professional needs. This model of education can create a tension between maintaining academic standards in HE and meeting 'consumer' priorities. Nonetheless, it is acknowledged that ensuring that the needs of students and employers are met in a sustainable way is critical to programme development in order to maximise student recruitment, retention and achievement, and contribute to the professionalism of the workforce in CYPS.

To engage successfully in flexible modes of delivery there are a number of personal attributes that you will need. You need to be:

- organised;
- an independent learner;
- motivated;
- proactive;
- enthusiastic; and
- committed. (Durrant, Rhodes and Young, 2009)

You will also need to have **self-regulation** (the ability to independently plan, monitor and assess your own learning), time management and ICT skills. These skill sets are invariably developed as a student progresses through the course, particularly as many learners on work-based programmes are mature students returning to study, or those with little experience of managing the demands of study and work/placement simultaneously. This may appear to be a barrier to learning in the early phases of a programme; however, on many work-based courses you will find that study skills such as these are included as a feature of your course (see Chapter 1). Additional guidance, tutorial support and technical assistance may also be offered in the initial phases of a programme so that you can access flexible modes of delivery successfully (Hill, 2006).

Activity: Time management

Using a diary, record all of the work/leisure activities that you do in a one-week period. Make a note of all of the opportunities that you have to study in that one-week period.

Which of the modes of learning listed below would suit your circumstances? Use the definitions given to help you to select your preferences:

- Daytime – typically three hours (9.00–12.00 and 13.00–16.00).
- Evening – typically three hours (17.00–20.00).
- Weekend – typically Saturday (9.00–17.00).
- Distance learning – initial lecture, tutorial, online materials.
- E-learning – online materials, blogs, wikis.

As Nichols (2007) notes, presenting students with choices regarding when, where and how to learn can be daunting, particularly for those returning to study after several years or those engaging in placement-based courses for the first time. Flexible approaches of this nature require that you create and manage individual learning plans (ILPs), thus shifting responsibility for course design, within set parameters, to you as the learner. In order to construct an ILP you will need to be able to understand the differences between the modes of delivery and recognise the skills necessary to engage successfully with a module delivered in this way. It is worth noting that those practitioners/trainees attending the classroom might also encounter a different learning and teaching experience to those accessing e-learning materials online or distance learning packages and you may wish to take this into consideration when selecting the way that you will study.

Academic counselling to assist you in understanding the demands of the modes of study and signposting appropriate options to meet your individual needs is of paramount importance; on many work-based programmes this is a pre-requisite to commencing the course. However, it could be argued that this in some respects undermines the whole ethos of a flexible approach to learning whereby you as the student can/should determine your own pattern of study.

Reflective task: Thinking about the advantages and disadvantages of e-learning and classroom based learning

- Make a list of the advantages and disadvantages of e-learning and classroom based learning.
- What skills and knowledge would you need to access these different types of learning opportunities?
- Work with a colleague or peer and compare your findings. What are the similarities and differences?

In adopting this student-centred approach, and allowing you to select the way that you study and have greater control of your learning, you as the learner must also recognise and consider your individual academic needs when selecting how, when and where to study. Consideration needs to be given to what is appropriate in terms of your personal attributes, skill sets and academic ability in order that you might achieve your academic potential and to avoid 'setting yourself up to fail'.

As O'Donnell *et al.* (2009) highlight, students' needs and abilities are diverse, hence 'one size does not fit all', and you may find some of the different types of delivery more useful than others in facilitating the learning process.

Case study: Thinking about flexible study patterns

Critically reflect on the different case studies below. How could the individual needs of these students be matched to flexible learning modes? What are the barriers to meeting these individual requirements? What strategies can be used to address these issues?

Case Study 1: Early years worker

Claire is working in a private day care nursery as a room leader in the baby unit. She manages a group of staff caring for infants aged 3–12 months. She completed her Level 3 BTEC qualification two years ago but needs to improve her qualifications if she is to advance her career; her long-term aim is to become an EYT. Claire works different shifts each week. Her shift patterns are 7.30–16.00 and 8.30–18.30 with an hour break for lunch. Claire still lives at home with her parents and enjoys playing netball for her local team at the weekends.

Case Study 2: Teaching assistant

Mohammed works as a teaching assistant in a large inner city primary school with children in Year 6 and is the coach for the school football team. Mohammed has been at the school for seven years and works from 08.30–16.00 and one evening 16.00–17.30 each week. Mohammed recently completed his HLTA and has ambitions to become a primary school teacher. He currently covers classes twice a week when the Year 6 teacher is on PPA.

Case Study 3: College adviser

Jo has been working at the college for ten years and has had a range of roles during this time. She currently acts as an adviser for students on a range of personal issues, signposting students to appropriate agencies. As part of her job Jo keeps a database of student details that she updates frequently. She works 08.30–17.00 but often stays much later to deal with 'student issues'. She completed her NVQ qualification 10 years ago but needs to update her qualification if she is to gain promotion at the college. Jo is part of the local theatre group who meet weekly.

Case Study 4: Health care assistant

Peter is a health care assistant at a health centre; he completed his Advanced Diploma in Childcare and Education 12 years ago but is keen to update his qualification. Peter visits parents and their new-born infants in the home to offer support, advice and guidance in the child's first year and also works alongside the health visitors in weekly clinics in the health centre. He works from 08.30–17.30 each day. Peter is the sole carer for his son who is six years old.

Employer involvement

While employer involvement is an essential feature of work-based learning programmes it has been noted that the commitment of employers can be difficult to secure (Smith and Betts, 2003). The priorities of employers and employees in CYPS may differ significantly and this may impact on the accessibility of the various modes of delivery for those in training/work. The business needs and organisational aims of employers often appear to those training/working in CYPS to supersede the learning needs of students, despite the benefits to service provision of well qualified and trained staff (Gleeson and Kemp, 2004). Therefore it is crucial to secure the commitment of your employer/manager of the setting if you are studying on a work-based course as they are the 'gatekeepers' to quality work-based learning opportunities and often influence the study patterns of learners and opportunities in the setting to complete assessments. Employers may act as work-based mentors in the setting to help you in your programme of study and might:

- enable some flexibility in your working patterns to allow for study time;
- support professional development planning;
- contribute to fees;
- offer advice on work-based assessments; or
- direct you to sources of information (professional/academic) to support your studies.

Learning, teaching and assessment

Traditionally in education the relationship between the learner and teacher has been through a pedagogic approach whereby the teacher gives students a structure and high levels of support that fosters the confidence in learners to engage in study (Hase and Kenyon, 2000). The teacher decides what the learner needs to know and how the knowledge and skills necessary will be taught.

The variety of teaching methods used to facilitate learning on work-based programmes that include a range of different modes of delivery and provide a flexible curriculum are based on the notion of reflective practice (see Chapter 10) and self-directedness. By providing this flexible learning curriculum, there is necessarily a shift from a pedagogical approach, where you as the student are dependent and passive in the learning process, and the mantle of responsibility for learning lies with the teacher, to an andragogical model that expects you as the student to take control of your own learning, recognising the limits of your knowledge and motivating yourself to learn (Knowles, 1970; Paraskevas and Wickens, 2003).

Reflective task: Defining the differences between pedagogy and andragogy

Pedagogy offers students a clear framework for their studies. It is governed by the teacher and gives students a structure and high levels of support that fosters the confidence in learners to engage in study. A pedagogical approach is based on the following:

- the student is dependent and has little experience;
- students need extrinsic motivation and are motivated by external pressures, competitiveness and the consequences of failure;
- the teacher directs students in order to learn and progress and learning is a process prescribed by the teacher; and
- the teacher assumes full responsibility for learning and evaluates the process.

Andragogy emphasises the self-direction of motivated students and encourages a critical reflective approach to learning. An andragogical approach is governed by the following:

- the student is self-directed, reflective and responsible for their own learning;
- the students have a wealth of diverse quality experiences and are a rich resource for each other;
- the student wants to improve their performance and can identify gaps in their knowledge;
- learning is relevant to work/training situations;
- students are intrinsically motivated to learn; and
- the teacher acts as a facilitator.

Using the information above, reflect on these different approaches to learning and teaching. What are the advantages/disadvantages of each approach? Reflect on your personal abilities, skills and attributes. Which approach would suit your individual study needs at this point in time? Why?

Reece and Walker (2007) argue that the shift from pedagogy to andragogy could create some difficulties for students, many of whom will only have experienced learning and teaching that is prescribed by the teacher. Arguably an approach that is governed by the teacher might, in the early phases of the course, give students a structure and the high levels of support that fosters the confidence in learners to engage in study at higher education institutes (HEIs). However, it is acknowledged that passive learning of this nature that is teacher dependent is not generally conducive to adult learning and will not facilitate the notion of reflective practice that underpins work-based learning approaches (Scales, 2008).

Hence, within the higher education classroom, there has been a shift towards andragogic teaching methods such as the '**Socratic Seminar**' that employs strategies such as discussions, simulations, case studies and role-playing that are perceived to be fundamental to the learning process and you will encounter these types of learning and teaching approaches on most work-based courses. These methods emphasise active learning and the sharing of knowledge in order to help learners to progress from the recognition and recall of knowledge to the higher-order complex thinking tasks required in real life of analysis, evaluation and synthesis as identified by Bloom (1960) in his Learning Taxonomy (Petty, 2004).

Activity: Thinking about learning and teaching approaches

Work with a colleague/peer to thought shower how you might use the following learning and teaching approaches to enhance practice as a practitioner/trainee in the workplace:

Method	What is it?	Example
Case study	An examination of a real or simulated problem structured so that learning can take place	A young person is self-harming and confides in a mentor at college. Are/ should the parents be informed?
Simulation	A replication of a real or possible situation	Prioritising or time management in a simulated situation
Role play	Practitioners/trainees act out a role in events	An incident where a child/young person is disadvantaged due to race, gender or disability
Discussion	Students are actively involved in talking to each other about issues that concern all parties	Exploring attitudes such as the treatment of young offenders with medication to prevent re-offending

---

Communities of practice

This social learning model, which includes the use of andragogic learning and teaching methods, was initially proposed by Lave and Wenger (1990) and views learning as a collective process that takes place in a 'community of practice'. Wenger (1998: 73) argues that there are three strands of this approach that enables learning to take place through these communities of practice:

- *Mutual engagement.* Shared practice (the same job and challenges) means that everyone encounters similar issues, ideas and problems thus everyone is keen to engage in the learning process.
- *A joint enterprise.* Community members who share a profession thus respond to situations in a similar way and often have shared aims, ideals and challenges and a mutual understanding.
- *A shared repertoire.* Everyone uses the same terminology and has similar ways of doing things that has been adopted by the community, hence participation is open to all. (Faulconbridge, 2005: 125)

Learning is seen as occurring when individuals 'compare and enrich interpretations' (Wenger, McDermott and Snyder, 2002: 64) and unconsciously learn from discussion, hence co-constructing learning. This particular model is considered as particularly pertinent in the teaching of work-based programmes such as Foundation Degrees and Higher Apprenticeships as there is an emphasis on work-based experiential learning with learning being seen as a social activity. There is a range of ways that you can be part of communities of practice to support your studies; these include setting up a wiki, discussion board or Facebook page to share ideas and experiences with others on your course. You could also organise a study group to share knowledge and discuss the learning that is taking place on the course that you are on.

Activity: Exploring communities of practice

Wenger (2006: 1) suggests that 'communities of practice are groups of people who share a concern or a passion for something they do and learn how to do it better as they interact regularly'.
   Visit http://tinyurl.com/ar9f9hs to develop an understanding of the characteristics of communities of practice. Make personal notes to support your understanding.

As a student on a work-based learning programme, you would be expected to go beyond the acquisition of knowledge and skills and develop the capacity to critically reflect upon practice, challenging accepted theories, views and opinions, and acting proactively to improve practice in CYPS (see Brookfield's *Four Lenses*, 1995). Furthermore, as an active learner you would be expected to demonstrate the ability to reflect upon and question personal values and assumptions that influence your views and opinions, and hence practice with children and young people (Argyris and Schön, 1996).

   The wide range of learning, teaching and assessment methods used on work-based programmes are designed to support you in developing these attributes and, as an active learner, help you to become a 'capable' person (Stephenson and Weil, 1992) with the ability to use the competencies that you have to work effectively with a range of professionals across CYPS. Examples of these different assessment methods are offered in Figure 3.1.

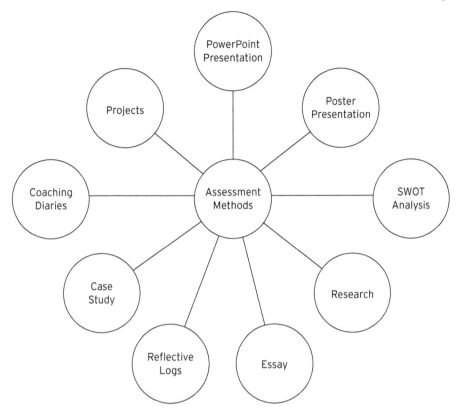

Figure 3.1 Assessment methods for work-based learning

Conclusion

This chapter has explored the flexible teaching approaches that are used to facilitate learning on many work-based degree programmes. While a range of flexible teaching strategies have been discussed, it is essential to acknowledge that all those training or working in CYPS have different academic, personal and professional circumstances and you have to ascertain the model that is appropriate to meet your individual needs.

Areas for further consideration

There are a number of other areas for consideration which you may wish to explore as part of your own personal study. The suggestions below merely offer a select number of aspects which will help to further develop your understanding of work-based learning:

Accessing available funding	Building professional relationships with peers in the classroom
Work-based learning and the 'critical friend'	Challenging one's own professional practice
Learning to learn	Professional Development Portfolios

Further reading

Books

Moon, J. (1999) *Reflection in Learning and Professional Development: Theory and practice.* London: RoutledgeFalmer.
This book explores reflection and its value in improving learning and professional practice. Chapter 3 - Reflection in Experiential Learning - considers the role of reflection in learning from experience, and in professional practice.

Reece, I. and Walker, S. (2007) *Teaching, Training and Learning.* 6th edn. Tyne and Wear: Business Education Publishers.
This book explores teaching, training and learning in the lifelong learning sector. Chapter 1.4 - Models of Learning - is particularly interesting as it examines a range of learning theories and identifies the characteristics of an andragogical approach to learning and teaching.

Academic publications

Li, L., Grimshaw, J. M., Neilsen, C., Judd, M., Coyte, P. C. and Graham, I. D. (2009) Evolution of Wenger's Concept of Community of Practice. *Implementation Science*, 4(11), 1–8. [Online]. Available at: http://tinyurl.com/bfcthdz (Accessed: 11 January 2013).
This paper explores the experiences of health professionals in the workplace engaging in learning and information sharing through informal groups and networks. Communities of practice are investigated in terms of knowledge exchange and building a sense of belonging within teams/networks and groups.

McGrath, V. (2009) Reviewing the Evidence on How Adult Students Learn: An examination of Knowles' model of andragogy. *Adult Learner: The Irish Journal of Adult and Community Education.* pp. 99–110. [Online]. Available at: http://tinyurl.com/bzos59k (Accessed: 10 January 2013).
This article reviews how adults learn by exploring the learning theory proposed by Knowles known as andragogy. The use of student experiences to contribute to the learning process in the classroom is examined.

Website

The Department for Education (DfE): a resource that will keep you up to date with changes at a national level. Available at: www.dfe.gov.uk.
Please note that although this is an education website, information regarding changes in services across the 0–19 sector can be found at this site.

References

Argyris, C. and Schön, D. (1996) *Organisational Learning II.* Reading: Addison-Wesley.

Beaney, P. (2006) *Researching Foundation Degrees: Linking research and practice.* London: Foundation Degree Forward.

Blatchford, P., Webster, R. and Russell, A. (2012) *Challenging the Role and Deployment of Teaching Assistants in Mainstream Schools: The impact on schools.* [Online]. Available at: http://tinyurl.com/a5kbs9x (Accessed: 10 December 2012).

Brookfield, S. (1995) *Becoming a Critically Reflective Teacher.* San-Francisco: Jossey-Bass.

Butt, G. and Lance, A. (2009) 'I am not a teacher': some effects of remodelling the roles of teaching assistants in English primary schools. *Education 3-13: International Journal of Primary, Elementary and Early Years Education*, 37 (3), 219-231.

Children's Workforce Development Council (2010) *Common Core of Skills and Knowledge*. [Online]. Available at: http://tinyurl.com/byafaaq (Accessed: 20 December 2012).

Department for Children, Schools and Families (2005) *Children and Young People's Workforce Strategy: A strategy to build a world-class workforce for children and young people*. [Online]. Available at: http://tinyurl.com/8dv89gw (Accessed: 20 December 2012).

——(2008) *2020 Children and Young People's Workforce Strategy*. [Online]. Available at: http://tinyurl.com/cu97k7u (Accessed: 20 December 2012).

Department for Education (2011) *Positive for Youth: A new approach to cross-government policy for young people aged 13 to 19*. London: Crown. [Online]. Available at: http://tinyurl.com/aw6h6gs (Accessed: 10 January 2013).

——(2012a) *Foundations for Quality: The independent review of early education and childcare qualifications* (Nutbrown Review). [Online]. Available at: http://tinyurl.com/ax7jby3 (Accessed: 10 January 2013).

——(2012b) *Early Years Professional Status Standards*. [Online]. Available at: http://tinyurl.com/98dw43g (Accessed: 18 December 2012).

——(2013) *More Great Childcare: Raising quality and giving parents more choice*. [Online]. Available at: http://tinyurl.com/cyz4ny4 (Accessed: 17 May 2013).

Department for Education and Skills (2002) *Time for Standards: Reforming the schools workforce*. London: HMSO.

——(2003) *Every Child Matters: Change for Children*. London: HMSO. [Online]. Available at: http://tinyurl.com/6dnfz93 (Accessed: 10 December 2012).

——(2004) *The Children Act*. [Online]. Available at: http://tinyurl.com/aml2pgj (Accessed: 20 December 2012).

——(2005) *Children's Workforce Strategy: A strategy to build a world-class workforce for children and young people*. [Online]. Available at: http://tinyurl.com/8dv89gw (Accessed: 18 December 2012).

Durrant, A., Rhodes, G. and Young, D. (2009) *Getting Started with University-Level Work Based Learning*. Middlesex: Middlesex University Press.

Edmond, N. and Price, M. (2009) Workforce remodelling and Pastoral Care in Schools: a diversification of roles or a de-professionalisation of functions? *Pastoral Care in Education: An International Journal of Personal, Social and Emotional Development*, 27 (4), 301-311.

Faulconbridge, J. R. (2005) *Local-global Geographies of Tacit Knowledge Production in London and New York's Advertising and Law Professional Service Firms*. PhD Thesis: Loughborough University.

Gleeson, D. and Keep, E. (2004) Voice without Accountability: the changing relationship between employers, the State and education in England. *Oxford Review of Education*, 30 (1), 37-63.

Hase, S. and Kenyon, C. (2000) From Andragogy to Heutagogy. Southern Cross University: *ultiBASE Articles*. [Online]. Available at: http://tinyurl.com/bs2xk9d (Accessed: 20 December 2012).

Hill, J. (2006) Flexible Learning Environments: Leveraging the affordances of flexible delivery and flexible learning. *Journal of Higher Education*, 31 (3), 187-197.

Knowles, M. (1970) *The Modern Practice of Adult Education: Andragogy versus Pedagogy*. New York: Cambridge Books.

——(1978) *The Adult Learner: A Neglected Species*. Houston, TX: Gulf Publishing Co.

——(1980) *The Modern Practice of Adult Education: From pedagogy to andragogy*. 2nd edn. New York: Cambridge Books.

Lave, J. and Wenger, E. (1990) *Situated Learning: Legitimate peripheral participation*. Cambridge: Cambridge University Press.

Nichols, M. (2007) Comparing Modes of Study: A perspective on Hagel and Shaw's 'Students Perceptions of Study Modes'. *Distance Education*, 28 (3), 371-376.

O'Donnell, V. L., Tobbell, J., Lawthom, R. and Zammit, M. (2009) Transition to Postgraduate Study: Practice, Participation and the Widening Participation Agenda. *Active Learning in Higher Education*, 10 (26), 26-40.

Paraskevas, A. and Wickens, E. (2003) Andragogy and the Socratic Method: The Adult Learner Perspective. *Journal of Hospitality, Leisure, Sport and Tourism Education*, 2 (2), 4-13.

Petty, G. (2004) *Teaching Today*. 3rd edn. Cheltenham: Nelson Thornes.

Quality Assurance Agency for Higher Education (2010) *Foundation Degree qualification benchmark*. 2nd edn. Gloucester: QAA. [Online]. Available at: http://tinyurl.com/cpyr6wc (Accessed: 20 January 2012).

Reece, I. and Walker, S. (2007) *Teaching, Training and Learning: A Practical Guide*. 6th edn. Tyne and Wear: Business Education Publishers.

Scales, P. (2008) *Teaching in the Lifelong Learning Sector*. Berkshire: Open University Press.

Smith, R. and Betts, M. (2003) Partnerships and the Consortia Approach to United Kingdom Foundation Degrees: A case study of benefits and pitfalls. *Journal of Vocational Training*, 55 (2), 223-238.

Snape, D., Parfrement, J. and Finch, S. (2007) *Evaluation of the Early Years Sector-Endorsed Foundation Degree Findings from the Final Student Survey*. London: DfES.

Stephenson, J. (1994) 'Capability and Competence: Are they the same and does it matter?' *Capability*, 1(1), 3-4.

Stephenson, J. and Weil, S. (1992) *Quality in Learning: A capability approach in higher education*. London: Kogan Page.

Sylva, K., Melluish, E., Sammons, P., Siraj-Blatchford, I. and Taggart, B. (2004) *The Effective Provision of Pre-School Education (EPPE) Project: Final Report*. London: DfES.

Thurgate, C., MacGregor, J. and Brett, H. (2007) The Lived Experience: delivering a foundation degree in health and social care. *Journal of Further and Higher Education*, 31 (3), 215-223.

Training and Development Agency for Schools (2006) *Professional Standards for Higher Level Teaching Assistants*. [Online]. Available at: http://tinyurl.com/aqyqflg (Accessed: 18 December 2012).

——(2007) *Higher Level Teaching Assistant Handbook* [Online]. Available at: http://tinyurl.com/be9yzhd (Accessed: 7 January 2013).

——(2009) *A Foundation Degree Framework for the Children's Workforce in Schools*. London: TDA.

Wenger, E. (1998) *Communities of Practice: Learning, Meaning and Identity*. Cambridge: Cambridge University Press.

——(2006) *Communities of practice – a brief introduction*. [Online]. Available at: http://tinyurl.com/ar9f9hs (Accessed: 21 January 2013).

Wenger, E., McDermott, R. and Snyder, W. M. (2002) *Cultivating Communities of Practice*. Boston, Massachusetts: Harvard Business School Press.

4 'The Researcher and the Researched': Ethical research in Children's and Young People's Services

Simon Brownhill

Introduction

In all sectors across Children's and Young People's Services (CYPS) there are an increasing number of practitioners and those training who are actively engaged in work-based research to support continuing and initial professional development, inform change, and improve provision and practice. From early years practitioners seeking to establish the most effective ways of inducting new children into their settings, to youth practitioners evaluating the delivery of programmes to support 'at risk' groups, research allows people to:

- find something out;
- evaluate something;
- find out if something works; or
- improve your own or others' practice. (adapted from Thomas, 2009: 4)

While this research is seemingly of both personal and professional benefit, it has resulted in 'a growing awareness of ethical issues' (Burton, Brundrett and Jones, 2008: 51) as human rights, data protection and public accountability become ever emphasised and scrutinised features of today's society.

Reflective task: Gaining an awareness

Download a free copy of either:

- *The Ethics of Social Research with Children and Families in Young Lives: Practical experiences* by Morrow (2009) - available at http://tinyurl.com/82j3pw9; or
- *Research with Children and Young People: Exploring the tensions between ethics, competence and participation* by Skelton (2008) - available at: http://tinyurl.com/c2kr6bs.

Reflect on its content, identifying *five* key pieces of information which support you in your knowledge and understanding of the increased attention paid to the ethics of social research (research involving people) over the last few decades.

This chapter will focus its attention on exploring select ethical concepts including privacy, incentives and the right to withdraw, which shape the way that ethical research is undertaken across the 0–19 sector. While the participation and protection of research participants is a key consideration within this chapter, an exploration of the need to also protect the researcher is made to promote a 'heightened [sense] of knowing and doing' (Murray and Lawrence, 2000: 21) for all involved in research activity. The chapter begins by highlighting research legislation which underpins and informs quality ethical practice with children, young people, families and communities.

Research legislation

There are numerous national research governance policies and relevant legislation which you should be aware of prior to engaging with any kind of research work. The Social Research Association (SRA) (2003: 15) supports this by stating that:

> Researchers have an obligation to ensure that they are informed about the appropriate legislation of the country in which they are conducting research and how that legislation might affect the conduct of their research. Researchers should not knowingly contravene such legislation.

In the United States, 'human research is governed by specific legislation in the form of the National Research Act (1974) coupled with quasi-official guidelines contained in the Belmont Report (1978)' (Denscombe, 2005). In the United Kingdom, national legislation includes the Human Rights Act (1998), the Data Protection Act (1998), the Freedom of Information Act (2000) and the Health and Social Care Act (2008). The *Code of Practice for Research* (UK Research Integrity Office [UKRIO], 2009) and the *Research Governance Framework for Health and Social Care* (Department of Health [DoH], 2008) serve as examples of pertinent legislation which have 'been designed to encourage good conduct in research and help prevent misconduct' (UKRIO, 2009: 4). While it is not essential that you should acquire an extensive knowledge of the above, it is strongly advocated that you should demonstrate an *awareness* of national policy and legislation by actively searching for and engaging with relevant documentation.

Activity: Engaging with national policy and legislation

Select any two of the national policies/legislation which are pertinent to the service you work/ train in, making personal notes to demonstrate your awareness and engagement with this documentation:

Policy/Legislation	Web link
Human Rights Act (1998)	Available from www.legislation.
Data Protection Act (1998)	gov.uk/ using the *Search* facility
Freedom of Information Act (2000)	to locate the pertinent Act
Health and Social Care Act (2008)	
Code of Practice for Research (UKRIO, 2009)	http://tinyurl.com/7deojxl
Research Governance Framework for Health and Social Care (DoH, 2008)	http://tinyurl.com/35q3wkv

You may wish to search and reflect on the content of the *Executive Summaries* of the policies/ legislation above (also available online).

Because of the kind of research you are likely to undertake, careful consideration is needed to 'protect the interests, status, values and beliefs of all participants and organisations... from harm (e.g. physical, social, psychological, professional)' (Sharp, 2009: 22). Efforts to assure this are influenced not only by legislation but by two key ethical principles which are fundamental to all research activity – *beneficence* and *non-maleficence*.

Beneficence and non-maleficence

The terms above are likely to be new to you. In simple terms they refer to the notion of 'doing' – *doing good* (beneficence) and *not doing harm* (non-maleficence). Tooth, Lutfiyya and Sokal (2007: 4) state that 'the principle of **beneficence** imposes a duty to benefit others and, in research ethics, a duty to maximize net benefits'. This encourages you to think about the *value* of your research, not just for yourself but for those participating in your project. **Non-maleficence** is defined by Haight (2006: 8) as 'the ethical principle that holds that [researchers] must not make matters worse'. In the medical profession the notion of *not doing harm* is one which is required of all doctors; this requirement is one which should also apply to *your* research as it urges you to think about the *potential harm* your research could cause, not only to yourself but for those taking part, the setting and the wider community.

Case study: Thinking about beneficence and non-maleficence

Reflect on the case studies below, considering the *value* of Hassan's proposed research (Case Study 1) and any *potential harm* which may be caused by Maggie's proposed research (Case Study 2).

Case Study 1:

Hassan is working as a student Teaching Assistant in a Year 4 class (8-9 year olds) in a large inner city primary school. Many of the children at the school speak English as an Additional Language (EAL) and staff attribute this as a contributing factor to the low attainment in **oracy** (speaking and listening) across the school. Hassan wants to undertake some research to find ways to promote oracy development through outdoor physical activity, particularly as the school is trying to address worrying trends relating to levels of childhood obesity in the local community.

Case Study 2:

Maggie has been working as a full-time member of a Youth Offending Team (YOT) for 15 years. She enjoys what she calls 'the lovely multi-agency make-up' of the team she works in but has recently begun to feel that the needs of victims and their families are not being met; she believes that certain team members from the police and health services are more interested in supporting those who are at risk of reoffending. Maggie wants to undertake some research to gauge the commitment of team members to the overarching aims and objectives of the YOT by getting the team to reflect on their practice, highlighting any aims or objectives they feel are not being fully embraced through their team contributions.

It is recommended that when you start thinking about the research you would like to undertake you make reference to Table 4.1. It offers some supportive reflective questions to help you think critically about the notion of 'doing' linked to your potential project.

Table 4.1 Thinking critically about 'doing good' and 'not doing harm' when engaged in research activity

Doing good (beneficence)	*Not doing harm* (non-maleficence)
Will my research help to improve my own and others' *knowledge/understanding/skills/attitudes*?	Does my research carry any *physical risks* for participants (e.g. physical activity, consumption of a substance, e.g. food or drink)?
Is my research hopefully going to improve *practice* in my setting/placement?	Might my research cause *personal/professional tensions* between staff members/service users?
Might my research change *policy* in my place of work/placement?	Is my research likely to *invade a participant's privacy* or *breach assurances of confidentiality*?
Could my research *positively address an issue* in my setting/placement?	To what extent will my research *challenge people's perceptions* or *values*?
Will my research *give participants 'a voice'*?	Are there any *psychological risks* involved in my research (e.g. emotional discomfort, stress)?

Once you have considered the principles of beneficence and non-maleficence, reference should be made to relevant guidelines that 'identify certain norms and standards of behaviour that researchers are expected to follow' (Connolly, 2003: 4). It is to these *ethical guidelines* that this chapter turns its attention.

Ethical guidelines

There are many examples of ethical guidelines which are offered by professional societies, organisations and research associations to help those undertaking research to shape their professional code of conduct (see, for example, The British Psychological Society [BPS], 2010; NSPCC, 2011). Ethical guidelines have long been recognised as a central element in scientific and medical research (see the World Medical Association [WMA], 2005; the Nursing and Midwifery Council, 2008). Within an educational context valuable ethical guidelines are offered by the British Educational Research Association (BERA) (2011) and the Scottish Educational Research Association (SERA) (2005). For those working with young people within a sporting context, e.g. extended school sports leaders and health and fitness providers, reference to *The BASES* ([The] British Association of Sport and Exercise Sciences) *Expert Statement on Ethics and Participation in Research of Young People* (2011) is strongly recommended. The SRA (2003) and the Joint University Council Social Work Education Committee (JUCSWEC) (2002) offer valuable guidelines which serve as useful prompts and pointers for those within a health and social care context. Those who work with young people are likely to be aware of the National Youth Agency's (NYA) (2004) *Ethical Conduct in Youth Work* but it is important to remember that these values and principles relate to the professional working behaviours of youth practitioners as opposed to ethical behaviours linked to research activities (for information, see Banks, 2010; Bradford and Cullen, 2011).

The select guidelines offered above are by no means designed to be 'authoritarian or rigidly prescriptive' (SRA, 2003: 11) in content, but serve to be informative and useful for researchers. What is important to remember is that these ethical guidelines will not give you *the* answer with regard to addressing the 'ethical dilemmas' that are specific to your research project; it is ultimately *you* who will have to make decisions linked to these (obviously with support from your tutors/supervisors at college/university). Menter *et al.* (2011: 53) claim that all institutions (colleges, universities, other agencies that carry out research) have 'instituted a framework for scrutinising and checking that research designs have been developed in line with good ethical practice'. This means that it is most likely that you will have to write an *ethics proposal* that gives details about your research project. You will only be able to initiate work on your research project once you have been given ethical approval by your institution's Ethics Committee. Talk to your tutors/supervisors about the process of gaining institutional ethical approval for your research project in terms of the documentation which needs to be completed and timeframes when these committees meet; your tutors/supervisors will also be able to make you aware of any policies or Codes of Practice from your institution which you may have to read and reflect on as part of the ethical approval process.

It is appreciated that new researchers may be a little overwhelmed by some of the content of the ethical guidelines which have been previously highlighted; it is recommended that you make reference to the remainder of this chapter *before* exploring relevant ethical guidelines so that you have an informed and digestible overview of a range of ethical considerations which are likely to impact on your research work in CYPS.

Ethical considerations

Silverman (2011) gives mention to a number of *ethical dimensions* which need to be considered by researchers to ensure levels of respect and honesty to research participants are adhered to. Dimensions (which for the purposes of this chapter will be referred to as 'considerations') that will be explored in this chapter, in turn, include:

- informed consent;
- privacy – anonymity and confidentiality;
- incentives;
- the right to withdraw; and
- the protection of the researcher.

Informed consent

Greig, Taylor and MacKay (2007: 174) highlight that 'one of the common factors in all ethical considerations... is the need to gain informed consent from research participants'. **Informed consent** means participants are given 'sufficient and accessible information' (Gray, 2009: 75) about the research project so that they can make an *informed* decision about whether to take part or not. Informed consent is particularly important for research undertaken in CYPS because your research is likely to involve participants who may be considered 'vulnerable', e.g. children (largely because of their age) and some categories of adult, including those with disabilities, those who are ill, and those who have undergone traumatic or adverse emotional events such as domestic abuse (see Stafford and Smith, 2009). The consent of participants can be obtained in two different ways:

- *verbal means* including face-to-face discussions, telephone conversations and meetings; and
- *written means* including letters, information sheets, forms, notes, reply slips and statements.

This raises an interesting consideration about what you should say/write to gain the informed consent of participants.

Reflective task: What do they need to know?

Take a piece of paper and write down as many things that *you* would want to know about a research project if you were approached to take part in one. Compare your list to the suggestions offered below:

The aim(s) of the research	Name(s) of the person undertaking the research and their organisation base (college/university/setting)	Who is being invited to take part in the research and why
The kind of information being sought	The amount of time required of participants to take part in the research	Who will have access to the research data once it is collected
How the privacy of participants will be preserved	Contact details of the researcher so participants can make contact with them if necessary	Who should the research data be returned to and when (*if using a postal questionnaire*)

Any information you present to participants should be clear, concise and succinct; if you are vague or confusing about your research then you are likely to put people off taking part. This level of clarity is especially important when trying to gain the informed consent of certain groups of people. For example:

- Young children, young people with disabilities, and family members with low **literacy** skills may be unable to read any written research documentation you prepare. Think carefully about the most appropriate way of gaining informed consent from these different groups.
- If your research involves young children who attend the private day nursery you work/train at, who should give informed consent – the children themselves? Their parents/carers? The manager/owner of the setting? *Good practice advocates all three!*
  - You should seek permission to undertake your research from your employers/placement (the 'gatekeepers') *before* you approach parents/carers and children.
  - UNICEF (2002: 5) suggest that while parental(/carer) consent is important it 'is not an adequate standard in light of the rights of the child'; this means that researchers should gain informed *assent (Declaration of Helsinki* – WMA, 2008) which means that children themselves agree to take part in the research.
- Research which involves young people does not necessarily need parental consent *if* the young person has 'sufficient maturity to understand the nature, purposes and likely outcome of the proposed research' (Greig, Taylor and MacKay, 2007: 177). If this is difficult to ascertain do seek the consent of both the young person and their parents/carers.

One of the reasons why participants decide not to be involved in research is because they are anxious about their loss of privacy and the assurances (or lack of) that are offered by researchers to protect this. In an effort to ensure that this does not impact on participants being involved in your research an exploration of this ethical consideration is offered below.

Privacy

Howe and Moses (1999: 25) consider privacy as having 'an intrinsic value tied to human dignity and security' and acts as a basic human need. There are two ways in which we can protect participants' privacy: *anonymity* and *confidentiality*.

1 Anonymity

Anonymity means 'without a name' and refers to the way in which your research is written up. Denscombe (2010: 65) suggests researchers avoid presenting research findings (e.g. in projects, dissertations, theses, or reports) 'which allow individuals or organizations to be identified by name'. This raises an important point: anonymity does not just serve to protect the real names of people but operates to protect the names of settings (e.g. your place of work/placement), businesses and organisations (e.g. the institution you are studying at) which may be involved in your research. All research participants have the right to remain anonymous and there are a number of reasons for this (e.g. personal, professional, legal, child protection) which participants *do not have to disclose to you*. What is important is that you are aware of different strategies to preserve participants' true identities.

Research participants can also be anonymised through the use of **pseudonyms**. A pseudonym is a 'name change' – the children's book *Alice's Adventures in Wonderland*, for example, was written by Reverend Charles Lutwidge Dodgson who wrote under the pseudonym Lewis Carroll.

Case study: Using pseudonyms

Critically reflect on the way pseudonyms are used to protect the identities of colleagues and the setting in the case study below.

Fiona is an infant teacher in a small rural primary school. She works in close proximity with six other teaching colleagues. Fiona undertook a small piece of research to compare the views of her colleagues about a new strategy for teaching phonics which was being piloted by the local authority. By conducting individual interviews Fiona found that there was a clear divide in opinion about the value of the strategy and its impact. In an effort to protect the identity of her colleagues Fiona replaced their names with gender appropriate alternatives when quoting from their respective interview transcript: Ruth became *Dawn*; Lynda became *Sally*. Fiona took great care to protect the name of her school where she undertook the research, replacing it with a rather generic invented name – *Rushwood Primary School*.

Angrosino (2007) describes pseudonyms as an example of a **code** that researchers can use when describing people; other codes include digits (*1, 2, 3*) or letters of the alphabet (*A, B, C*). Take care when using letters of the alphabet as there is sometimes a tendency for new researchers to use the initials of a participant as the code, e.g. *Barry Prichard* is replaced with the letters *BP*; if your research seeks the views of colleagues in the social care setting where you work/are placed in and you use initials as your coding mechanism, you run the risk of inadvertently identifying participants, particularly if there is only one person in your setting that has the initials BP – Barry thus becomes easily recognisable!

Activity: Addressing problematic issues which threaten anonymity

Select one of the two scenarios below and work with your colleagues/peers to thought shower what you could do to manage the particular issue being presented. Share your thoughts with your tutors or undertake some professional/academic readings to support your practical management of the issue being proposed:

1   If you are sending out an anonymous questionnaire to workers in several residential children's homes and you would like to send those completing it a summary of your main findings, how will you know who to send it to if they do not disclose their name and address?
2   If you are conducting a focus group discussion with a group of youth work volunteers and only one of the participants is male how will you ensure that their contributions are not easily distinguishable?

Henn, Weinstein and Foard (2006) argue it is extremely problematic to assure research participant anonymity, largely because of the close proximity between the researcher and the research participants. It is thus deemed necessary for researchers to assure participants of a high degree of *confidentiality*.

2 Confidentiality

Babbie (2010: 67) states that '[a] research project guarantees **confidentiality** when the researcher can identify a given person's responses but essentially promises not to do so publically'. This means that only you are able to identify the responses of individuals in your project; those outside of your research (e.g. tutors, supervisors, colleagues, peers) should not be able to 'connect' research participants with their responses. Lewis (in Richie and Lewis, 2003) offers further insight into this by highlighting the need for researchers to avoid the following in their research reporting:

● *Direct attribution* – comments linked to a name or a location, e.g. the identity of participants or the place where the research was conducted.
● *Indirect attribution* – reference to a collection of characteristics that might identify an individual or small group, e.g. a newly employed drug and alcohol worker in a particular local authority or mature male foster carers in the Manchester area.

The inadvertent disclosure of this information to others can be potentially harmful to participants, e.g. damaging a family member's personal reputation or the professional standing of a practitioner. It is, however, important to remember that participants may inform you of something which implicates either them or another person, examples of which include illegal activities, serious physical or mental health problems, child abuse or neglect. The data collected for your project does not enjoy 'legal privilege' which means that you have a duty of care to inform others *if necessary*. The decision to breach assurances of confidentiality should be made in consultation with your tutor or supervisor to ensure that appropriate procedures are followed and necessary individuals are informed. It is thus suggested that when seeking consent you need to explain the *limits of confidentiality* linked to your research – see http://tinyurl.com/cgfcemf for further information.

Activity: Collecting, storing, and using shared information

The confidentiality of participants is usually achieved by restricting the access other people have to the research data you have collected. All researchers are bound by the legal requirements established in the Data Protection Act (1998) in relation to the storage and use of personal data. Select one of the three readings below, identifying practical ways to assure a 'lock-and-key mentality' (Descombe, 2010: 66) with regard to the safe keeping of the data collected from your research:

- Book chapter: Respect for rights: privacy and confidentiality (Chapter 3) In *The Ethics of Research with Children and Young People* (Alderson and Morrow, 2011 – see pp. 36-39).
- Academic guidance: *Data Protection in Research* (Canterbury Christ Church, 2006) –available at: http://tinyurl.com/bmz6gwy.
- Online resource: *The practical guide to data protection* (Harding, 2003) – available at: http://tinyurl.com/blqaswa.

One of the ways to recruit research participants is through the use of *incentives*. It is important, however, to consider the ethical issues relating to their usage.

Incentives

Take a moment to ask yourself the following: *why would children, young people and/or families want to take part in your research?* There are many reasons why people give their consent to take part in research activity; these include:

- being interested and curious about the research focus (intrinsic motivation);
- wanting to help and support others (you) in their professional development;
- keen to 'do their bit';
- feeling obliged to be a participant;
- seeking the kudos of being involved in research activity; or
- because of the **incentives** being offered to them (extrinsic motivation).

There is evidence to suggest that the use of incentives is an effective way of increasing participation rates in research (Galea and Tracy, 2007). Consider what you could offer people as an incentive for engaging in your research.

Activity: Suitable incentives for children, young people and adults

Reflect on the table of incentives offered below and identify those which you feel would be suitable for children, young people and adults. Consider the reasoning behind the decisions you make.

Ball point pens	Sweets	Money
Voluntary work	Key rings	Stickers
Donations to charity	Vouchers	Books
Raffle/lottery tickets	Movie passes	Stamps

Incentives generally fall into two particular categories: *non-monetary* (e.g. pens or key rings) and *monetary* (e.g. cash or vouchers). Incentives are used either as compensation for the time or effort given by individuals/groups of people, or they can be given as a way of thanking those for their involvement in your research. While many of the incentives offered in the table above are *tangible* in nature (i.e. physical and touchable), incentives can also be *intangible*, for example feeling good about oneself for taking part in the research. Selecting the right type of incentive will improve the likelihood of certain participants taking part in your research; for children, tangible, non-monetary incentives are certainly more enticing, whereas intangible or monetary incentives are likely to encourage young people/adults to become willing participants. For an interesting 'progression' of age appropriate incentives (0–18 years), see Rice and Broome (2004: 169).

While increased participation rates help to strengthen research findings and demonstrate an active and positive interest in your research, it is important to consider the implications of using incentives in research work. For example:

- What are the *cost* implications of using monetary incentives?
- Who is going to *pay* for the tangible incentives and where will the money come from?
- What are the *time* implications of offering, for example, voluntary work to participants in different settings?

The use of incentives, particularly those which are tangible and monetary in nature, also raise a number of ethical considerations which both novice and experienced researchers need to consider.

 Reflective task: Is the use of monetary or other non-monetary incentives ethical?

The Council of American Survey Research Organizations (CASRO) (2002, cited in Seale, 2004) interprets the use of tangible incentives as unacceptable forms of bribery; Christians (in Denzin and Lincoln, 2000: 138) considers any offers of incentive as 'physical/psychological coercion'.

Would you see yourself as *bribing* children to take part in your research about their health practices at home if you offered them sweets? Would you really be *coercing* young people to take part in your research about the emotional support offered by social workers with movie tickets or DVDs? Share and discuss your thoughts with your colleagues/peers. See Grant and Sugarman (2004) for further information.

Another important ethical consideration you should be aware of is the *right to withdraw*.

The right to withdraw

Case study: The right to withdraw

Suzie, a teenage pregnancy worker, is conducting a focus group with six young mothers in a Children's Centre. During the discussion, which focuses on perceptions of what it is like to be a 'new young mum', Suzie notices that one of the participants (referred to here as Z) is avoiding eye contact with her and the other participants; Z makes no contribution to the focus group and is visibly tense if she is invited to share her opinions.

It should be clear from reading the above that Z is uncomfortable about taking part in the research. There are a number of potential reasons for this:

1   Z lacks confidence in speaking in a group situation;
2   Z does not want to share her personal views with others for fear of 'getting it wrong';
3   Z may have other things on her mind which are distracting her (her baby may be unwell, for example);
4   Z feels unable to contribute anything new to the discussion.

Suzie could have alleviated Z's anxieties by reminding Z of her right to withdraw from the research. The right to withdraw means that participants can leave the research project *at any time* - before they take part in the research, actually during it or retrospectively. Good practice suggests that participants should be made aware of this through verbal and written means which are appropriate to the participant (see page 50). Interestingly, Edwards (2005) argues that participants should not necessarily have unconditional or absolute rights to withdraw; a viewpoint that is opposed by Chwang (2008) and substantiated by the *Declaration of Helsinki* (WMA, 2008: 3). With varying assessments being made about participants' right to withdraw, new researchers typically have many questions about this ethical consideration, examples of which are offered in Table 4.2 with a response to support your understanding of the practicalities of the right to withdraw.

Table 4.2 The practicalities of the right to withdraw

Question	Response
Can I ask the participant who withdraws from my research to re-engage at a later date?	No - their decision should be fully accepted and binding.
Should I ask the participant why they want to leave?	No - they should be able to leave your research without giving a reason.
What do I do with the data I have gathered from the participant who wants to withdraw?	This data (both hard copy and electronic form) needs to be either returned to the participant or securely disposed of, e.g. shredded, permanently deleted from your computer or memory stick.
Will I get a lower mark for my research project if someone leaves?	No - be honest about participants leaving in your research write-up, reflecting on the possible reasons as to why this happened and what you have learned as a result of this.

One of the fears of research participants is what will happen if they do decide to withdraw from research they initially agreed to be a part of. For example, if a parent decided to withdraw their teenage daughter from a piece of action research her sports coach was conducting, the parent (*and* possibly the teenager) may worry that the sports coach will not continue to offer a quality experience/education for their daughter because of his annoyance that they chose to take their daughter out of his research. While it is inevitably disappointing and frustrating when someone withdraws from your research, you must ensure that you remain professional, assuring participants that their decision will not adversely affect your relationship with them and the quality of the service you provide. The right to withdraw, in essence, allows participants to protect themselves if they feel that the research they are involved in is in some way harmful. But how do researchers protect themselves?

The protection of the researcher

While there are many potential risks for participants to be involved in research, the same applies to the researchers themselves. This is an area of consideration which few academics reflect on but it is considered imperative that you demonstrate a duty of care to your own personal safety. Consider the value of the following practical suggestions to assure personal protection:

- Invite a peer or a colleague to sit in on any interviews you conduct and act as a note taker where possible/appropriate. Do seek permission for them to be present otherwise this may be unsettling for your interviewee(s).
- Consider working in pairs. If you are the sole researcher for your research project always maintain telephone contact with colleagues and family members if there are any difficulties.
- Check the maintenance of your car before you travel to a public venue if you decide to conduct part of your data gathering in a public place such as a public house or a participant's house.
- If you feel *at risk* at any time during the gathering of your research data then terminate this with immediate effect.

Conclusion

This chapter has sought to raise your awareness of a range of ethical issues which influence the way quality research in CYPS should be conducted. While underlying principles and guidelines have been discussed, you should be mindful that there is no 'one way' to deal with ethical considerations. Indeed, it is important to acknowledge the uniqueness of your research project and how ethical considerations pertinent to your research will need to be shaped and reshaped in response to dilemmas, circumstances and events as your project develops. This is what makes ethical research both exciting and a challenge!

Areas for further consideration

There are a number of other areas for consideration which you may wish to explore as part of your own personal study. The suggestions below merely offer a select number of aspects that will help to further develop your understanding of ethical research in CYPS:

Covert or deceptive research	Giving advice
Debriefing	Environmental protection
External researchers coming into the setting and conducting research	Ethical tensions surrounding the dual practitioner-researcher role

Further reading

Books

Alderson, P. and Morrow, V. (2011) *The Ethics of Research with Children and Young People*. 2nd edn. London: Sage.
This book offers a comprehensive guide to the relevant laws, guidelines and current debates involved in conducting research with children and young people.

Mauthner, M., Birch, M., Jessop, J. and Miller, T. (eds) (2002) *Ethics in Qualitative Research*. London: Sage.
An informative book which considers the gap between the concrete practice of doing research and the theoretical principles formulated in ethical guidelines. See http://tinyurl.com/d56b9lp for an interesting book review by Brinkmann.

Academic publications

Morrow, V. (2008) Ethical dilemmas in research with children and young people about their social environments. *Children's Geographies*, 6(1), 49-61. [Online]. Available at: http://tinyurl.com/d5m4ba9 (Accessed: 29 March 2012).
This paper highlights some of the debates about the extent to which research with children differs from research conducted with other groups of people. Ethical dilemmas raised during the author's undertaking of research involving 12-15 year olds are explored.

Stuart, J. and Barnes, J. (2005) *Conducting Ethical Research*. NESS. [Online]. Available at: http://tinyurl.com/c6wj5yv (Accessed: 29 March 2012).
This comprehensive document outlines many of the ethical issues which need to be considered by researchers when undertaking research that involves families and children. Exemplar research letters, consent forms and information sheets are included on pages 25-33.

Website

The Research Ethics Guidebook: a resource for social scientists. Available at: www.ethicsguidebook.ac.uk/ A great website which offers useful signposts for researchers to detailed information about applying for ethics approval, negotiating ethics at different stages of the research process, and dealing with ethics dilemmas that arise during a project.

References

Alderson, P. and Morrow, V. (2011) *The Ethics of Research with Children and Young People.* 2nd edn. London: Sage.

Angrosino, M. (2007) *Doing Ethnographic Observational Research.* London: Sage Publications.

Babbie, E. (2010) *The Practice of Social Research.* 12th edn. Belmont, CA: Wadsworth.

Banks, S. (ed) (2010) *Ethical Issues in Youth Work.* 2nd edn. Oxon: Routledge.

Bradford, S. and Cullen, F. (eds) (2011) *Research and Research Methods for Youth Practitioners.* London: Routledge.

British Educational Research Association (BERA) (2011) *Ethical Guidelines for Educational Research.* Available at: www.bera.ac.uk/ (Accessed: 4 March 2012).

Burton, N., Brundrett, M. and Jones, M. (2008) *Doing Your Education Research Project.* London: Sage Publications.

Canterbury Christ Church (2006) *Data Protection in Research.* [Online]. Available at: www.canterbury.ac.uk/Research/Documents/DataProtection.pdf (Accessed: 30 March 2012).

Christians, C. G. (2000) Ethics and Politics in Qualitative Research. In: Denzin, N. K. and Lincoln, Y. S., *Handbook of Qualitative Research.* 2nd edn. Thousand Oaks: Sage Publications Inc.

Chwang, E. (2008) Against the Inalienable Right to Withdraw from Research. *Bioethics,* 22(7), pp. 370–378.

Connolly, P. (2003) *Ethical Principles for Researching Vulnerable Groups.* [Online]. Available at: www.ofmdfmni.gov.uk/ethicalprinciples.pdf (Accessed: 26 February 2012).

Council of American Survey Research Organizations (CASRO) (2002) Code of Standards and Ethics for Survey Research. In: Seale, C. (ed.) (2004) *Social Research Methods: a Reader.* London: Routledge.

Data Protection Act (1998) [Online]. Available at: www.legislation.gov.uk/ukpga/1998/29/contents (Accessed: 30 March 2012).

Denscombe, M. (2005) Research Ethics and the Governance of Research Projects: The Potential of Internet Home Pages, *Sociological Research Online,* 10(3). [Online]. Available at: www.socresonline.org.uk/10/3/denscombe.html (Accessed: 26 February 2012).

——(2010) *Ground Rules for Social Research.* 2nd edn. Berkshire: Open University Press.

Department of Health (DoH) (2008) *Research Governance Framework for Health and Social Care.* [Online]. Available at: http://webarchive.nationalarchives.gov.uk/+/www.dh.gov.uk/en/Aboutus/Researchanddevelopment/AtoZ/Researchgovernance/DH_4002112 (Accessed: 30 March 2012).

Edwards, S. J. (2005) Research participation and the right to withdraw. *Bioethics,* 19(2), pp. 112–130.

Freedom of Information Act (2000) [Online]. Available at: www.legislation.gov.uk/ukpga/2000/36/contents (Accessed: 30 March 2012).

Galea, S. and Tracy, M. (2007) Participation Rates in Epidemiologic Studies. *AEP,* 17(9), pp. 643–653. [Online]. Available at: http://depts.washington.edu/epidem/Epi583/January20-08.pdf (Accessed: 26 March 2012).

Grant, R. W. and Sugarman, J. (2004) Ethics in Human Subjects Research: Do Incentives Matter? *Journal of Medicine and Philosophy,* 29(6), pp. 717–738. [Online]. Available at: www.waisman.wisc.edu/events/ethics/sprin06-sem2-incentives-compensation.pdf (Accessed: 26 March 2012).

Gray, D. E. (2009) *Doing Research in the Real World*. 2nd edn. London: Sage.

Greig, A., Taylor, J. and MacKay, T. (2007) *Doing Research with Children*. 2nd edn. London: Sage.

Haight, A. (2006) *The Ethics of Gifted Education: What can we learn from medical ethics?* Paper presented to the 10th Conference of the European Council for High Ability, Lahti, Finland, 15 September. [Online]. Available at: www.brookes.ac.uk/schools/education/rescon/cpdgifted/docs/research/A_Haight_ethics-of-gifted-education.pdf (Accessed: 7 March 2012).

Harding, D. (2003) *The Practical Guide to Data Protection*. [Online]. Available at: www.research-live.com/features/the-practical-guide-to-data-protection/2001021.article (Accessed: 30 March 2012).

Health and Social Care Act (2008) [Online]. Available at: www.dh.gov.uk/en/Publicationsandstatistics/Legislation/Actsandbills/HealthandSocialCareBill/index.htm (Accessed: 30 March 2012).

Henn, M., Weinstein, M. and Foard, N. (2006) *A Short Introduction to Social Research*. London: Sage.

Howe, K. R. and Moses, M. S. (1999) Ethics in educational research. *Review of Research in Education*, 24(1), pp. 21–60.

Human Rights Act (1998) [Online]. Available at: www.legislation.gov.uk/ukpga/1998/42/contents (Accessed: 30 March 2012).

Joint University Council Social Work Education Committee (JUCSWEC) (2002) *Code of Ethics for Social Work and Social Care Research*. [Online]. Available at: www.juc.ac.uk/swec-res-code.aspx (Accessed: 4 March 2012).

Lewis, J. (2003) Design Issues. In: Richie, J. and Lewis, J. *Qualitative Research Practice: A guide for social science students and researchers*. London: Sage.

Menter, I., Elliot, D., Hulme, M., Lewin, J. and Lowden, K. (2011) *A guide to Practitioner Research in Education*. London: Sage Publications.

Morrow, V. (2009) *The Ethics of Social Research with Children and Families in Young Lives: Practical Experiences*. Working Paper No.53. Oxford: Young Lives. [Online]. Available at: www.younglives.org.uk/files/working-papers/wp53-the-ethics-of-social-research-with-children-and-families-in-young-lives-practical-experiences (Accessed: 26 February 2012).

Murray, L. and Lawrence, B. (2000) *Practitioner-Based Enquiry: Principles of Postgraduate Research*. London: Falmer Press.

National Society for the Prevention of Cruelty to Children (NSPCC) (2011) *Ethical issues in research with children: a reading list*. [Online]. Available at: www.nspcc.org.uk/Inform/research/reading_lists/ethical_issues_in_research_with_children_wda55732.html (Accessed: 4 March 2012).

National Youth Agency (NYA) (2004) *Ethical Conduct in Youth Work: A statement of values and principles from The National Youth Agency*. Leicester: The National Youth Agency. [Online]. Available at: http://nya.org.uk/dynamic_files/workforce/Ethical%20Conduct%20in %20Youth%20Work%20 (Reprint%202004).pdf (Accessed: 4 March 2012).

Nursing and Midwifery Council (2008) *The code: Standards of conduct, performance and ethics for nurses and midwives*. [Online]. Available at: www.nmc-uk.org/Nurses-and-midwives/The-code/The-code-in-full/ (Accessed: 4 March 2012).

Rice, M. and Broome, M. E. (2004) Incentives for Children in Research. *Journal of Nursing Scholarship*, 36(2), pp. 167–172.

Scottish Educational Research Association (2005) *Ethical Guidelines for Educational Research*. [Online]. Available at: www.sera.ac.uk/docs/00current/SERA%20 Ethical%20GuidelinesWeb.PDF (Accessed: 4 March 2012).

Sharp, J. (2009) *Success with your Education Research Project*. Exeter: Learning Matters Ltd.

Silverman, D. (2011) *Interpreting Qualitative Data*. 4th edn. London: Sage.

Skelton, T. (2008) Research with children and young people: exploring the tensions between ethics, competence and participation. *Children's Geographies*, 6(1), pp. 21-36. [Online]. Available at: www.tandfonline.com/doi/pdf/10.1080/14733280701791876 (Accessed: 29 March 2012).

Social Research Association (SRA) (2003) *Ethical Guidelines*. [Online]. Available at: www.the-sra.org.uk/documents/pdfs/ethics03.pdf (Accessed: 26 February 2012).

Stafford, A. and Smith, C. (2009) *Practical Guidance on Consulting, Conducting Research and Working in Participative Ways With Children and Young People Experiencing Domestic Abuse*. Edinburgh: Scottish Government Social Research.

The British Association of Sport and Exercise Sciences (BASES) (2011) *The BASES Expert Statement on Ethics and Participation in Research of Young People*. [Online]. Available at: www.bases.org.uk/Ethics-and-Participation-in-Research-of-Young-People (Accessed: 4 March 2012).

The British Psychological Society (2010) *Code of Human Research Ethics*. Leicester: The British Psychological Society. [Online]. Available at: www.bps.org.uk/sites/default/files/documents/code_of_human_research_ethics.pdf (Accessed: 4 March 2012).

Thomas, G. (2009) *Doing Your Research Project*. London: Sage Publications.

Tooth, J., Lutfiyya, Z. and Sokal, L. (2007) *Partnership Research in Education: An Ethics Protocol*. [Online]. Available at: www.edu.gov.mb.ca/k12/iru/library_publications/partnership_research_in_education.pdf (Accessed: 7 March 2012).

UK Research Integrity Office (UKRIO) (2009) *Code of Practice for Research: Promoting good practice and preventing misconduct*. London: UK Research Integrity Office. [Online]. Available at: www.ukrio.org/ukR10htre/UKRIO-Code-of-Practice-for-Research1.pdf (Accessed: 30 March 2012).

UNICEF (2002) *Children Participating in Research, Monitoring and Evaluating (M & E) - Ethics and Your Responsibility as a Manager*. Geneva: UNICEF.

World Medical Association (WMA) (2005) *Medical Ethics Manual*. [Online]. Available at: www.whcaonline.org/uploads/publications/em_en.pdf (Accessed: 4 March 2012).

——(2008) *Declaration of Helsinki: Ethical Principles for Medical Research Involving Human Subjects*. [Online]. Available at: www.wma.net/en/30publications/10policies/b3/17c.pdf (Accessed: 29 March 2012).

Section 2
The Learner

5 Gifted and talented learners

Lynn Senior

LEARNING OBJECTIVES

After studying this chapter, you will be able to:

✔ Define what is meant by the terms *gifted* and *talented*.
✔ Identify some of the characteristics associated with gifted and talented children and young people.
✔ Identify the government initiatives and legislation pertinent to the gifted and talented agenda in schools and settings.
✔ Explore some of the strategies for working with gifted and talented children and young people.

Introduction

When working as a practitioner or trainee in the 0–19 sector you will undoubtedly encounter children or young people with a range of abilities. While those children and young people at the 'lower end' of the ability spectrum may be, and quite rightly, supported with extra resources and appropriately trained manpower, those children and young people deemed to be at the other end of the spectrum may experience less support (Eyre, 1997). This chapter explores the concept of supporting those children and young people who are deemed to be gifted and talented (G&T) and considers how we as practitioners or those training can meet their needs within the notion of 'inclusive education'.

It should be noted that the discussion in this chapter is more focused on educational contexts as the notion of gifted and talented has limited relevance to other areas in the 0–19 sector such as health or social services. However, this is not to say that practitioners and those training outside of the education arena will not come into contact with children and young people who are considered gifted and talented; it is thus considered useful for all readers to actively engage with the content of this chapter.

The chapter begins with an explanation of the numerous definitions of gifted and talented and provides a historical and current perspective on the legislation and practice underpinning provision for this often overlooked group. As with much educational provision, a lack of government legislation and issues of rather 'muddled thinking' around gifted and talented has existed for some time; however, current policy and thinking dictates that provision for this group of children and young people is integrated into 'mainstream' education, with funding going directly to head teachers or practitioners with the aim to support needs locally. The chapter prompts the reader to reflect on this and to consider the importance of their role within the context of the National Occupational Standards framework (UKCES, 2008) and the Common Core of Skills and Knowledge (CWDC, 2010). While issues surrounding identification and identification strategies of G&T are considered, the chapter focuses on the significance of identification for inclusion, the environment and approaches available for practitioners and those training to utilise seeing as 'gifted pupils have the right to an appropriate education' (Clark and Callow, 2002: 33). Further exploration is given to supporting gifted and talented children and young people found within the early years, primary, secondary, and post-16 sectors, as well as those with multiple special needs.

Definitions

Before considering what we mean by the term, it is worth noting that gifted and talented as a concept has been the topic of much debate throughout the years (Gagne, 1993; Hoge and Cudmore, 1986), with many articles critiquing the methods of identification (Frasier and Passow, 1994) and indeed the ways in which these young people are treated throughout their educational career (Rogers, 2007). Due to word constraints of the chapter, you are encouraged to explore the *Further readings* offered at the end of this chapter to gain an understanding of this debate.

Gifted and *talented* are two words that are used synonymously to identify children and young people who appear to be working beyond the expected norms for their age group. However, when considering what we actually mean when we label a child and young person 'gifted' or 'talented' it is more beneficial to break down the label into its two distinct parts. So what do we mean by a *gifted* child or young person? Gagne (2003: 61) states that '**Gifted** children and young people are those whose potential is distinctly above average in one or more of the following domains of human ability: intellectual, creative, social and physical'; he continues by defining the **talented** child and young person as one 'whose skills are distinctly above average in one or more areas of human performance' (p. 109). This is quantified with the notion that a gift is a superior natural ability whereas a talent is a skill that has been well developed. From this it could be argued that while a talent implies that the child and young person has a gift, a gift does not necessarily indicate a talent.

Gagne (2003) argues that someone can start with a gift but only develops the talent through a variety of factors, including family, school, internal motivations and personal factors. He considers these factors to fall into two distinct groupings: *intrapersonal* and *environmental*. Examples of intrapersonal factors would include the motivation of the child or young person, their temperament and personality, their ability to self-manage, and their adaptability to situations. Environmental factors on an individual's ability to develop talent are external to the child or young person and include their family and cultural background, the influence of other people, the availability of activities to the child or young person, and life events.

However, the key word of Gagne's definition on page 66 is *potential*. He argues that being smart is not enough; a child or young person needs support and guidance to achieve his/her gifted potential. It is at this point that we can start to see how we as practitioners or trainees could influence or impact upon a child or young person labelled 'gifted' or 'talented' as it would appear we have a role to play in nurturing gifts as both secondary and external forms of reference.

Activity

Use Gagne's (2000) Differentiated Model of Giftedness and Talent – available at http://tinyurl.com/b7ef36j – to reflect on the provision within your setting.

- How does the model and practice compare?
- What conclusions can you draw?
- How does future practice need to change within your setting as a result?

Further definitions include the definition put forward by the DfES (2003) in its White Paper *Excellence in Cities*. This definition breaks down the two terms into specific subjects with *gifted* being applied to the top 5–10 per cent of pupils per school measured by actual or potential achievement in the main curriculum subjects, and *talented* being applied to the top 5–10 per cent of pupils per school measured by actual or potential achievement in the subjects of Art, Music or PE. Some LAs and academic institutions, e.g. Lancashire and Oxford Brookes, also expand the label to include the word *able*, with the connotation that able children and young people have the potential to achieve at a higher level than the majority of their peers within 'academic subjects'.

Reflective task

Consider the definition put forward by the DfES – what issues or problems can you see with such a definition? What would be your preferred definition of gifted and talented for children and young people? Why? Discuss your thoughts with colleagues/peers.

Other definitions that have arisen from the House of Commons (1999: 69–70) include a 'child and young person with a measure cognitive ability two standard deviations above the mean (approximately IQ 130 and above) might be considered highly able'. Definitions such as this call into question the use and role of IQ within the definition of ability, with some psychologists favouring a quantitative interpretation in the form of a numerical statement, while others prefer a more qualitative approach, through nature and nurture, for example the use of Multiple Intelligences as described by Gardner (2011). Finally in this section, it is worth considering the views of the Potential Plus UK (2013) (previously the National Association of Gifted Child and Young Person – NAGC) who prefer the term *High Learning Potential* (HLP) to gifted and talented. We shall return to this later in the chapter.

Legislation and government initiatives

While *gifted and talented* as a concept has been discussed for many years, it is important to reflect on the most recent legislation and initiatives that have been put in place within the UK education context. Under the Labour government the White Paper *Excellence in Schools* (1997) set out the principles upon which the government saw the development and improvement of education within the UK. This paper set out plans to give every child and young person, regardless of ability, a firm educational foundation, and while not being distinct, the gifted and talented concept fell within the umbrella term of *special educational needs* and the requirement to raise standards in both teaching and achievement for these children and young people.

Following the White Paper, the Excellence in Cities (EiC) programme was launched in 1999 to promote inclusion, raise standards and resolve educational problems faced in inner city schools and other urban areas. The programme tackled underachievement through the provision of learning mentors, learning support units and provision for gifted and talented children and young people. In 2007 the Centre for British Practitioners (CfBT) Education Trust secured a £42-million contract to run the programme *Young, Gifted and Talented*. It was designed for the top 10 per cent of pupils aged 4–19 and worked via the internet with local 'hubs' run through universities. However, the EiC programmes and centrally funded initiatives have not been continued following the 2010 election and the change of government. More recently, the coalition government (2010) has introduced the 'Pupil Premium', which is additional funding that is being given to schools to support disadvantaged children. Visit the following website – http://tinyurl.com/az3stsb – which provides details of a Pupil Premium case study on a gifted and talented programme run in Devon. In addition, the coalition government has committed itself to supporting schools to provide stretch and challenge for all pupils including the most academically able. To do this several initiatives have been introduced, some of which are listed below:

- Introduction of new teaching standards that include a clear expectation of the need to support and challenge high achieving students (http://tinyurl.com/aok2afe).
- Introduction of a new OFSTED framework with a focus on the progress of high achieving students.
- Revision of the National Curriculum to allow schools to give more time to create educational opportunities that stimulate and stretch all students (currently in progress).
- Revised performance tables to include the progress made by students with different attainment levels to allow parents/carers to see how well the school caters for children with varying abilities.

The present UK government has also continued the Dux award scheme which rewards high performing students in Year 9 by providing funding to allow one student from each secondary school to visit a Russell Group university with the view that this will encourage higher aspirations – for further information see http://tinyurl.com/b3fljqw.

Table 5.1 highlights some of the initiatives that have been implemented over the last two decades. Consider how they have impacted upon gifted and talented education to date.

Table 5.1 Select Initiatives 1997–2012

Year	Direct Policies	Indirect Policies	Consultations	Govt. Initiatives	Non-govt. Initiatives
1997	Excellence in Schools DfES White Paper				
1999	Excellence in Cities DfES White Paper				
2002				National Academy of Gifted and Talented Youth (NAGTY) at the University of Warwick	
2003		Every Child Matters DfES			
2005	Higher Standards, Better Schools for All DCSF White Paper				
2007		The Child and Young Person's Plan DCSF	2020 Vision DCSF Review Group		
				Young, Gifted and Talented Academy (YG&T) CfBT Education Trust for DCSF Sept 2007 – March 2010	
2008					International Gateway for Gifted Youth (IGGY) at the University of Warwick
2010	With the end of YG&T's contract, responsibility for G&T devolves to schools with Ofsted inspection				
2012	Pupil Premium		Sutton Trust report 'Educating the Highly Able'	Dux Award	

Characteristics of the g&t child and young person: how can we identify g&t?

The identification of children and young people who fall under the umbrella term 'gifted and talented' is crucial if we are to ensure that their needs are met and that the correct guidance and provision is in place to support these needs. Early research has indicated that practitioners and those training will not automatically identify children or young people with high levels of ability (Denton and Postlethwaite, 1985). It could be argued that this early research is still valid today with some children being dismissed as non-communicative or problematic rather than being gifted or talented in a particular area. This issue of identification becomes more complex when considering that no single, simple, or indeed *uniform* definition of gifted and talented exists! This is compounded further when the notion of ability is also considered within definitions, as ideas of ability are often linked to cultural values that change over time. Within nurseries, schools and colleges the first step to identifying those who are gifted and talented is to create an institution-wide definition that fits within the ethos of the establishment and provides a working consensus leading to effective provision for the child and young person identified. Eyre (1997) believes that for identification strategies to be effective they need to be embedded within educational systems that will have an impact upon practice and to ensure that the quality of learning and teaching is improved. Organisations such as MENSA have checklists for parents/carers, practitioners and trainees to use as guidance to help to identify the gifted child and young person – see www.mensa.org.uk/. Characteristics of a gifted child or young person include:

- an unusual memory;
- intolerance of other children or young people;
- an awareness of world events;
- prefers to spend time with adults or in solitary pursuits; and
- extrovert/introvert. (Extract from MENSA checklist, Press Office, 2007 – available at http://tinyurl.com/8dxqqu6)

As has already been discussed, the identification of gifted and talented children and young people is problematic; in an effort to support practitioners the Qualifications and Curriculum Authority (QCA) published guidelines in 2007, both generic and subject specific, to help the recognition of such children and young people. These standards are still valid for use in schools and settings and at the time of writing had not been updated. In addition, the National Quality Standards in Gifted and Talented Education (2005) also gave descriptors for identification purposes.

 Activity

Look at the descriptors provided within the National Quality Standards in Gifted and Talented Education (2005). These standards can be found at http://tinyurl.com/c8w5r36. Consider how these descriptors link to your understanding of gifted and talented within your setting/placement.

Betts and Neihart (1988) identify six types of gifted children and young people with particular needs:

- the successful;
- the challenging;
- the underground;
- the dropouts;
- the double-labelled; and
- the autonomous learner.

Table 5.2 on the following three pages provides further information on how Betts and Neihart characterised these six types. Montgomery (1996) builds on these six types by describing the gifted and talented *underachiever* whose characteristics include aggressive behaviour, poor attitudes towards school, not working well in group situations, lack of concentration and poor execution of work.

Reflective task

- What do you consider to be the strengths in the different forms of identification discussed in this section?
- What are the disadvantages and limitations?
- How does your workplace/placement use these methods of identification to describe its gifted and talented children and young people?

As alluded to earlier on in this chapter, the Potential Plus UK (2013) prefers to use the term *High Learning Potential* (HLP) instead of 'gifted'. They assert that the distinguishing feature shared by all children and young people with HLP is asynchronous development whereby the intellect develops faster and further than other attributes such as social, emotional and physical development. They also identify some defining characteristics for the child and young person with HLP in that they enjoy learning at a much faster pace, can process information to a much greater depth and can be quite intense, especially in terms of energy (*high*), imagination (*vivid*), intellectual ability (*high*), sensitivity (*high*) and emotion (*high*). They also identify a child and young person with HLP as one who is a perfectionist, who equates success to self-worth.

Table 5.2 Six types of gifted children and young people with particular needs (Betts and Neihart, 1988)

Feelings and attitudes	Behaviours	Needs	Adults' and peers' perceptions of type	Identification	Home support	School support
THE SUCCESSFUL - Boredom - Dependent - Positive self-concept - Anxious - Guilty about failure - Extrinsic motivation - Responsible for others - Diminish feelings of self and rights to their emotion - Self critical	- Perfectionist - High Achiever - Seeks teacher approval and structure - Non-risk taking - Does well academically - Accepts and conforms - Dependent	- To see deficiencies - To be challenged - Assertiveness skills - Autonomy - Help with boredom - Appropriate curriculum	- Loved by teachers - Admired by peers - Loved and accepted by parents	- Grade point average - IQ Tests - Teacher nominations	- Independence - Ownership - Freedom to make choices - Time for personal interests - Risk taking experiences	- Accelerated and enriched curriculum - Time for personal interests - Compacted learning experiences - Opportunities to be with intellectual peers - Development of independent learning skills - In-depth studies - Mentorships - College & career counselling
THE CHALLENGING - Boredom - Frustration - Low self-esteem - Impatient - Defensive - Heightened sensitivity - Uncertain about social roles	- Corrects teacher - Questions rules, policies - Is honest, direct - Has mood swings - Demonstrates inconsistent work habits - Has poor self-control - Is creative - Prefers highly active & questioning approach - Stands up for convictions - Is competitive	- To be connected with others - To learn tact, flexibility, self-awareness, self-control, acceptance - Support for creativity - Contractual systems	- Find them irritating - Rebellious - Engaged in power struggle - See them as creative - Discipline problem - Peers see them as entertaining - Want to change them - Don't view as gifted	- Peer recommendations - Parent nomination - Interviews - Performance - Recommendation from a significant, non-related adult - Creativity Testing - Teacher advocate	- Acceptance and understanding - Allow them to pursue interest - Advocate for them at school - Modelling appropriate behaviour - Family projects	- Tolerance - Placement with appropriate teacher - Cognitive & social skill development - Direct and clear communication with child - Give permission for feelings - Studies in-depth - Mentorships build self-esteem - Behavioural contracting

Type	Behaviours	Needs	Perceived by others	Identified by	Support (home/family)	Interventions (school)
THE UNDERGROUND - Unsure - Pressured - Confused - Guilty - Insecure - Diminished feelings of self and right to their emotions	- Denies talent - Drops out of G/T and advanced classes - Resists challenges - Wants to belong socially - Changes friends	- Freedom to make choices - To be aware of conflicts - Awareness of feelings - Support for abilities - Involvement with gifted peers - Career/college info - Self-acceptance	- Viewed as leaders or unrecognised - Seen as average and successful - Perceived to be compliant - Seen as quiet/shy - Adults see them as unwilling to risk - Viewed as resistive	- Gifted peer nomination - Home nomination - Community nomination - Achievement testing - IQ Tests - Performance - Teacher advocate	- Acceptance of underground - Provide college & career planning experiences - Time to be with same age peers - Provide gifted role models - Model life-long learning - Give freedom to make choice	- Recognise & properly place - Give permission to take time out from G/T classes - Provide same sex role models - Continue to give college & career information
THE DROPOUTS - Resentment - Angry - Depressed - Explosive - Poor self-concept - Defensive - Burn-out	- Has intermittent attendance - Doesn't complete tasks - Pursues outside interests - "Spaced out" in class - Is self-abusive - Isolates self - Is creative - Criticises self & others - Does inconsistent work - Is disruptive, acts out - Seems average or below - Is defensive	- An individualised programme - Intense support - Alternatives (separate, new opportunities) - Counselling (individual, group, and family) - Remedial help with skills	- Adults are angry with them - Peers are judgmental - Seen as loners, dropouts, dopers, or air heads - Reject them and ridicule - Seen as dangerous and rebellious	- Review cumulative folder - Interview earlier teachers - Discrepancy between IQ and demonstrated achievement incongruities and inconsistencies in performance - Creativity testing - Gifted peer recommendation - Demonstrated performance in non-school areas	- Seek counselling for family	- Diagnostic testing - Group counselling for young students - Non-traditional study skills - In-depth studies - Mentorships - Alternative out of classroom learning experiences - G.E.D.

Table 5.2 continued

Feelings and attitudes	Behaviours	Needs	Adults' and peers' perceptions of type	Identification	Home support	School support
DOUBLE LABELLED - Powerless - Frustrated - Low self-esteem - Unaware - Angry	- Demonstrates inconsistent work - Seems average or below - May be disruptive or acts out	- Emphasis on strengths - Coping skills - G/T support group - Counselling - Skill development	- Seen as "weird" - Seen as "dumb" - Viewed as helpless - Avoided by peers - Seen as average or below in ability - Perceived to require a great deal of imposed structure - Seen only for the disability	- Scatter of 11 points or more on WISC or WAIS - Recommendation of significant others - Recommendation from informed special ed. teacher - Interview - Performance - Teacher Advocate	- Recognise gifted abilities - Challenge them - Provide risk-taking opportunities - Advocate for child at school - Do family projects - Seek counselling for family	- Placement in gifted programme - Provide needed resources - Provide alternative learning experiences - Begin investigations and explorations - Give time to be with peers - Give individual counselling
AUTONOMOUS - Self-confident - Self accepting - Enthusiastic - Accepted by others - Supported - Desire to know & learn - Accepts failure - Intrinsic motivation - Personal power - Accepts others	- Has appropriate social skill - Works independently - Develops own goals - Follows through - Works without approval - Follows strong areas of passion - Is creative - Stands up for convictions - Takes risks	- Advocacy - Feedback - Facilitation - Support for risks - Appropriate opportunities	- Accepted by peers and adults - Admired for abilities - Seen as capable and responsible by parents - Positive influences - Successful - Psychologically healthy	- Grade point average - Demonstrated performance - Products - Achievement Testing - Interviews - Teacher/Peer/Parent self-nominations - IQ tests - Creativity Testing	- Advocate for child at school and in community - Provide opportunities related to passions - Allow friends of all ages - Remove time and space restrictions - Do family projects - Include child in parent's passion	- Allow development of long-term integrated plan of study - Accelerated and enriched curriculum - Remove time and space restrictions - Compacted learning experiences with pretesting - In-depth studies - Mentorships - College & career counselling and opportunities - Dual enrolment or early admission - Waive traditional school policy and regulations

Meeting the needs of the gifted and talented

As previously highlighted, children and young people who are considered to be gifted and talented are a diverse and disparate group and therefore meeting their needs can be seen by some practitioners and trainees as 'challenging'. However, it must be noted that most gifted and talented pupils have no more individual needs than the majority of their peers who do not fall into the gifted and talented bracket. In common with all children and young people, those who are gifted and talented need to be in an environment conducive to learning, work on activities that meet their learning needs, along with opportunities for further socialisation and emotional development. There are different ways this can be facilitated; these are discussed below.

1 The environment

All children and young people need an environment, both at home and in the educational setting, in which they can feel secure and confident in their own ability. For a gifted and talented individual this requirement is no different to that of their peers. In addition, they will need a level of challenge that provides them with the intellectual stimulation that they need to grow. However, practitioners and those training in the sector need to ensure that the environment is sensitive to an individual who may be perceived as a 'know-it-all' to their less able peers; in doing so this enables the gifted child or young person to demonstrate his or her ability with confidence. This would also apply to the gifted and talented child/young person who is underachieving for whatever reason.

2 Learning needs

While the legislation and initiatives surrounding the curriculum frameworks for gifted and talented are in flux it is worth remembering that materials were available under the former Labour government that provided information and materials designed to extend and stretch the more able. *Key Messages for Teaching Gifted and Talented Pupils* was published in 2004 and both the QCA and the DfES contributed advice to this.

Activity

Go to the following website and download the *Key Messages* document highlighted above: http://tinyurl.com/cbk4ynm

Identify *three* strategies that you could embrace as part of your professional practice working with children and young people in your setting. Share these with colleagues/peers and evaluate the impact of them following their implementation.

As a practitioner/trainee it is important to remember to ensure that realistic targets are set to meet the learning needs of any child and young person, regardless of whether they are labelled gifted and talented or not. These targets should then be reviewed on a regular basis. One of the ways in which you could do this is to develop Individual Learning Plans (ILPs) or Multi-Element Plans (MEPs). ILPs were initially developed for Skills for Life learners to enable them to monitor progress towards their final goal. Essentially an ILP is produced as a result of initial and diagnostic assessment of the learner and is drawn up in negotiation with the learner (where appropriate) to set their individual goals. The negotiation element of the ILP process is crucial in that it allows the learner to take control of their own learning, while at the same time allowing you as the practitioner or trainee to challenge and stretch the learner's aspirations. As a tool the ILP has become an essential process in what is referred to as 'the learning journey' (DfES, 2004). This journey is summarised as:

- sign posting/referral;
- screening;
- initial assessment;
- diagnostic assessment;
- ILP;
- summative assessment;
- formative assessment. (Senior, 2009)

Activity

There are many different examples of learning plans that can be used to support children and young people. You may wish to visit the Quality Improvement Agency (QIA) website – http://tinyurl.com/cdhjycj – to consider further how you could use them to maximum benefit for you, the learner and the setting.

3 Social and emotional needs

Again, as with all children and young people, the G&T child and young person will have social and emotional needs. As educational establishments and practitioners/trainees we have a very important part to play here as we are secondary forms of reference within a child and young person's socialisation. That is to say that our values, attitudes and beliefs will impact upon the development of the child and young person in our care. As already discussed there is no uniform definition or characteristic that can be attributed to a gifted and talented child and young person, and as a practitioner or trainee we need to be aware of the many facets of personality that may manifest. The six types identified by Betts and Neihart (1998), as described on pages 72-74, is a useful starting point for any practitioner wishing to understand further the needs of their different children and young people. However, it must be noted that these characteristics are in part stereotypical and may not fully describe your learner.

Regardless of personality and characteristics it could be argued that one of the most important forms of socialisation for the gifted and talented child and young person is the ability to work in teams and to value the contribution of less able peers, while at the same time not being the dominant team member, just because they can. Several strategies for encouraging this skill can be adopted, including using a learning mentor to support the child or young person. **Mentoring** is a process that creates relationships between experienced and the less experienced people with a view to helping the less experienced person to develop. Other published definitions follow similar themes to this, with Pollard (in DfES, 2004: 19) defining mentoring as: 'The provision of support for the learning of one person through the guidance of another person, who is more skilled, knowledgeable and experienced in relation to the context of the learning taking place'.

To put it in its simplest form a mentor is someone available to learn from. In addition to mentoring the practitioner may opt for a **coaching** role rather than a mentoring role; although these terms are often interchangeable, Maclennan (1995: 4) defines coaching as:

> The process whereby one individual helps another; to unlock their natural ability; to perform, to learn, and achieve; to increase awareness of the factors that determine performance; to increase their sense of self-responsibility and ownership of their performance; to self-coach to identify and remove barriers to achievement.

Further to this, Hersey and Blanchard (1995) use a categorisation of learners to help direct how we as practitioners should coach children and young people to achieve their full potential. The two types of learners that we are concerned with when considering gifted and talented are those that fall into the categories of:

- *High Competence, Variable Commitment* - these learners are relatively experienced and competent with the subject and subject knowledge, but may lack confidence to work without the support of the coach, or they may lack the motivation.
- *High Competence, High Commitment* - experienced and confident in their ability.

As the coach to this diverse range of learners you have several different approaches available to you to support their learning. Three examples are listed below:

1 *Guiding* - two-way communication. The learner still needs direction as they lack experience and some commitment. The practitioner allows the learner to make choices and decisions, but will challenge if the learner is going off track.
2 *Supporting* - less direction needed, but still offering a lot of support. The learners are now making their own decisions. They need less direction because they have the necessary skills, but still need a coach to boost their confidence and/or motivation level.
3 *Delegating* - the coach needs to give little direction or support. This is for learners who have a high competence and high confidence/motivation level. The learner decides when the coach needs to be involved.

Case Study: *Learning Mentor/coach*

Brigit has just joined your Key Stage 1, Year Two class. She is deemed to be a gifted and talented youngster and although very quiet and shy in class her parents' carers insist that she is not like that at home. They have requested that she is provided with a learning mentor to help her overcome her problems and to ensure she develops to her full potential.

Consider the following:

- What style of mentoring discussed above do you think would be the most appropriate given the information about this learner?
- What personal or practical skills would you need to be able to mentor her effectively?

Working with the gifted and talented child or young person

All practitioners across the 0-19 age phase must show the G&T child and young person they are valued, giving them appropriate academic challenge and also chances to be together to feel less isolated. This section considers possible strategies that could be used in a typical learning and teaching environment.

Differentiation

Differentiation refers to an adjustment of all relevant parts of the curriculum in response to children's and young people's different learning needs and preferences (Porter, 2005). These adjustments can be to any of the four aspects of curriculum: *the environment, the content, the teaching and learning activities* and *the products*. For example, a gifted and talented child/young person may need additional resources or an accelerated pace of activity. In addition they may benefit from being placed in different areas of the classroom and with different children and young people for different activities. Within the school sector it is quite common to find ability groupings across year groups whereby children and young people are placed into ability streams, which may be different for different subjects. In the early years sector it is more common to find multi-age groupings. As a strategy this can have the effect of enabling younger and older children to mix and create friendships with peers at the same development level.

Other aspects of differentiation that are important for the gifted and talented child/young person include the differentiation of learning and teaching. All child and young people learn through active engagement and activity, and the key to effective differentiation is knowing your child or young person and recognising any problems or frustrations they have with tasks.

Activity

Several models for teaching and supporting gifted children and young people exist. Take a look at Bloom's Taxonomy wheel (available at http://tinyurl.com/bddw3xn) – how could you differentiate based on this model? What could your setting/placement put in place to ensure that it uses differentiation effectively?

Personalised learning

Personalised learning for gifted and talented children and young people was envisaged in *Better Schools for All* (DfES, 2006) and was predicated on 'a highly structured and responsive approach to each child and young person's learning, in order that all are able to progress, achieve and participate'. The Personalised Learning (PL) framework is presented in Figure 5.1. Further information about this can be found at http://tinyurl.com/a23sb27

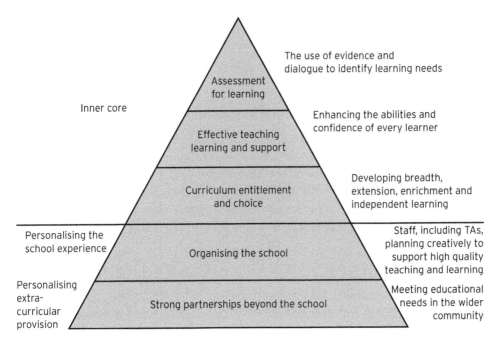

The use of evidence and dialogue to identify learning needs

Assessment for learning

Inner core

Enhancing the abilities and confidence of every learner

Effective teaching learning and support

Curriculum entitlement and choice

Developing breadth, extension, enrichment and independent learning

Personalising the school experience

Organising the school

Staff, including TAs, planning creatively to support high quality teaching and learning

Personalising extra-curricular provision

Strong partnerships beyond the school

Meeting educational needs in the wider community

Figure 5.1 The Personalised Learning (PL) framework

Involving parents and carers

Parents and carers play an essential role in the development of their gifted and talented child or young person. The list below highlights some of the ways in which you can involve them in their child/young person's education:

- encourage parents and carers to share information;
- put parents and carers in touch with support organisations;
- encourage parents and carers to extend their child's/young person's strengths outside of school, e.g. attending football clubs, French clubs, libraries, museums and relevant competitions;
- make available the school's/setting's policy on gifted and talented pupils/learners;
- ensure that parents and carers know who they may contact with any concerns or queries; and
- be aware of and sensitive to the pressure from parents and carers about their gifted and talented child/young person.

Case studies

Reflect on the two case studies below and consider what strategies you would use to support both of these children:

1   Jessica (aged 10) is gifted in maths, ICT and English (she has a reading age of 14). Jessica is often found chatting during class and disrupting other children when she should be working. She appears to be bored and gets through her work very quickly.
2   Jeremy is a talented 10 year old. He excels in art and can play a variety of musical instruments very well. He struggles with English and maths but enjoys ICT sessions. He says very little and rarely asks for help.

Organisations to help with gifted and talented children

Several organisations exist to support parents/carers, practitioners and children/young people who are gifted and talented. Potential Plus UK – www.nagcbritain.org.uk – is an independent charity that works with families to support both the family and the child and young person. MENSA also offer support on identifying gifted and talented children and young people, supporting those identified. For further information, consider visiting www.mensa.org.

Conclusion

While this chapter set out to provide an overview of gifted and talented, as a practitioner/ trainee you should be mindful that there is no definitive definition. Some accepted definitions and characteristics that are displayed by children/young people who are deemed to be gifted or talented do exist. However, all children/young people will be different and recognition of their gift/talent may not be easy, nor will the development of strategies to ensure they achieve their potential.

Despite this, as a practitioner/trainee you have an obligation to ensure that all children/ young people, regardless of their age or ability, succeed and grow while in your care, be it pre-school, nursery, school or college. As such, the gifted and talented debate should be at the forefront of your daily working practice.

Areas for further consideration

There are a number of other areas for consideration which you may wish to explore as part of your own personal study. The suggestions below merely offer a select number of aspects which will help to further develop your understanding of gifted and talented in CYPS:

Gifted and talented and homework	Gifted and talented and ICT
Gifted and talented summer schools	Gifted and talented and learning styles
Gifted and talented and creativity	Gifted and talented and critical thinking

Further reading

Books

Callaghan, C. and Hertzberg Davis, L. (2012) *Fundamentals of Gifted Education*. London: Routledge.
This text provides a framework that can be used to plan effective programmes for the gifted and talented, surrounding issues such as philosophy, curriculum, social and emotional development.

Strip, C. (2000) *Helping Gifted Children Soar: A practical guide for parents and teachers*. Scottsdale: Gifted Psychology Press.
Although an American text and written from an American perspective, this text contains practical ideas for helping gifted and talented children and young people achieve their full potential.

Academic publications

Rogers, K. B. (2007) Lessons Learned about Educating the Gifted and Talented: A synthesis of the research on educational practice. *Gifted Child Quarterly*, 51 (4), 382–396.
This article discusses the lessons learned from research on the education of the gifted and talented suggests. Although several of the lessons arise from traditional practice in the field, the article also considers some of the currently researched differences in how the gifted learner intellectually functions.

Reis, S. M. and Renzulli, J. S. (2003) Current research on the social and emotional development of gifted and talented students: Good news and future possibilities. *Psychology in the Schools*, 41 (1), 119–130.
In this article, research about the social and emotional development of gifted and talented students is summarised and suggestions are made about strategies to enhance these students' school experiences. Suggestions are provided for assessment and educational programming based on students' strengths and interests that may result in helping talented students realise their potential.

Website

TES Gifted and talented teaching resources – available at http://tinyurl.com/aqvhsmp.
This website has a wide selection of teaching resources created by practitioners to support those who plan, teach and assess children and young people who are gifted and talented.

References

Betts, G. and Neihart, M. (1988) Profiles of the gifted and talented. *Gifted Child Quarterly*, 32 (2), 248–253.
Children's Workforce Development Council (CWDC) (2010) *Common Core of Knowledge and Skills*. [Online]. Available at: www.childrensworkforcematters.org.uk/common-core (Accessed: 30 December 2012).
Clark, C. and Callow, R. (2002) *Educating the Gifted and Talented*. London: David Fulton.
Denton, C. and Postlethwaite, K. (1985) *Able Children: Identifying them in the classroom*. Windsor: NFER/Nelson.
DfEE (1997) *Excellence in Schools*. London: DfEE.
DfES (2003) *Excellence in Cities and Education Action Zones: management and impact*. HMI 1399. London: DfES.
——(2005) *Higher Standards: Better Schools for All*. HMI- HC631. London: DfES.
Eyre, D. (1997) *Able Children in Ordinary Schools*. London: David Fulton/Nace.
Frasier, M. M. and Passow, A. H. (1994) *Towards a New Paradigm for Identifying Talent Potential*. Research Monograph 94112. NRC/GT: University of Connecticut.

Gagne, F. (1991) Toward a differentiated model of giftedness and talent. In Colangelo, N. and Davis, G. A. (eds) *Handbook of Gifted Education*. Boston: Allyn and Bacon.

——(1993) Constructs and models pertaining to exceptional human abilities. In Heller, K. A., Monks, F. J. and Passow, A. H. (eds) *International Handbook of Research and Development of Giftedness and Talent*. Oxford: Pergamon Press.

——(1999) My Convictions About the Nature of Abilities, Gifts, and Talents. *Journal for the Education of the Gifted*, 22 (2), 109–136.

——(2000) A Differentiated Model of Giftedness and Talent (DMGT). [Online]. Available at: www.curriculumsupport.education.nsw.gov.au/policies/gats/assets/pdf/poldmgt2000rtcl.pdf (Accessed: 10 September 2013).

——(2003) Transforming gifts into talents: The DMGT as a developmental theory. In N. Colangelo and G. A. Davis (eds) *Handbook of Gifted Education*. 3rd edn. Boston: Allyn & Bacon. pp. 60–74.

Gardner, H. (2011) *Frames of Mind: The Theory of Multiple Intelligences*. New York: Basic Books.

Hoge, R. D. and Cudmore, L. (1986) The use of teacher-judgment measures in the identification of gifted pupils. *Teaching & Teacher Education*, 2 (2), 181–196.

Mensa (2013) [Online]. Available at: www.mensa.org/ (Accessed: 28 January 2013).

Montgomery, D. (1996) *Educating the Able*. London: Cassell.

——(ed) (2000) *Able Underachievers*. London: Whurr.

Potential Plus UK (2013) [Online]. Available at www.nagcbritain.org.uk (Accessed: 28 January 2013).

Rogers, K. B. (2007) Lessons Learned About Educating the Gifted and Talented: A Synthesis of the Research on Educational Practice. *Gifted Child Quarterly*, 51 (4), 382–396.

Senior, L. (2009) *Essential Skills for the 14–19 Diploma Teacher*. Harlow: Pearson.

UKCES (2008) *National Occupational Standards framework* [Online]. Available at: http://nos.ukces.org.uk/Pages/index.aspx (Accessed: 28 January 2013).

6 Special educational needs and disabilities: Supporting the needs of children and young people through inclusive practice

Rosemary Shepherd

LEARNING OBJECTIVES

After studying this chapter, you will be able to:

✔ Identify national policies and relevant legislation associated with the inclusion agenda to support learners with a special educational need or disability.
✔ Evaluate the importance of providing an inclusive educational setting.
✔ Consider some of the key special educational needs and disabilities found in educational settings.

Introduction

Most practitioners and those training in educational settings will have some experience of supporting children and young people with a **special educational need** or **disability** (SEND) and will, no doubt, have explored ways to support such learners. Some of these children and young people will have been supported through systems that have been introduced through government policies and strategies, while others will have been supported through the conscientious efforts of caring professionals.

This chapter will initially consider government policies and strategies in order to provide some context on how children and young people with a SEND are currently managed and included in mainstream education. The societal attitude towards such learners is steadily changing as people become more aware of the needs of such learners, partly due to the various organisations and charities such as the British Dyslexia Association (BDA) and National Autistic Society (NAS) that have helped people to gain a better understanding of what it means to have a SEND, as well as the government's drive to educate learners with SEND in mainstream schools (DfE, 2012).

The attitudes of professionals towards children and young people with a SEND has not always been satisfactory; the main reason, according to Abbott (2006: 630), is that many professionals have felt 'ill-equipped to meet the wide range of learning difficulties in today's classrooms and negative feelings persist [including] a sense of fear ... about [the professional's] ability to deal with pupils who have certain characteristics'.

We still have much to learn about managing the learning of children and young people with a SEND as well as ensuring that we provide each learner with an equal opportunity to reach their potential. This chapter will support practitioners and those training as they work towards achieving inclusion and helping children and young people to reach their potential. All sectors within CYPS are likely to encounter and work with children, young people and families with a SEND. The focus of this chapter is on SEND in educational settings to help focus the discussion. It is hoped that readers in other areas of the 0–19 workforce will recognise how advocated practice relating to working with and supporting children and young people with SEND can be transferred and adapted within their own individual contexts.

The government's case for change

The UK educational system is currently experiencing radical change, largely brought about by the effects of a global economic recession and a change in government in May 2010 which brought about a barrage of reforms to the education system and its services to support children, young people and their families (Ekins, 2012). As part of this accumulation of reform, the Green Paper *Support and Aspiration: A new approach to special educational needs* (DfE, 2011) has promised a wide range of changes in SEND provision in order to accelerate the government's case for change (DfE, 2012) which discussed the following three areas:

1   That every child deserves a fair start in life, with the very best opportunity to succeed.
2   Disabled children and children with SEN often feel frustrated by a lack of the right help at school or from other services.
3   The circumstances of children, young people and their parents can differ greatly; from young people requiring a few adjustments in class to children with life-limiting long-term conditions requiring a much longer term arrangement.

The government suggests that the life chances for approximately two million children and young people in England are 'disproportionately poor' because they have been identified as having a special educational need (SEN), or a disability (DfE, 2012).

Reflective task: *Gaining an awareness of needs*

Consider the children or young people in your setting/placement who may fall into the category of having a special educational need or disability.

- In what ways do you think children and young people might be disadvantaged because they have a SEND? Think about academic difficulties, play situations in and out of the classroom, emotional and social situations, and physical difficulties.

Consider what provision is already in place to ensure that each child's/young person's learning needs are provided for.

The government (DfE, 2012) suggests that poor provision for children and young people with a SEND, particularly those with complex needs such as autism, dyslexia, dyspraxia or **Attention Deficit Hyperactivity Disorder** (ADHD), is likely to significantly affect their quality of life. Parents and carers seeking to support their children often find the whole system around managing the needs of their child or young person difficult to penetrate, or gain access to in order to ensure effective learning opportunities for those they care for. In addition to this, the government suggests that the systems and provisions that are put in place by the educational setting to support such children and young people with a SEND do not necessarily provide the appropriate support needed. They claim that such systems can often appear unfriendly and difficult to access (DfE, 2012), and can be confusing to families who may have an in-depth knowledge and understanding of their child's or young person's needs but limited knowledge of the systems that should be supporting them. The Lamb Inquiry (2009: 3), which considered the voices of parents, found that parents believed 'good, honest and open communication [to be] one of the important components of building confidence and good relationships'. With this in mind the inquiry suggested that 'parents need to be listened to more and brought into a partnership with statutory bodies in a more meaningful way' (p. 3) in order that the parent's knowledge is used effectively in the educational setting. Such knowledge and understanding displayed by the **parent/carer** may appear to be undermined by professionals if communication is not maintained and invitations to contribute to multi-element planning are not offered. This can lead to parents/carers feeling frustrated, reproachful and critical towards the systems used when the child or young person does not progress well academically, socially or emotionally within the setting.

Such provisions and systems within the educational setting can also be particularly confusing and/or inaccessible to parents/carers whose child or young person is diagnosed with a SEND at the secondary or post-16 stage of education. The diagnosis of a SEND itself can be a debilitating experience to both the family and the child or young person, as they are expected to negotiate a system that uses language and terminology that may not appear to be looking directly to support them.

Activity: *Engaging with terminology*

Consider the following terms used by SEND professionals in educational settings; can you offer an explanation for each?

Accommodations	Curriculum-based assessment	Multi-element plan
Reasonable adjustment	Functional environment	Fine motor
Articulation	Assistive technology	Personalisation
Acuity	Executive functioning	Differentiation
Mainstreaming	Screening	Functional performance

Here are a couple of online glossaries to help you:

- www.disabilityrights.org/glossary.htm
- www.fetaweb.com/06/glossary.sped.legal.htm

How could you support a parent or carer who is seeing/hearing some of these terms for the first time on their child's/young person's multi-element plan (MEP)?

While professionals seek to manage the terminology used within their setting and ensure that such terms are understood and implemented correctly, practitioners and those training are also faced with a deluge of national and local policy with its high expectations of implementation.

The impact of the medical and social model on legislation for special educational needs and disability

Over the last 40 years reforms in SEND have been built upon legislation in order to ensure the inclusion of the learner in educational settings (Hodkinson and Vickerman, 2009). Prior to the 1970s, a child or young person with a SEND would not necessarily have been 'integrated' into an educational setting if it was thought that the child was not able to adapt to the setting. Gibson and Blandford (2005) explain that the term **integration** was used in the Warnock Report in 1978, which recommended that children and young people with a SEND could be placed into a mainstream classroom; however, the level of integration was seen as a 'limited form of education provision' (p. 9) that allowed the child or young person to be included in the physical environment of the mainstream classroom. The onus, interestingly, was on the child or young person with the SEND to make any necessary adaptations according to their needs to fit into the rigour of mainstream learning. This view of integration is now considered to form part of what is called the needs model of disability and integration, where as a consequence of the 1970 Education Act all children and young people were considered to be 'educable' (Thompson, 2010).

During the time period from the 1870 Education Act to the present day the educational provision for children and young people with SEND has been split into three time periods and three models of disability:

1   Medical model of disability and segregation (1870–1970).
2   Needs model of disability and integration (1971–1989).
3   Social model of disability and inclusion (1990–present). (Adapted from Gibson and Blandford, 2005)

Prior to 1970 and the onset of the needs model and integration introduced by the Warnock Report (1978), the impairment attached to the child or young person was thought to be the individual's problem and not viewed as an issue to concern anyone other than the individual affected. Reiser (2010) informs us that this view of disability is seen as the medical model of disability, where 'the impairment is focused on, rather than the needs of the person'. An example of medical model thinking can be seen where a child using a wheelchair is unable to gain access to a classroom because the doorway is too narrow. The medical model would suggest that the child cannot access the classroom because of the wheelchair, rather than the problem being the width of the doorway. The social model of disability, in contrast, which was developed during the 1990s by disability rights activists, would see the width of the doorway as the disabling barrier. The social model suggests that it is society that disables people, sometimes through fear or prejudice but often through the design of curriculum or environment that is designed to meet the needs of the majority of people who are not disabled. Table 6.1 demonstrates the differences in thinking between the medical and social model and the differences that can be made to remove some of the disabling barriers from an educational setting.

Table 6.1 Medical model thinking and Social model thinking: a comparison (adapted from Reiser, 2010 – see http://tinyurl.com/ams5l9w)

Medical model thinking	Social model thinking
Child is faulty	Child is valued
Diagnosis	Strengths and needs defined by self and others
Labelling	Identify barriers and develop solutions
Impairment becomes focus of attention	Outcome based programme designed
Assessment, monitoring, programmes of therapy imposed	Resources are made available to ordinary services
Segregation and alternative services	Training for parents/carers and professionals
Ordinary needs put on hold	Relationships nurtured
Re-entry if normal enough or permanent exclusion	Diversity welcomed, child is included
Society remains unchanged	Society evolves

Interestingly, the term inclusion did not arrive until the Salamanca Statement was issued by UNESCO in 1994 which called on all governments in the United Nations to 'adopt as a matter of law or policy the principle of inclusive education' (p. ix) with the suggestion that it should be the educational setting that should adapt or change in order to accommodate the learner with a SEND. The Salamanca Statement and Framework of Action that was formulated at the conference suggested that schools should assist children and young people with a SEND to become economically active and provide them with the skills needed in everyday life, offering training in skills that respond to the social and communication demands and expectations of adult life (UNESCO, 1994).

As surprising as some of these concepts appear to us now in the twenty-first century, it is useful to consider the context in which these reforms and models were acknowledged and the radical changes that have taken place in a reasonably short time. In order to put the policy into some perspective, take some time to consider Table 6.2, which gives an indication of the range of policy that has involved the move from integration to the inclusion of children and young people with a SEND.

For more information on these and additional policies, you may like to follow the following web link to help you map out the historical context further: http://tinyurl.com/b76cuvu.

The response to the consultation of the 2011 Green Paper *Support and Aspiration: A new approach to special education needs* has been produced in the form of the report *Next Steps*

(May 2012) with legislation due in early 2014. The *Next Steps* response outlines the government's vision for an educational system in which:

- children's special educational needs and disabilities are picked up early and support is routinely put in place quickly;
- staff have the knowledge, understanding and skills to provide the right support for children and young people who have SEN or are disabled wherever they are;
- parents and carers know what they can reasonably expect their local school, local college, local authority and local services to provide, without them having to fight for it;
- for more complex needs, an integrated assessment and a single Education, Health and Care Plan from birth to 25; and
- greater control for parents over the services they and their family use. (DfE, 2012)

Table 6.2 From integration to the inclusion of children and young people with a SEND: Policy/Legislation 1970–2012

Policy/Legislation	Details
1970 Education Act	All children and young people now considered to be educable
1978 The Warnock Report	Promoted integration into mainstream schooling for all with a SEND
1981 Education Act (conditions for Local Authorities)	Requirement to identify needs of learners with SEND and put a statement in place of how needs were to be met
1994 Salamanca Statement and framework	Adopt inclusive education, the setting expected to adapt rather than the learner
1997 Green Paper *Excellence for All Children: Meeting Special Educational Needs*	New Labour government – evolution of inclusive education. Inclusion firmly on the political agenda
2001 Special Educational Needs and Disability Act (SENDA)	Curriculum 2000 – revised National Curriculum to secure learning for all learners – followed by the SEN Code of Practice to strengthen the rights of all to be educated in mainstream schooling
2004 Children Act – Legislative support for *Every Child Matters*	To promote cooperation between agencies to ensure the **safeguarding** of children and young people
2011 Green Paper *Support and Aspiration: A new approach to special educational needs*	To provide a streamlined assessment and Education Healthcare Plan to bring all services together
2012 Next Steps	Implementation of new code of practice due in 2014

So what changes can we expect to see in the future? The *Next Steps* response informs that educational settings will be provided with:

1   a single assessment process which is more streamlined, better involves children, young people and families and is completed quickly;
2   an Education, Health and Care Plan which brings services together and is focused on improving outcomes; and
3   an offer of a personal budget for families with an Education, Health and Care Plan.

Reflective task: *Next steps and the impact on your setting*

- What differences or impact will the government's changes have on your educational setting/placement?
- Think about the current system where the local authority produces a statement of special educational needs and disability. Will streamlining this process benefit those with a SEND or overlook/discriminate against any children or young people on the borderline?
- What might be the benefits of an Education, Health and Care plan in your setting/placement?
- How effective is the notion of providing funding for parents/carers and how might such funding be designated?

Consider visiting the following web link – http://tinyurl.com/b2y2g8n – paying particular attention to pages 4–11 of the online document. Reflect back on your responses to the questions above in light of your engagement with the online reading.

Now that we have considered some of the governmental policies that feed into our practice we need to consider in more depth the notion of inclusive practice. Inclusive practice started to gain some initial recognition in the Warnock Report (1978); however, it was not fully introduced into our terminology until the Salamanca Statement (1994). Interestingly, the term **inclusion** is still a much-debated term and remains undefined.

Defining inclusive practice

Inclusive education has been emerging since the Warnock Report in 1978 and has been a focus of debate for most of this time. You may feel that your practice is as inclusive as the next practitioner's/trainee's, but how do you know you are 'being inclusive' and how do you ensure that inclusivity is present in your setting/placement? Avramidis *et al.* (2002: 158) inform us that the word inclusion is perceived by most people as a 'bewildering concept which can have a variety of interpretations and applications'. So, if we all have different interpretations of what inclusion is, how do we know it is happening in our setting/placement? It is difficult to imagine that we all understand the term and implement inclusion to all of our learners in the same way; although you may provide a good standard of learning for each individual, there is still considerable debate about whether inclusion is actually achievable (Norwich, 2002).

Reflective task: *Considering your own views on inclusion*
Reflect on your own personal views of inclusion and learning.

1   What is your definition of inclusion?
2   Where did you develop this definition of inclusion? Was it developed through personal experience, professional experience, qualifications, and/or research?
3   How does your definition of inclusion compare to your colleagues/peers?

Consider the following definitions of inclusion; do any of these definitions match your ideas of inclusion?

1   Ainscow *et al.* (2006: 2) suggest that inclusive practice requires 'significant changes to be made to the content, delivery and organisation of mainstream programmes' and is 'a whole school endeavour which aims to accommodate the learning needs of all students'. The discourse on inclusion has moved beyond simply focusing on the response to individuals to explore how settings, policies, cultures and structures can recognise and value diversity. Ainscow *et al.*'s view of inclusion points us in the direction of not just focusing on individual learning needs but suggests the requirement of making significant changes to our teaching programmes to ensure that we are teaching to a wider range of needs. What impact would this have in your setting/placement? Working with children or young people on a one-to-one basis in a smaller setting may involve only limited changes to content and delivery. However, working with a larger group of learners with a range of SENDs would involve the use of differentiation during the planning of content and during the actual delivery of the lesson to ensure that the different levels of need are accommodated for.

Activity: *Comparing planning needs for different settings*

Consider how differentiation in planning for content and delivery is applied in the following settings:

- pupil referral unit;
- youth detention centre;
- mainstream school classroom;
- hospital classroom;
- add your setting.

What impact do you think this has on your/others' workload?
   What impact do you think this use of differentiation has on (your) learners?

2   A further definition of inclusion is taken from the Centre for Studies in Inclusive Education (2002: 2) who suggest that inclusion is about all 'children and young people – with and without disabilities or difficulties – learning together in ordinary pre-school provision, schools, colleges and universities with appropriate networks of support'. Inclusion means 'enabling all students to participate fully in the life and work of mainstream settings, whatever their needs' (p. 2). There are many different ways of achieving this and an inclusive timetable might look different for each pupil/student.

   Again, a similar opinion in terms of accommodating learning needs, this statement assumes that all children and young people in a setting can learn together, and that the appropriate networks of support are in place for each individual learner, and that there is funding to support this.

3   Finally another definition of inclusion used in Farrell (2010: 105) suggests that inclusion is 'all children [being] educated together in the same mainstream classrooms, following the same curriculum, at the same point in time, and experiencing teaching essentially the same as other children'.

In this definition we can draw on the word 'same' being used four times. Does this mean that education is equal for each learner or is this closer to assuming a 'one size fits all' teaching approach? There are, of course, many other definitions of inclusion. However, from these definitions alone, it can be seen that the views from professionals on the idea of inclusion is complex, and that there is no one definition that tells us exactly what inclusion is. With this in mind, and as we consider our different learning settings, we would need to evaluate how our inclusive policies can be formed by taking information from an informed range of understanding, identifying where such knowledge can be applied to ensure that we are making the reasonable adjustments where we can in order to meet the needs of the children or young people in our settings.

Ensuring inclusive practice

Inclusive education is considered by Winter and O'Raw (2010) to be at the centre of human rights and equal opportunities. The use of inclusion in an educational setting challenges all those policies and practices that serve to exclude some children or young people from their right to education. The term 'inclusion' shifts the focus of adaptation from the child to the educational setting, unlike integration (remember the Warnock Report in 1978) which does not specify what should be done. The term inclusion is often used to describe the extent to which a child or young person with a SEND is involved as a full member of the educational setting with full access to and participation in all aspects of education. It is thought that inclusion better conveys the right to belong to the mainstream and a joint endeavour to end discrimination and to work towards equal opportunities for all (Centre for Studies in Inclusive Education, 2002).

Reflective task: *Demonstrating your awareness of needs*

Reflect on your planning for effective learning and inclusion. When you plan your session/lessons/activities do you:

- Think about setting suitable learning challenges for all learners?
- Consider what the diverse learning needs of the children/young people you work with might involve?
- Explore how you could overcome any barriers to learning?
- Consider alternative assessment/s?

Developing knowledge and understanding of the key SENDs in 0-19 settings

Following the introduction of the 2001 SEN Code of Practice (DfES, 2001a), and in response to the requests from professionals in local authorities, schools, health and social services who needed more explicit guidance on evaluating and implementing the policy into their settings, the government provided an SEN toolkit (DfES, 2001b) which provided suggestions and practical advice on how to implement the Code of Practice. Broken up in 12 different sections, each part of the toolkit – available at http://tinyurl.com/byop6uu – was seen to be relevant to certain groups of professionals. In addition to the toolkit the government also produced a report entitled *Data Collection by Type of Special Educational Needs* in 2003, which was consequently updated in 2005 (DfES, 2005). Although the main areas of difficulty or special need are set out in the 2001 SEN Code of Practice (DfES, 2001a), the DfES (2005) publication provided more detailed information. The government sub-divided some of the broader areas of SEND into the categories used by Ofsted as shown in Table 6.3.

Table 6.3 Categories of SEND (adapted from DfES, 2005 and Gibson and Blandford, 2005: 21)

Category	Areas of need
A	**Cognition and learning needs** • Specific learning difficulty • Moderate learning difficulty • Severe learning difficulty • Profound and multiple learning difficulty
B	**Behavioural, emotional and social developmental needs** • Behaviour, emotional and social difficulty
C	**Communication and interaction needs** • Speech, language and communication needs • Autistic spectrum disorder
D	**Sensory and/or physical needs** • Visual impairment • Hearing impairment • Multi-sensory impairment • Physical disability

Case study

Consider the following case study of Ahrif in a Year 7 mainstream educational setting. Can you identify any characteristics that might lead you to suspect any of the SENDs identified in Table 6.3?

Upon arriving in the ICT lab, Ahrif (age 11) raced over to switch on the nearest computer, eager to get started on his favourite computer software. The log on screen soon became the treasured board game he had been constructing in great detail for the past two weeks. The teacher called out to the class that no computers were to be switched on yet and that all learners were to stop what they were doing and listen carefully. Ahrif obediently turned towards the teacher, leaving the computer on standby. During the process of instruction, Ahrif accidently caught the mouse with his elbow which brought up the screen he had been working on. The teacher was disappointed with Ahrif and following school procedures for pupils who are disobedient, gave Ahrif a lunchtime detention. Ahrif tried to explain that he had already switched the computer on previous to the instructions not to, but this brought about a lengthier detention. Ahrif continued to try and explain, growing more anxious by the second, flapping his arms and glaring in embarrassment. Ahrif continued to profess his innocence which brought about even more direct discipline from the teacher in terms of detention time and the threat of calling a senior member of staff, which resulted in Ahrif swearing angrily at the teacher, pushing his desk out of the way and storming out of the classroom.

- Which SEND do you think is being displayed by Ahrif?
- Where do you think this SEND fits into the categories taken from the *Data collection by Type of Special Educational Needs* suggested by the DfE (2005)? A, B, C or D? All of them?
- What are the risks of trying to identify and manage a SEND incorrectly: a) for the professional; and b) for the child/young person?

The situation above resulted in the young man being excluded from his educational setting for three weeks and being placed in another school's behavioural unit which caused much distress and confusion for both Ahrif and his family. A diagnosis of **Asperger's Syndrome** was reached not long after this incident when Ahrif had turned 12. However, there could be other characteristics from other types of SEND in this case study, e.g. behaviour, emotional and social difficulty or speech, language and communication needs and sensory needs.

Hannell (2006) reminds us that most professionals working with children and young people will sometimes have concerns about a learning or behavioural difficulty, and may need to make a decision about whether to seek further advice or make a referral so that a correct diagnosis can be made and a multi-element learning plan (MEP) put into place. To support the professional, Hannell (2006) has produced a range of checklists which may help in differentiating lesson content, and providing opportunities for the learner to participate more fully in the class; consider using and adapting these in your own practice. In addition to Hannell's suggestions, Manchester City Council produced a report (2010) giving guidance for professionals on the identification, assessment and strategies to support young people from minority ethnic groups who may also have a special educational need or disability.

Activity: *Browse the link*

The following web link takes you to the report *Minority ethnic pupils and special educational needs: Guidance and self-evaluation for schools on identification, assessment and strategies for minority ethnic pupils who may also have a special educational need* (Manchester City Council, 2010) - http://tinyurl.com/aqxfl8f

The report explains the process that professionals need to take in order to identify difficulties with the progress in children and young people with a particular emphasis on minority ethnic pupils and gives suggestions on referrals around the following:

1   learners' communication;
2   learning;
3   social, emotional and behaviour needs;
4   physical and sensory needs.

Actively engage with the report by annotating it, making notes, highlighting it and summarising sections.

- How useful are these suggestions to your setting/placement?
- Are they only useful for professionals managing the SENDs of minority ethnic pupils?
- Could you add any further suggestions to support the children or young people in your setting/placement?

By engaging with this chapter it is hoped that you are becoming a little more familiar with a range of SENDs. The following case study is offered to see if you are able to identify the SENDs which Sophie has.

Case study

Sophie, aged 15, is studying art and is obsessed with drawing Manga characters in great detail. She has created over 50 comics and has collected hundreds of Manga books and films and series. Although her drawings are of excellent standard, her sentence structure is often confused with many spelling errors. During class, Sophie tries to listen and make notes but struggles to remember what the teacher has said, and during practical work finds it difficult to follow and remember instructions. She seems to find it difficult to understand what is expected of her. Sophie is afraid to ask for help and does not usually like working with others. The teacher has noticed that sometimes Sophie looks blank and that her eyes flutter as she gazes out of the window. Sophie appears to be quite anxious and often arrives late to class.

It is possible that Sophie is showing signs of **dyslexia**, **epilepsy** and either **dyspraxia** or **autism**, due to her literacy difficulties, short-term memory problems, obsession with comics and her blank gaze (this is often referred to as *petite mal*). However, these are only the author's initial thoughts – you may identify different conditions. There may be overlapping conditions, which Dittrich and Tutt (2008: 3) refer to as 'co-morbidity' or 'co-existing disorders', which are the terms used when the same child or young person has more than one SEND. It is essential to note here that it is not our role as professionals to diagnose a SEND but rather to be able to identify the barriers to learning so that the necessary provision can be put in place to support the child or young person.

The twice exceptional child: gifted and talented children with disabilities

Interestingly, a report from the Council of Curriculum, Examinations and Assessment (CCEA) (2006: 65) suggests that children and young people who are gifted and also have a SEND tend to be recognised first for their disability and 'more frequently, emphasis is placed on remediating the disability than on nurturing the child's individual gifts and talents and in some cases the disability may entirely obstruct recognition of talent'. An estimate given by Evans (2009) suggests that there are likely to be between 5–10 per cent of gifted pupils who could have a learning difficulty and that 2–5 per cent of pupils with disabilities may also be gifted. Without good observation and an understanding of both gifted and talented and SEND education, such learners could find their gift or talent is overlooked.

Activity: *Gifted, talented and SEND*

What if a child or young person in your setting is displaying some of the characteristics you have identified as a SEND but they are also displaying a gift or talent? Sophie appears to have a talent for art and Ahrif could be gifted in managing computer software.

Which do you think would be observed and managed first in your educational setting/placement – would it be:

- the gift;
- the talent;
- the SEND?

What might be the result for the child or young person's learning if only their SEND is focused upon? What might be the result if the gift or talent is valued and the SEND disregarded?

For more information on gifted and talented children and young people, please see Chapter 5.

Strategies to manage SEND in an educational setting

There are many books, articles and websites that provide ideas and strategies for the effective learning management of children and young people with a SEND. However, getting some of the basics right initially can go a long way to supporting a range of SENDs in the learning environment. Some of the key areas that need addressing to provide a more inclusive educational setting are to ensure that there is a range of support workers who are trained to work one-to-one or in small groups with the children or young people with SEND. Using resources that have been adapted to meet the needs of each child or young person can also serve well to ensure that those who are struggling with a concept, whether they have a SEND or not, have the opportunity to experience inclusion and complete the given task.

An area of particular and current interest in educational settings is the range of ICT applications on offer. Often referred to as assisted ICT, the use of ICT can provide a range of opportunities for children and young people with SEND so that they can engage in **multi-sensory learning** which can enable them to express themselves through the use of light, touch or sound. SCoTENS (n.d.; see http://tinyurl.com/bg3n57a) suggests that 'pupils with visual problems can be helped through the use of different coloured screens and fonts'. Speech-to-text software can support pupils with dyslexia and a variety of software programmes can be set at different levels in order to engage pupils with different levels of learning difficulty. The use of careful questioning to identify that learning is taking place has also been found to benefit children and young people with a SEND, and to check that the curriculum content is being presented at the right level. Too often a child or young person with a SEND can experience failure because they have 'misunderstood or overly completed a task' (Betts, Betts and Gerber-Eckard, 2007: 52).

Reflective task

Consider the SENDs in the grid below. Where possible we need to meet individual needs, but there are some strategies that we could put in place that could meet the needs of most/all learners with or without a SEND.

- Which strategies are you using already?
- Which of the following might you need to adopt?

Special educational need or disability	Some of the characteristics	Useful strategies
Autism/Asperger's Syndrome/High Functioning Autism	Social/communication difficulties. Misunderstanding/rigid thinking. Obsessions.	One to one and small group structured teaching. Visual timetables and use of visuals (picture exchange communication system - PECS) to explain what to do next. Give opportunity to move around.
Dyslexia	Short term memory difficulties. Difficulty with literacy, reading, writing and spelling.	One to one structured, progressive teaching. Use a variety of teaching approaches to engage the senses e.g. speaking, listening, seeing, movement and touch.
Dyspraxia	Difficulty with coordinated movement (motor coordination). Slow to develop motor milestones and handwriting.	Give opportunity to move around. Practise fine motor skills. Build self-esteem. Use short, clear sentences when instructing.
ADHD	Always on the go. Acts impulsively. Often blurts out inappropriate comments. Talking incessantly.	Keep instructions simple and clear. Position close to a supervising adult. Give firm reminders of what is required. Provide a place of safety to retreat and calm down. Provide opportunities to move around.

(adapted from Terrell and Passenger, 2011)

Many of the strategies for managing the learning of children and young people with SEND are common sense; however, by creating an environment that already includes many of these inclusive teaching strategies, we can then make any reasonable adjustments not already in place, as required.

Conclusion

As the government moves forward with its changes within the special educational needs and disability sector, the notion of inclusion will undoubtedly still be up for debate. As the focus on special educational needs and disability finds itself high on the government agenda for change, we can look forward to a new era of SEND provision and policy that provides a more effective learning experience for those of our learners who need and deserve the best education that can be provided for them.

Further reading

Books

Terrell, C. and Passenger, T. (2011) *Understanding ADHD, Autism, Dyslexia and Dyspraxia*. Dorset: The British Medical Association/Family Doctor Publications.
This book offers a clear guide to the definition of a range of SENDs, strategies to support the child or young person, and case studies which put the SEND into context, both in the home and the educational setting.

Hannell, G. (2006) *Identifying Children with Special Needs: Checklists and Action Plans for Teachers*. London: Sage.
An informative book which contains a range of checklists and action plans to support the identification and learning management of children and young people with a SEND.

Academic publications

Leatherman, J. and Niemeyer, J. (2005) Teachers' Attitudes Toward Inclusion: Factors influencing classroom practice, *Journal of Early Childhood Teacher Education*, 26 (1), 23–36. [Online]. Available at: http://tinyurl.com/b6p7ok2 (Accessed: 19 May 2013).
This paper demonstrates the wholehearted commitment of professionals in terms of inclusion, but also highlights the difficulties experienced by professionals and those new to the sector who are faced with teaching children and young people with SEND.

Barnes, P. (2008) Multi-agency working: what are the perspectives of SENCOs and parents regarding its development and implementation? *British Journal of Special Education*, 35(4), 230–240.
This paper discusses the notion of multi-agency working and how professionals are working to ensure that children and young people with SEND are supported through educational, social and health care agencies.

Web link

The inclusive learning and teaching handbook – available at: http://tinyurl.com/bc9jsvt.
This web link offers a handbook that is focused on students with SEND in higher education. However, it contains some useful ideas and strategies to support a range of settings in managing the learning needs of learners with SEND.

References

Abbott, L. (2006) Northern Ireland head teachers' perceptions of inclusion. *International Journal of Inclusive Education*, 10 (6), 627–643.

Ainscow, M., Booth, T. and Dyson, A. (2006) *Improving Schools, Developing Inclusion*, London: Routledge.

Avramadis, E., Bayliss, P. and Burden, R. (2002) Inclusion in action: an in-depth case study of an effective inclusive secondary school in the south-west of England. *International Journal of Inclusive Education*, 6 (2), 143–163.

Barnes, P. (2008) Multi-agency working: what are the perspectives of SENCOs and parents regarding its development and implementation? *British Journal of Special Education*, 35 (4), 230–240.

Betts, S. W., Betts, D. E. and Gerber-Eckard, L. N. (2007) *Asperger Syndrome in the Inclusive Classroom: Advice and strategies for teachers*. London: Jessica Kingsley Publishers.

Centre for Studies in Inclusive Education (2013). [Online]. Available at: www.csie.org.uk/ (Accessed: 20 May 2013).

Council of Curriculum, Examinations and Assessment (CCEA) (2006) *Gifted and talented children in (and out) of the classroom*. [Online]. Available at: www.nicurriculum.org.uk/docs/inclusion_and_sen/gifted/gifted_children_060306.pdf (Accessed: 30 January 2013).

DfES (2001a) *Special Educational Needs Code of Practice*. [Online]. Available at: www.education.gov.uk/publications/standard/publicationDetail/Page1/DfES%200581%202001 (Accessed: 20 May 2013).

——(2001b) SEN toolkit. [Online]. Available at: www.education.gov.uk/publications/standard/publicationDetail/Page1/DfES%200558%202001 (Accessed: 20 May 2013).

——(2005) *Data Collection by Type of Special Educational Needs*. [Online]. Available at: http://webarchive.nationalarchives.gov.uk/20130401151715/https://www.education.gov.uk/publications/standard/_arc_Governancemanagementandfinance/Page6/DFES-1889-2005 (Accessed: 20 May 2013).

Department for Education (2011) *Support and aspiration: A new approach to special educational needs and disability*. [Online]. Available at: www.education.gov.uk/consultations/downloadableDocs/SEND%20Green%20Paper.pdf (Accessed: 30 August 2013).

——(2012) *The Government's case for change*. [Online]. Available at: www.education.gov.uk/childrenandyoungpeople/send/b0075291/green-paper (Accessed: 12 May 2013).

Dittrich, W. and Tutt, R. (2008) *Education Children with Complex Conditions: Understanding overlapping and co-existing developmental disorders*. London: Sage.

Ekins, A. (2012) *The Changing Face of Special Educational Needs: Impact and Implications for SENCOs and their schools*. Abingdon: Routledge.

Evans, L. (2009) *Links between SEN and gifted & talented: part 1*. [Online]. Available at: www.teachingexpertise.com/e-bulletins/links-between-sen-and-gifted-and-talented-6636 (Accessed: 12 May 2013).

Farrell, M. (2010) *Debating Special Education*, Oxon: Routledge.

Gibson, S. and Blandford, S. (2005) *Managing Special Educational Needs*. London: Paul Chapman Publishers.

Gillard, D. and Horsington, C. (2012) *The History of Education in England*. [Online]. Available at: www.educationengland.org.uk/ (Accessed: 12 May 2013).

Grandin, T. (2011) *The way I see it: A personal look at Autism and Asperger's*. 2nd edn. Arlington TX: Future Horizons.

Hannell, G. (2006) *Identifying Children with Special Needs, Checklists and Action Plans for Teachers*. London: Sage Publications.

Hodkinson, A. and Vickerman, P. (2009) *Key Issues in Special Educational Needs and Inclusion*. London: Sage.

Lamb, B. (2009) *Lamb Inquiry: special educational needs and parental confidence*. [Online]. Available at: http://webarchive.nationalarchives.gov.uk/20130401151715/https://www.education.gov.uk/publications/eOrderingDownload/01143-2009DOM-EN.pdf (Accessed: 12 May 2013).

Leatherman, J. and Niemeyer, J. (2005) Teachers' Attitudes Toward Inclusion: Factors influencing classroom practice. *Journal of Early Childhood Teacher Education*, 26 (1), 23–36. [Online]. Available at: www.tandfonline.com/doi/pdf/10.1080/10901020590918979 (Accessed: 19 May 2013).

Manchester City Council (2010) *Minority ethnic pupils and special educational needs: Guidance and self-evaluation for schools on identification, assessment and strategies for minority ethnic pupils who may also have a special educational need.* [Online]. Available at: www.mewan.net/senco/getfile.php?src=60/EMA+and+SEN+Guidance.pdf (Accessed: 12 May 2013).

Norwich, B. (2002) Education, inclusion and individual differences: Recognising and resolving dilemmas. *British Journal of Education Studies*, 50(4), 482–592.

Reiser, R. (2010) *Disability Equality*. [Online]. Available at: www.worldofinclusion.com/index.htm (Accessed: 30 August 2013).

Stowe, C. (2000) *How to reach and teach children and teens with Dyslexia*. San Francisco: Jossey-Bass.

Terrell, C. and Passenger, T. (2011) *Understanding ADHD, Autism, Dyslexia and Dyspraxia*. Dorset: The British Medical Association/Family Doctor Publications.

Thompson, J. (2010) *The Essential Guide to Understanding Special Educational Needs*. Harlow: Pearson.

United Nations Educational, Scientific and Cultural Organisation (UNESCO) (1994) *The Salamanca Statement and framework for action on special needs education*. [Online]. Available at: www.unesco.org/education/pdf/SALAMA_E.PDF (Accessed: 12 May 2013).

Warnock, M. (1978) *The Warnock Report: Special Educational Needs*. London: Her Majesty's Stationery Office. [Online]. Available at: www.educationengland.org.uk/documents/warnock/ (Accessed: 10 February 2013).

Winter, E. and O'Raw, P. (2010) *Literature Review of the Principles and Practices relating to Inclusive Education for Children with special Educational Needs*. [Online]. Available at: www.ncse.ie/uploads/1/NCSE_Inclusion.pdf (Accessed: 12 May 2013).

7 Children, young people and risk - *just about managing?*

Sarah McMullen

LEARNING OBJECTIVES

After studying this chapter, you will be able to:

✔ Recognise the difference between 'risk' and being 'at risk'.
✔ Understand risk factors and responses.
✔ Identify the professional responsibilities that a practitioner/trainee has to themselves as well as children and young people at risk.
✔ Evaluate different approaches to risk management in professional practice with children and young people.

To begin with it is necessary to acknowledge that as professional practitioners/trainees we must be careful when using definitions and categorisations to describe the behaviour of children and young people. These definitions can be disempowering and consequently put children and young people further at risk. In spite of this, being absolutely clear about what we mean by a phrase or term when we use it, in association with practice with children and young people, is equally as important.

Introduction

In professional practice with children and young people a great deal of emphasis is placed on *identifying* risks (sexual, psychological, physical and emotional), *assessing* risk (the level of harm that it may produce) and *responding to* risk (planning, minimising, avoiding, modifying and managing). To be able to do this effectively, practical and emotional strategies, tools and resourcefulness are needed by practitioners/trainees. Understanding the outcomes of risk is an important starting point. These outcomes will enable you to recognise some of the factors which the children and young people you are working/training with are experiencing in relation to risk. This understanding can lead you to see risk as something that can be dangerous and developmental. Your response to a child or young person at risk can then be something that does not just *manage* the risk that they are living with or engaging in, but also enables possible opportunities for social and emotional *development* as an alternative response. This chapter is about developing the outcomes of risk, not just about managing them.

Professional responsibilities and risk

As has been previously suggested, practitioners and trainees who work/train with children and young people are often expected to identify, assess and respond to risk in practice. A practitioner/ trainee can feel under a lot of pressure to 'get it right' and not to miss anything that may leave a child or young person in harm's way or at risk. Practitioners and trainees should be trained/taught about the importance of responding to risk in practice, for example through implementing **child protection** procedures when there is evidence that the emotional, psychological and physical welfare of the child or young person is at risk. We as practitioners/trainees should also learn in supported environments strategies for coping at an emotional level when exposed to situations where we too feel vulnerable. Some of our coping strategies come from our natural **resilience**; some come from professional knowledge that can create a learnt form of resilience, and some is based on reflexivity in and on practice (Schön, 1996). It is our training, our experience and our level of resilience that enables us to work with children and young people at risk effectively.

Furlong and Cartmel (2006) argue that people are increasingly moving away from the old securities that kept them and the world in which they live feeling safe, and are putting more energy and focus upon the prevention and exclusion of the new risks which are becoming embedded individually in their lives. Children and young people, however, have a less developed sense of vulnerability and perceived risk; this can mean that as professionals we have to be aware of our own vulnerability within a situation as well as the vulnerability of the child or young person at risk. In order to do this, we have to have professional knowledge about the following: clear boundaries, accessible support, knowledge of child protection and health and safety procedures, a consistent approach and a degree of **emotional intelligence** (Goleman, 1998). We also have to have demographic, environmental, family and individual knowledge of the child or young person that we are to support; this knowledge can lead us to identify the factors that cause risk for the child or young person that we are there to support.

Reflective task

Think about the ways in which you have been exposed to risk in your personal or professional life and how well you have survived it:

1   What was the risk?
2   Was the risk experienced through a situation you found yourself in or through a choice that you made?
3   How did you respond to the risk?
4   Did you seek help or support to deal with the risk?
5   By reflecting back (Schön, 1996), what have you learnt about yourself as a result of your experience of risk?

Understanding risk in professional practice with children and young people

At one level, how risk is experienced and lived by us all is a defining feature of our daily lives; the impact of it and our approach to it is dependent on who we are and the resources we have available to us. At another level, we frequently read or hear about dreadful acts of violence, natural disasters, and acts of terrorism or incomprehensible accidents that have harmed people or put them at extreme risk. When we hear that children and young people are affected, we are often more shaken than if just adults were involved. This reaction, it is argued, is because children and young people are more vulnerable to experiencing danger and consequently risk. As adults we feel compelled to protect them and angry when they have not been protected. As adults we have more understanding and awareness of the consequences of risk, and so in the main we try to avoid or manage them. Children and young people rarely have this understanding and awareness. Because of this, early years providers, schools, after-school clubs, colleges and youth work providers work hard to raise children's and young people's awareness of healthy relationships and lifestyles, in an attempt to build awareness and a level of resilience to risk. However, too much knowledge and awareness of risk can create barriers and almost be damaging in its own right. It can leave a child too scared to risk being away from their parents/carers (their protectors) and miss out on a friend's sleepover or trips away. It can leave a young person in an abusive relationship as they are too scared of risking the unknown to leave. A young person who is too concerned about the risks of living away from home may not go on to further study or move away to get a job. A child who only ever gets their parents'/carers' attention when they have broken a known rule may grow up with very low self-esteem and confidence – they know what they cannot do but not what they can do. Too much knowledge and awareness of risk can also remove all barriers; it can influence children and young people to seek kicks and highs through dangerous activities and relationships, making the risk of danger seem exciting and almost a rite of passage.

 Activity

In June 2012, the BBC News website published this article:

Police warn Jersey teenagers about Facebook lifts page
Jersey teenagers are breaking the law and putting themselves at risk by charging for lifts to strangers, the States of Jersey Police has said. The comments come after a page was set up on social networking site Facebook, where anyone can post their numbers and ask for a lift home. Acting Chief Inspector Mary Le Hegerat said it was dangerous and the drivers were breaking the law by accepting money. The Jersey Lifts page has 996 members so far. Those who had joined the group on the page complained that taxis were too expensive and there were no late buses.

If you were working with some of the young people using this service, how would you plan a piece of work that enabled them to identify, assess and respond to the potential risks of this service?

'Risk' and 'at risk'

Risk can be exciting, challenging and controlling; it can build and reduce opportunity and choice. It can nurture confidence, increase danger, and enable political, educational and social development. It can be minimised, increased and managed. It can be at the heart of harm; it can enable emancipation. It can foster resilience; it can be fundamental to change and the outcome of inequality and circumstance. Despite the plethora of definitions of what risk can be, the term is most often used in both our personal and professional lives in the context of danger or harm. Historically, risk has been part of everyday life for some time. It is argued that in centuries past people believed that danger was everywhere and they constructed systems based on this belief to control and reduce danger. Not 'buying into' these systems was considered laying oneself, as Lupton (2013: 3) suggests, at the 'mercy of fate, to relinquish any senses of control' or in other words individuals were putting themselves at unnecessary risk by not taking control of all the aspects of their lives. Nowadays, having control over your life and the impact of influences on it is still considered important and a means of survival; although the dangers we face today have changed, the need to protect ourselves and others from risk and harm has not.

Hepburn and White (1990: 5) suggest that the term '**at risk**' is 'particularly applied to young people whose prospects for becoming productive members of society look dim', as they will consistently experience what Bell and Bell (1993) describe as either dangerous or life-threatening risk in a cyclic manner. Extremes such as thrill seeking, drug and substance misuse, having unprotected sex, befriending strangers on-line, poverty, social exclusion, homelessness, involvement with the social justice system, repeated patterns of unhealthy relationships and unemployment all fall into this category. Vulnerable or young people considered at risk fall into one of the following four categories:

1   They take control of their life.
2   They try to take control over parts or all of their life.
3   They do not want to take control over parts or all of their life.
4   They have no control over any part of their life.

These differences are caused by a variety of different factors (which we will explore later in this chapter). However, they can all lead to the same consequence: exposure to risk.

Activity

The term 'at risk' is used as a broad statement and includes a wide range of children and young people. Some examples include children and young people who:

- are disabled;
- have mental ill health difficulties;
- are from black and ethnic minority groups;
- are refugee and asylum seekers;

- are in care (children's homes, foster and adoption);
- are known to the criminal justice system or at risk of offending;
- are homeless;
- are excluded from school or non-attenders;
- mis-use drugs or alcohol;
- are young carers or parents;
- have absent parents;
- are living in areas of economic deprivation and poverty;
- are living in rural isolation.

> Adapted from *Making Connections Toolkit, Including Young People* (engage, 2006).

Choose three of the 'at risk' factors above (or use your own) and write a list of the types of risk that children or young people may face associated with each factor. For example, if a young person has mental ill health difficulties they may feel isolated, lack confidence, have few social networks and struggle with their attendance at school or college. They may harm themselves or become addicted to high risk-taking activities such as drink driving and unprotected sex as ways of trying to 'feel better'.

Risk-taking behaviour

Through the past decade a range of national policy has been actively created to respond to the impact of risk and risk-taking behaviour in the lives of children and young people. Policies such as *Every Child Matters* (DfES, 2003), *Youth Matters* (DfES, 2005) and *Youth Matters: Next Steps* (DfES, 2006) have been instrumental in shaping professional practice for children and young people. These policies have provided a pooled programme of change to improve outcomes for all children and young people. However, in recent years, youth policy in particular has either been lacking or diverted to policy on prevention of crime and youth justice. Because of this, dealing with troubled or troublesome children and young people is now a major policy concern in practice. Even the most recent policy in support of engaging with young people at risk – *Positive for Youth* (DfE, 2011) – looks to minimise the impact of risk on others, but provides very little in the way of clear strategies or guidance for practitioners to tackle the existence of risk in the lives of the young people they are working with.

A child or young person's idea of what risk is and the impact it can have is often based on their personal and situational experience of life. Because of this they may not see the circumstances that they grow up in and the ways in which they live their lives as consciously or unconsciously contributing towards the difficulties that they face or their behaviour. Abbott-Chapman and Denholm (2001) and Bell and Bell (1993) focus some of their thinking on behaviours of children and young people at risk. Abbott-Chapman and Denholm (2001) discuss levels of risk perception and levels of risk participation in the behaviour of children and young people. They suggest that some of the highest risk-taking activities identified in their research (sharing needles and starving or slimming) had very low levels of participation, suggesting that some of the greatest risk-taking behaviours were the ones that were least engaged in. Bell and Bell (1993), on the other hand, categorise levels of general risk taking behaviour demonstrated by children and young people at risk. These include creative and developmentally enhancing behaviours (e.g. rock climbing, canoeing), dangerous behaviours (e.g. joy riding, unprotected sex, petty crime), and life threatening behaviours (e.g. fighting with knives or guns, gang membership). These categories are quite simplistic but they enable us to have a measurable starting point when trying to categorise the risks and associated behaviours we see in practice. Creative and developmentally enhancing levels of risk are crucial in enabling children and young people to learn about areas such as working together with others, assessing levels of risk, health and safety and emotional comfort levels. They also enable an understanding of resilience and building confidence and esteem. The dangerous and life threatening levels of risk (Bell and Bell, 1993) that children and young people engage in can unfortunately normalise danger and destructive behaviour. It is argued widely that the destructive individual factors involved in risky behaviour have outcomes that include low academic performance, poor self-esteem, underestimating one's own vulnerability, a lack of skills to resist peer pressure, seeking immediate rather than deferred rewards, poor personal attachments and low aspiration.

Case study

On 21 November 2012 the BBC News website published the following case study to try and highlight a survivor's story of abuse after being lured by drink and drugs.

A report from the Children's Commissioner for England has suggested that thousands of children are sexually abused by gangs and groups each year. This is one child's story.

Things were going well for Emma until, at the age of 12, she was raped by an older male friend. And then, on her 13th birthday, she was lured into a dangerous world of drink and drugs by some older boys. 'They took us out in their cars and gave us whizz [amphetamines], weed and drink. Then they started texting us and wanting us to come out all the time. I would stay out all night and come home at 5am. I don't know why I did it, I guess it was exciting. It was tearing my family apart, I know that now.' Sometime later Emma was at the house of a friend when some boys and men turned up with drink and drugs. 'I don't know how it happened, but I ended up in a room on my own with one of them. He raped me and then other men came in. They took turns. I just laid there. Inside I was in bits, I just felt so empty. I saw some money on the side and managed to drag myself up and snatch it. I ran out of the house and got a taxi home. I told my mum when I got in – it was awful. I felt so dirty, I couldn't shower, I had to wait for the police and have all these tests. I had bruises all over.'

Consider the following:

- In what ways was Emma's behaviour risky?
- What were the risks she faced?
- Who did her behaviour affect?
- As a professional practitioner/trainee how would you support Emma?

Fear, resilience and risk

Because there is such a diverse attitude to risk and risk-taking behaviour, a balanced understanding of the characteristics of risk is important when approaching risk in professional practice with children and young people. Two of these elements are fear surrounding risk and the qualities of resilience to survive risk. Fear surrounding risk is there partly because not enough is known about certain risks; it is also partly there because so much is known about certain risks and it is also partly there because not all risks are manageable. Fear can be paralysing; it can restrict a person's world dramatically, limit potential and be the root of bigotry and oppression, but it can also be the impetus to act. If we relate fear to risk, one argument would be that fear of risk is broad and accepted; the nature and experience of fear, however, is individual. It is for these reasons that fear can either disable and de-motivate or enable and motivate the drive within a child or young person to engage in an activity. This is particularly true in the **transition** from childhood to adulthood, when identities are being shaped and motivations for exploring different aspects of life are being discovered. As a practitioner/trainee understanding the fear that is experienced by a child or a young person is crucial to understanding the motivations for certain behaviours (high and low levels of risk). If we can get to the heart of fear, we can sometimes get to the heart of how to enable change in the behaviour of a child or young person at risk, or demonstrating risky behaviour. The relationship between fear and resilience is strong. It can be fear of particular outcomes in life that build or destroy resilience. Risk-taking behaviours can be a sign of peer pressure, a lack of adaptability and consequently a lack of resilience. As practitioners/trainees we need to be aware that the demonstration of resilience and fear, in relation to risk, is specific to each individual. Resilience relates to levels of survival and strength and is at its strongest when coping strategies are developed and implemented, adaptability is fostered, and there is little hesitation in asking for help. Resilience can be at its weakest, however, when some of the individual dangerous and life threatening behaviours of risk are demonstrated.

Building resilience is something Norman (2000) suggests is a set of strategies that young people develop to manage their lives. It can also be a set of strategies that young people can be supported to learn and develop as these kind of strategies are not always the default position that a child or young person starts from. Much is written about resilience and risk and it is difficult to discuss the associations of risk to children and young people without including resilience. The focus of whether resilience is something that individuals have naturally, or whether it is something that is nurtured within an individual, has been the source of much academic and professional debate. Ungar (2004: 4) describes resilience as a social construction or a label that researchers have given individuals who 'survive and make their own sense of adversity' or risk. However, Gilligan (2001) suggests that resilience is the healing capacity within each child and their friendship groups. Clarke and Nicholson (2010: 9) suggest that resilience is about 'individual difference – why one person differs from another and why each of us is the person that we are'. Why one person is deeply harmed or harms someone else through engagement in risk, and why another person harnesses the risk and manages the impact of it on themselves and others, is the focus of identity and difference. These are recurring themes when discussing children, young people and resilience. Norman (2000: 3) suggests that 'resilience combines the interaction of two conditions: risk-factors that increase the vulnerability of individuals and the presence of personal, familial and community protective factors that protect against those vulnerabilities'. She goes on to suggest that the way in which a person will adapt or bounce back from adversity will be different in all of us; it will also vary with the individual over the course of their lifetime. Thomsen (2002: 9) argues that there are 'seeds of resilience within each person, essentially it is the person's ability to remain steady or to bounce back in spite of adversity'; however, is being able to bounce back always the most beneficial thing to do? Survivors of abuse may not necessarily agree; sometimes resilience can create more harm. Young people moving through the transition from childhood to adulthood can be prone to struggling with their emotions, as transitions through life are rarely linear and straightforward. As a result, young people can at times be in a state of emotional flux which makes trying to control or manage situations very difficult as decisions can be made based on feelings rather than facts or experience, thus at times creating more risk.

Risk factors and responses

As practitioners/trainees we need to have an awareness of the factors that cause risks as well as the types of risk-taking behaviours that can be demonstrated with these factors (Norman, 2000); only then will we begin to understand how to respond effectively and developmentally to risk.

Risk factors vary constantly for everyone and are dependent on so many different general influences: the social and political environment, the community, the family and the individual themselves. Specific factors that can be more exclusive to children and young people (Furlong and Cartmel, 2007; Fitch, 2009), include electronic social networks, crime, mental ill health, poverty, family, the environment, social exclusion, addiction and the individual themselves. The reason that some people suffer more as a result of exposure to risk factors is due to a lack of awareness of risk on one hand and peer, social, health, media, cultural, family and economic pressure on the other (Norman, 2000). For example,

- some children and young people are born into social and economic deprivation;
- some children and young people have care givers that are absent or that cannot look after them well enough;
- some children and young people are given money and material things instead of love and guidance;
- some children and young people are looked after wholly by professionals and some are carers themselves;
- some children and young people suffer poor mental and/or physical ill health and become cut off from their communities and friendship groups; the list goes on.

A commonality in professional practice with children and young people facing risk is that when risk factors are assessed, identified and responded to by professionals then the child or young person's opportunities and life chances will usually change dramatically. Effective professional intervention can change the outcomes of living with risk or being at risk for the better. This can be done by developing a greater understanding of how the risk factors that children and young people face are created and maintained, and the ways in which these can manifest themselves in their behaviour. McElwee (2007) suggests that there are factors that increase levels of conscious and unconscious harmful risk-taking behaviour, particularly among children and young people; these fall into four categories:

- Category 1: *The community*. Factors include normalisation and non-challenge of dangerous activity, low neighbourhood cohesion and extreme poverty.
- Category 2: *The family*. Factors include the normalisation of dangerous behaviour, avoidance of responsibility and a history of abusive family behaviour.
- Category 3: *Lack of engagement at school*. Factors include low commitment to achievement and anti-social behaviour.
- Category 4: *The individual or peer group*. Factors include normalisation of negative behaviour and influences and an 'innate sense of rebelliousness'. (McElwee, 2007: 31)

The importance of understanding young people and risk, and the difference between risks that can expand the social and emotional development of young people and risks that are life threatening is crucial when responding to risk. A developmental response would not be appropriate to a young person actively involved in drug trafficking, violent crime or child sex exploitation, for example. Equally, if risk is managed too zealously when a developmental approach could be more effective, then the outcomes can be as damaging as if they were not managed at all. For example,

- a new born child or toddler protected from seasonal illnesses and viruses could grow up with an underdeveloped immune system;
- a young person prevented from trying alcohol in a safe social environment may try it alone or with inexperienced friends and end up with alcohol poisoning;
- a young person who is prevented from exploring their sexuality or whose sexuality is made invisible by family members, may grow up with very low self-esteem, poor aspiration and express their pain through self-harm because their words are never listened to.

It is important to remember and be clear that some risks must have a managed response and some risks can have a developmental response. If we go back to the levels of risk that Bell and Bell (1993) suggest (see pages 104–5) and the categories of risk that McElwee (2007) argues (see above) and put them into a 'framework' (Table 7.1), it is possible to identify from: a) professional knowledge and experience; and b) the types of risk engaged in by the child or young person, the level of risk management as well as the possible level of social and emotional development and overall outcome that can take place.

Table 7.1 Management and development of risk framework

McElwee's Category of risk	Level of risk	Level of risk management	Level of possible social and emotional development	Probable outcome
Individual or Peer Group – negative behaviour and influences are normalised	**Everyday occurrences** – crossing the road, walking to school, playing in the park	**Low** – relies on the child or young person's general knowledge of road and stranger danger safety. Mild interventions required by parents, carers, school staff, youth workers	**Medium** – meet new friends, develop friendships, encouragement and support	**Low risk**
Individual or Peer Group – negative behaviour and influences are normalised	**Developmentally enhancing** – rock climbing, canoeing, orienteering, camping, trying new foods and alcohol	**Medium** – risk assessments to identify individual and overall risks required. Correct equipment required. Clear interventions required by parents, carers, school staff, youth workers	**High** – encouragement, support, new experiences, confidence, trust and possible friendship developed	**Medium to low risk**
Individual or Peer Group – negative behaviour and influences are normalised	**Dangerous risks** – joy riding, unprotected sex, drink driving, crime, addiction (gaming, gambling, sex) experimentation with drugs, too much 'junk' food and alcohol	**High** – Intervention to encourage change of behaviour. Definite interventions required by parents, carers, school staff, youth workers, social services	**Low** – Very few social development opportunities	**High risk to self and others**
Individual or Peer Group – negative behaviour and influences are normalised	**Life threatening risks** – fighting with knives or guns, gang membership, violent crime, addiction	**High** – Judicial intervention to remove individual from harming self and others, leading to change of behaviour. Support from parents, carers, youth workers, social services and probation officers	**Very low** – minimal social development opportunities	**Extremely high risk to self and others**

Activity

The Management and Development of Risk Framework (Figure 7.1) has identified some of the elements of risk in one of the four categories outlined by McElwee (2007) (community, family, lack of engagement at school and the individual or peer groups). Replicate this framework and share it with colleagues/peers, using one of these categories outlined by McElwee (2007) and your own experience (professional or personal). Discuss your findings with two or three colleagues/peers and compare what you have written.

Response to risk

Professional responses to risk need to come from professional knowledge (training, academic and policy), individual knowledge (of the child or young person and their circumstances) and experience (personal and professional with the aid of reflection and reflexivity). This knowledge needs to be demonstrated as a balance of guidance and support to enable and protect, not disempower and alienate. One of the approaches most effective in addressing risk and risk-taking behaviour with children and young people is the presence of a significant person in the child or young person's life. Positive attachments are crucial to an individual's development of 'self' and the acquisition of essential skills, morals and attributes. These attachments will enable a child or young person to move through the different stages, environments and phases of their lives more successfully. It is argued that there is a clear relationship between positive attachments and resilience in the face of difficulty and hardship. Ainsworth *et al.* (1978) argue that secure attachments are the ideal relationships for autonomy and success throughout life. A secure footing will not give all the answers, but it can enable confidence and belief in self, an understanding and awareness of self, knowledge of choice, and the value of asking for help. It is these qualities that can build resilient stepping stones in the lives of children and young people. Ainsworth *et al.* (1978) describe this as a secure foundation. Daniel and Wassell (2002) argue that attachments only fall into two camps: *secure* and *insecure*. Although this is a rather limited view of attachment, it is argued that anyone who does not feel completely secure in their primary or secondary attachments will in fact experience some degree of insecurity. The feelings of insecurity can provoke a variety of responses in all of us. For a child or young person, however, it can become another untamed emotion through which they see the harshness of the world. In the context of learning and education, in order for each child and young person to feel secure they need to be engaged with the subject as well as with the person delivering the subject. If a child or young person is demonstrating poor behaviour in a learning environment, it may be because they do not feel secure and are not being engaged with effectively by adults at home, or by the practitioners/trainees facilitating their learning. Consequently, they may feel unvalued and unrespected. Respectful and trusting relationships in any environment are crucial to encouraging children and young people to explore risky activities and respond in resilient ways. These relationships can harness fear, be developmental and safe. Children and young people will talk to people who they believe respect them; they will go to them when things go wrong or life gets difficult. The more consistent and supportive this relationship can become, the more the relationship can build trust and security. If children and young people do not trust adults then they are less likely to seek help from them; this can lead to greater exposure to risk. In the context of **informal education** (the practice delivered by professionally trained community and youth workers), risk can be acknowledged and resilience explored through a respectful and trusting acknowledgement of shared learning. The shared learning is between the young person and the informal educator. This can be approached through the context of conversations that start where a child or young person's feelings, experiences and frustrations all are at any given moment (Ingram and Harris, 2001; Batsleer, 2008; Smith and Jeffs, 2010; Sapin, 2013). Informal education is not driven by curriculum; it is driven by a dialogue between the child or young person and the informal educator. It opens the doorway to hear the whispers of vulnerability exhibited through loud disruptive behaviour in classrooms; it catches moments of helplessness through snatched conversation and builds the trust and security that enables the inadequacy or powerlessness felt by the child or young person to be explored safely and at their own pace. It fosters belief in an individual's ability to find the courage to change their behaviour for the sake of themselves, not just for the comfort of other people.

Many practitioners/trainees that work/train in formal or informal learning environments have their own approaches to building positive relationships with children and young people, which encourage participation in a learning environment. The professionally trained youth and community worker, for example, will not only use conversation as a vehicle to encourage engagement and participation, but as Batsleer and Davis (2010: 3) suggest, they will also seek to minimalise the 'usual barriers between an adult and a young person [as well as] those that arise because of the power and authority built into the role [of the youth worker]'. There is often a misconception that if one person has greater authority and power over another – teacher and child/young person; parent/carer and child/young person; social worker and child/young person; police officer and child/young person – then a respectful and positive relationship can be built. Doel and Sawdon (1999: 51–52) argue that it is the professional's denial of their own power and their 'inability to use it appropriately which poses the greatest threat to a group or a young person. Sometimes it is right to exercise this power and sometimes not, but it is never right to deny it'. Batsleer and Davis (2010: 3) go on to argue that 'setting boundaries for [children and] young people's behaviour or challenging them to stretch themselves beyond their starting points [comfort zones]' is the outcome of building mutually respectful, secure relationships with children and young people that are based on trust and not on power and authority.

Reflective task

Think of a time in a learning environment when you have:

1   Not felt engaged by the teacher or facilitator – how has this affected your engagement with learning?
2   Not felt respected by the teacher or facilitator – how has this affected your relationship with them?
3   Not trusted the teacher or facilitator – how has this affected how you have felt about yourself in this environment?

Discuss your answers with another colleague/peer that you trust and compare your experiences.

The lows and highs of risk

Stingfield and Land (2002: 3) suggest that the impact of risk can be brought into a learning environment at any age; they argue that 'the sheer abundance of potential risk factors now makes possible the classification of nearly every student as at risk at some point during his or her education'. The susceptibility of children and young people to risk is synonymous with growing up and developing a sense of understanding about self and the world in which they live. Bell and Bell (1993) suggest that risk-taking is an essential characteristic of the behaviour of children and young people. It is a process of self-exploration and identity through decision making and action. The cruel reality of risk is that if it is not responded to positively (by the risk taker or by a significant other in the risk taker's life) it can lead to greater levels of risk later on in life; it can also create risk and harm for others. There are, however, many young people who engage in high level risk-taking activities whose prospects are in fact very buoyant; consequently, as professionals, we need to be clear about when there is a need to step in to respond and enable and when there is a need to step aside and just be available. Quite simply, in the lives of children and young people there seems to be a clear distinction between those that do manage their exposure to risk, those that try to manage it, those that cannot manage it, and those that do not want to manage it. This is not an absolute or definitive proposition; it is merely the professional knowledge gained through many years of working with children and young people at risk.

Table 7.2 outlines the approaches taken to managing self-exposure to risk, the individual characteristics associated with each approach, the professional response, and the outcomes of each approach for the individual concerned.

Practitioners and those training may work with young people who demonstrate all four approaches to managing risk in their own lives (see Table 7.2). Risk approached in CATEGORY 1 could be described as being approached by someone with what Daniel and Wassell (2002) would describe as having a secure base; in educational practice practitioners and trainees can often see clear associations between the presence of a secure base, positive relationships and resilience in the face of adversity. However, having a secure base does not always mean that when risks are 'managed' they are avoided or adverse; some people thrive on taking risks – they love the thrill and high that the risk gives them and consequently they manage situations to ensure that they have as much exposure to particular risks as they need. People like this can be involved in extreme sports or high levels of sexual activity. On one hand their activity can be seen as simply meeting the physical and emotional needs that are in some way lacking in the rest of their lives; on the other hand they may just be pleasure and thrill seeking. The same incongruity to risk can be seen in gang membership, alcohol and drug misuse and crime. These young people can be just as motivated, aspirational, positive and able to find the people who will get them what they want; the outcomes here, however, can be much more damaging to themselves and other people, usually because their motivations do not come from a secure base. Our understanding as professionals therefore needs to take into consideration the fact that even if a young person is managing their own exposure to risk their risk-taking activity can still be harmful to themselves or other people.

Table 7.2 Exposure, responses and outcomes of risk

Approach to risk by the child or young person	Characteristics of individual	Professional response	Outcomes for individual
CATEGORY 1. **Takes control of the risks**	• Self-motivated • Positive attitude • Aspirational • Seeks help from useful people • Embraces change • Gets what they want	• Role model • Responsive • Supportive and encouraging	• Identifies and manages risk successfully
CATEGORY 2. **Tries to take control of the risks**	• Easily demotivated • Low self-confidence at times • Low aspiration • Low level mental ill health • Difficulty in maintaining relationships • Poor consistency • Scared of change	• Role model • Facilitates personal and social development opportunities • Consistent in approach • Supportive and encouraging	• Risks identified • Strategies to manage risk not well maintained without support
CATEGORY 3. **Does not want to take control of the risks**	• Unmotivated • Depressed • Unhelpful relationships and attachments • Lives from one high to the next • Has been badly let down • Resists change or manages it badly	• Role model • Facilitates personal and social development opportunities • Consistent in approach • Supportive and encouraging • Sign posts to other professionals for more support	• Vulnerable to risk
CATEGORY 4. **Has no control of risks**	• Oppressed • Depressed • Abusive relationships • Neglected • Cannot trust others • Longs for change, but too scared to make it happen	• Role model • Consistent in approach • Works with other professionals to support and encourage	• At risk to self and others

In CATEGORY 2 the young person who tries to take control of risk but does not always manage it successfully is often someone who has less of a secure base, fewer positive attachments, and is plagued by low levels of confidence and motivation – not surprisingly all of these factors are associated with poor mental ill health. Although Adair (1996) argues that deeply felt emotion can be a motivator and driver for practical change, the kinds of emotions felt by children and young people in these circumstances can be debilitating. In the case of managing risk there can often be a lack of consistency in the young person's approach to risk as emotions can come in waves, cloud judgements and be overwhelming.

Risk approached in CATEGORIES 3 and 4 can become manifested within a person and classifies them as someone who can be consistently vulnerable to risk or be 'at-risk' (Hepburn and White, 1990). This can be the result of many factors which have previously been discussed within this chapter. To understand the impact of being vulnerable to risk, it can be useful to reflect on the application of a definition of risk to our own lives.

Activity

Identify some of the risks that you have encountered in your life. Which of these risks do you believe you have had:

- A lot of control over?
- Little control over?
- No control over?
- Have not wanted to take control of?

Consider the following:

- What were the circumstances that enabled you to manage, or not manage, the risks you faced?
- Were you supported to manage these risks?
- How have the risks you have not managed well affected other people?
- What have you learnt from this?

Discuss the outcomes of this activity with a trusted colleague or peer.

Conclusion

In conclusion, within this chapter the concept of risk in relation to professional practice with children and young people has been considered. The responsibility of the practitioner/ trainee to keep themselves, as well as those they are working with, safe in practice has been discussed. Definitions of risk and at-risk have been outlined; some factors that cause risk and the behaviours associated with risk have also been explored. The concepts of fear and resilience in relation to risk have been investigated and some of the highs and lows of risk have been reflected upon. Finally, reflective questions and case studies have been presented throughout the chapter to enable you, the reader, to consider your own experiences of risk, by combining your current experience with further academic and professional knowledge. By no means is the discussion in this chapter definitive.

Areas for further consideration

There are a number of other areas for consideration which you may wish to explore as part of your own personal study. The suggestions below merely offer a select number of aspects which will help to further develop your understanding of risk when working with children and young people:

Explore the role of practitioner resilience further	Current child protection legislation
Access online risk assessment tools	An understanding of motivational theory
Reflection and critical thinking on one's own practice with vulnerable children and young people	The role of supervision to support resilience in practice

Further reading

Books

Geldard, K. (2009) *Practical Interventions for Young People at Risk*. London: Sage.
This book offers practical strategies for working with young people at risk. It suggests hands-on resources and guidance for working with key issues that young people at risk face; these include crime, poverty, mental ill health, addiction, depression, suicide and self-harm. Subjects such as anti-oppressive practice, culture, values and ethics are all considered as foundations of a multi-professional approach to practice.

Knight, S. (2011) *Risk and Adventure in Early Years Outdoor Play: Learning from Forest Schools*. London: Sage.
This book offers guidance on how to incorporate the wilder and riskier elements of outdoor play into the planning of those who work with children (0–8 years). It covers ways of using challenging and adventurous activities to their greatest advantage for children, as well as showing the practitioner the developmental significance of using risk in play.

Academic publications

Gilligan, R. (2000) Adversity, resilience and young people: the protective value of positive school and spare time experiences. *Children & Society*, 14 (1), 37–47.
This paper discusses the value of resilience when working with young people at risk. Social and development factors that shape a young person's degree of resilience are explored with specific reference to formal and informal educational experiences.

McElwee, N. (2007) *Chapter Two: From Risk to At Risk in At-Risk Children and Youth: Resiliency Explored*. USA: The Haworth Press. Note: This has been co-published simultaneously as Child and Youth Services, Vol. 29, No. 1/2, 2007.
This chapter explores how and why a child or young person might be considered at risk in a variety of educational, judicial, natural and medical environments.

Websites

An Introduction to Child Protection Legislation in the UK. Available at: http://tinyurl.com/73fzuqf
This NSPCC fact sheet gives a comprehensive guide to legislation surrounding child protection in the UK. It is an essential resource for all practitioners engaging in work with children and young people.

References

Abbott-Chapman, J. and Denholm, C. (2001) Adolescents' risk activities, risk hierarchies and the influence of religiosity. *Journal of Youth Studies*, 4(3), 279–291.
Adair, J. (1996) *Effective Motivation City*. London: Pan Books.
Ainsworth, M., Blehar, M., Aters, E. and Walls, S. (1978) *Patterns of Attachment: A Psychological Study of the Strange Situation*. Hillside NJ: Lawrence Erlbaum.

Batsleer, J. R. (2008) *Informal Learning in Youth Work*. London: Sage.

Batsleer, J. and Davies, B. (2010) *What is Youth Work?* Exeter: Learning Matters.

BBC News (2012) *A report from the Children's Commissioner for England has suggested that thousands of children are sexually abused by gangs and groups each year*. [Online]. Available at: www.bbc.co.uk/news/education-20421949 (Accessed: 25 May 2013).

——(2013) *Police warn Jersey teenagers about Facebook lifts page*. [Online]. Available at: www.bbc.co.uk/news/world-europe-jersey-18503105 (Accessed: 25 May 2013).

Bell, N. J. and Bell, R. W. (1993) *Adolescent Risk Taking*. London: Sage.

Clarke, J. and Nicholson, J. (2010) *Resilience, Bounce back from whatever Life Throws at You*. Surrey: Crimson Publishing.

Daniel, B. and Wassell, S. (2002) *Assessing and Promoting Resilience in Vulnerable Children: Adolescence. Vol. 3*. London: Jessica Kingsley Publishers.

Department for Education (2001) *Positive for Youth: a new approach to cross government policy for young people aged 13-19*. [Online]. Available at: www.gov.uk/government/publications/positive-for-youth-a-new-approach-to-cross-government-policy-for-young-people-aged-13-to-19 (Accessed: 25 May 2013).

Department for Education and Skills (2003) *Every Child Matters*. [Online]. Available at: www.education.gov.uk/consultations/downloadableDocs/EveryChildMatters.pdf (Accessed: 25 May 2013).

——(2005) *Youth Matters*. [Online]. Available at: www.infed.org/youthwork/green_paper_2005.htm (Accessed: 25 May 2013).

——(2006) *Youth Matters: Next Steps. Something to do, somewhere to go, someone to talk to*. [Online]. Available at: www.education.gov.uk/consultations/downloadableDocs/Youth%20Matters%20Next%20 Steps.pdf (Accessed: 25 May 2013).

Doel, M. and Sawdon, C. (1999) *The Essential Group Worker: Teaching and learning creative group work*. London: Jessica Kingsley Publishers.

Engage (2006) *Making Connections Tool Kit, Including Young People*. [Online]. Available at: www.engage.org (Accessed: 25 May 2013).

Fitch, K. (2009) *Teenagers at risk: The safeguarding needs of young people in gangs and violent peer groups*. NSPCC inform. [Online]. Available at: www.nspcc.org.uk/Inform/research/findings/teenagersatriskpdf_wdf64003.pdf (Accessed: 25 May 2013).

Furlong, A. and Cartmel, F. (2006) *Young People and Social Change*. Maidenhead: Open University Press.

——(2007) *Young People and Social Change*. 2nd edn. Maidenhead: Open University Press.

Gilligan, R. (2001) *Promoting Resilience: A Resource Guide on Working with Children in the Care System*. London: BAAF.

Goleman, D. (1998) *Working with Emotional Intelligence*. London: Bloomsbury Publishing.

Hepburn, L. and White, R. (1990) *School Dropouts: A two generation problem*. Public Policy Research Series. Athens, Georgia: The University of Georgia, Carl Vinson Institute of Government.

Ingram, G. and Harris, J. (2001) *Delivering Good Youth Work*. Lyme Regis: Russell House Publishing.

Jeffs, T. and Sith, M. (2010) *Youth Work Practice*. Basingstoke: Palgrave Macmillan.

Lupton, D. (2013) *Risk*. 2nd edn. London: Routledge.

McElwee, N. (2007) *At-Risk Children & Youth: Resiliency Explored*. London: Routledge.

McElwee, N., McArdle, S. and O'Grady, D. (2002) *Risk and Resilience? A Qualitative Study in County Wexford of Risk Factors for Young People. Wexford Area Partnership*. Impressions Print.

Norman, E. (2000) *Resiliency Enhancement: Putting the strengths perspective into social work practice*. New York: Columbia University Press.

Rak, C. F. and Patterson, L. E. (1996) Promoting Resilience in At Risk Children. *Journal of Counselling and Development*, 74(4), 368–373.

Robb, M. (2007) *Youth in Context: Frameworks, settings and encounters*. London: Sage.

Sapin, K. (2013) *Essential Skills for Youth Work Practice*. 2nd edn. London: Sage.

Schön, D. (1996) *The Reflective Practitioner: How Professionals Think In Action*. Ashgate: Arena Publishing.

Smith, M. and Jeffs, T. (2010) *Youth Work Practice*. 2nd edn. London: Palgrave Macmillan.

Stringfield, S. and Land, D. (2002) *Educating at Risk Students*. Chicago: University of Chicago Press.

Thomsen, K. (2002) *Building Resilient Students: Integrating resiliency into what you already know and do*. California: Corwin Press.

Ungar, M. (2004) *Nurturing Hidden Resilience in Troubled Youth*. Toronto: University of Toronto Press Incorporated.

Wolin, S. and Wolin, S. (1993) *The Resilient Self: How survivors of troubled families rise above adversity*. New York: Villard.

Wood, J. and Hine, J. (eds) (2009) *Work with Young People*. London: Sage.

Young, K. (2006) *The Art of Youth Work*. 2nd edn. Lyme Regis: Russell House Publishing.

Section 3
The Workplace

8 Skills and knowledge for effective practice

Deborah Hussain

LEARNING OBJECTIVES

After studying this chapter, you will be able to:

✔ Identify practice guidelines in relation to a range of professional roles.
✔ Define the skills and knowledge required by practitioners and those training who work within the 0–19 age range.
✔ Evaluate the applicability of practice guidelines in relation to current practice.
✔ Identify the skills developed as a practitioner/trainee that are transferable when applied to different age groups and working environments.

Introduction

This chapter will explore how the *Common Core of Skills and Knowledge* (DfES, 2005) establishes a baseline of skills and knowledge for all people working in the 0–19 sector. Consultation undertaken on the Green Paper *Every Child Matters* (DfES, 2003) identified that everyone working with children, young people and families should have a common set of skills and knowledge in order for them to work effectively. Throughout this chapter you will be given the opportunity to develop your knowledge and understanding of select standards, making links between the following:

● The Qualified Teacher Standards (DfE, 2012b);
● The Professional and National Occupational Standards for Youth Work (NYA, 2008);
● The National Standards for Head teachers (DfES, 2004);
● Early Years Professional Status Standards (Teaching Agency, 2012); and
● The National Occupational Standards for Supporting Teaching and Learning (TDA, 2010).

Through understanding a range of standards and how they link to the *Common Core of Skills and Knowledge* (DfES, 2005) you will be able to understand common key skills required in practice and how the roles undertaken in the Children's Workforce share a common goal to enable practitioners and those training to work effectively, thus improving outcomes for children, young people and families. Families should feel confident that the people supporting their children share a common core of skills, irrespective of role or setting.

Reflective task

Consider the setting that you are currently working in or are on placement at. What skills and knowledge do you need to have in order to work effectively there?

Make a list of all the skills and knowledge you identify with; as you read through this chapter visit the web links to specific standards and review your list accordingly. Use the areas identified below as a starting point:

Skill or knowledge	Positive aspects identified	Areas for development	Action taken
Children's and young people's development			
Oral communication			
Child protection			

Practice guidelines/standards

The Common Core underpins a number of workforce development activities. Local authorities have reported embedding the Common Core within:

- multi-agency training, providing common skills across different practitioners;
- recruitment, selection, induction and performance management;
- workforce development strategies; and
- training needs analyses (CWDC, 2008).

The *Common Core of Skills and Knowledge* (DfES, 2005 - see http://tinyurl.com/8nq7kv2) were developed by the DfES in partnership with service users, employers and workers. The Common Core reflects a set of common values that promote equality, diversity and challenge stereotypes with the aim of improving the life chances of children and young people. Linked closely to *Every Child Matters* (DfES, 2003; post 2010 referred to as *Helping Children Achieve More*) it acknowledges the important role that parents, carers and families have in helping children and young people work towards and achieve the ECM outcomes. The Common Core has six key areas of expertise:

- effective communication and engagement;
- child and person development;
- safeguarding and promoting the welfare of the child;
- supporting transitions;

- multi-agency working; and
- sharing information.

The focus of this chapter will be to explore the Common Core of Skills and Knowledge required as a baseline for all practitioners and those training to work with children and young people; however, these skills and knowledge are also identified in profession-specific standards.

The standards for Qualified Teacher Status were recently reviewed in 2012 by the DfE and set out the standards required of those wishing to teach – see http://tinyurl.com/dx794sk. Part One of the standards highlights eight standards with a focus on teaching. It links to an understanding of child development and learning. Part Two has a focus on personal and professional conduct linking to the Common Core in relation to communication and safeguarding. Reviewing the standards has seen an emphasis placed on 'quality' both within education and the wider workforce.

The Professional and National Occupational Standards for Youth Work (NYA, 2008 – see http://tinyurl.com/9lx7p2l) are clearly aimed at those working with young people. These are currently being reviewed but links to the Common Core are made in all six areas. This reflects the consultation that took place when identifying the Common Core of Skills and Knowledge, as these were developed to reflect the skills required for all practitioners working in the children's workforce.

The National Standards for Head teachers (DfES, 2004 – see http://tinyurl.com/8vf2mep) were developed after consultation with head teachers to reflect the skills required of a head teacher in the twenty-first century. Links made to the Common Core of Skills and Knowledge relate to head teachers having an understanding of child development, allowing children the opportunity to reach their optimum potential, and also the need to be excellent communicators with a range of professionals, sharing information and supporting transitions effectively.

The Early Years Professional Status Standards (Teaching Agency, 2012 – see http://tinyurl.com/9ln2cf3) were initially developed to allow early years practitioners to show their knowledge and understanding of supporting children and families from birth to five years, while leading and supporting other practitioners in developing practice skills. The original 39 standards have been reviewed (Teaching Agency, 2012) alongside the review of the EYFS (DfE, 2012a) and are now streamlined to eight standards with each standard broken down into sub-standards. These standards have been designed for people working with children from birth to five years and are linked to the Common Core of Skills and Knowledge by incorporating the six broad standards that include the requirement of practitioners to have a strong knowledge of child development, safeguarding and a strong link to effective communication and leadership. In September 2013 the EYPS was replaced with the Early Years Teacher. A new set of standards reflect the qualities required of an early years teacher – please see http://tinyurl.com/om6ot5a.

The National Occupational Standards for Supporting Teaching and Learning were developed by the TDA in 2010 (see http://tinyurl.com/94ojtam) in consultation with school leaders to establish national occupational standards for support staff in schools. Support staff in schools carry out a range of roles and responsibilities and the standards aim to identify what support staff need to do, know and understand in their roles. The standards are designed to allow school leaders to use them as a tool for school development. Prior to recruitment the school will be able to undertake a **skill mix** review, which helps identify the skill needs of the school, which will then be targeted through the recruitment process. For existing staff, performance reviews will allow both employers and employees the opportunity to review skills based on the standards and allow identification of any training needs that will support career progression. While there is commonality between the *Common Core of Skills and Knowledge* and the *National Occupational Standards for Supporting Teaching and Learning*, one major difference is the audience that the standards relate to. Clearly the *National Occupational Standards for Supporting Teaching and Learning* had a focus on support staff in schools whereas the *Common Core of Skills and Knowledge* were developed for the whole of the Children and Young People's workforce. The 69 units of the *National Occupational Standards for Supporting Teaching and Learning* reflect all six areas of the *Common Core of Skills and Knowledge*. Having identified national standards that inform and regulate practice, practitioners are required to develop skills to enable effective practice to take place.

Activity

Using the list you made in the first reflective task on page 122, consider once again the skills required in your current role; use the hyperlinks above to review the skills and amend your list accordingly. Consider any gaps that you have in the development of your knowledge and skills, taking time to consider the actions you will take to plan for your personal development.

Practitioners and those training need to develop a range of skills to be able to engage in effective practice. These skills include knowledge of child development, planning and curriculum design, safeguarding and child protection, inter-agency working and being an effective communicator. Effective communication will be the focus of the next section.

Effective communication

> Good communication is central to working with children, young people and their families. It involves listening, questioning, understanding and responding to children, young people and those caring for them. (CWDC, 2008)

For the purpose of this section of the chapter the focus will be on communication as considered in the *Common Core of Skills and Knowledge* and not communication in its broadest sense, e.g. media, web material, internet etc.

Effective communication requires skills of listening, observing, questioning, understanding and responding to what is being communicated to you. As a practitioner/trainee you will communicate with children, young people and the adults that care for them, as well as fellow workers and professionals from other organisations. It is therefore crucial that practitioners and those training are able to communicate effectively in order to meet the needs of the children and young people they support. From birth we are able to make our needs known by using a variety of communication techniques. A baby's first cry is the start of the communication process and will continue to develop into sophisticated speech as the child matures and learns new skills. As the child gets older it will learn to apply different communication techniques to different situations. Children learn from the **role models** around them (Dunhill, Elliott and Shaw, 2009) so it is important that practitioners and those training are able to model and nurture effective communication.

Social pedagogy would suggest the importance of being able to view the world from someone else's perspective as crucial for effective communication to take place (Petrie, 2011). To be able to understand someone else's perspective we need to create environments of safety and trust where the practitioner, child, young person and family feel confident to share thoughts, ideas and concerns. Great importance should be placed on the setting developing an ethos of mutual respect, shared values and trust where all practitioners and those training value the views and opinions of the communities they engage with.

The physical environment creates the atmosphere where you will engage with adults, children and young people. It is important that you create an inclusive environment, respecting and promoting the values of the setting and the communities that engage with the setting. If people feel comfortable and valued they will want to share thoughts, views and opinions and support the work of the setting. Take a moment to consider how you ensure that the environment you offer for service users reflects the values and backgrounds of the setting and the community.

In order to communicate effectively we need to develop good listening skills, becoming an active listener. According to Clark and Marsh (2011) there are six skills that are required of an active listener: *paying attention, holding judgement, reflecting, clarifying, summarising* and *sharing*. While these may appear obvious to those rooted in practice, developing positive active listening skills requires practice and time. Your frame of mind and body language will also influence the effectiveness of the conversation; remember that 60-70 per cent of the message being received by the listener is non-verbal! Avoid standing with your arms folded across your body as this creates a perceived barrier between you and everyone else. Be aware of how you are feeling as this could influence the way you respond to people.

There are times when communicating with children, young people and their family needs to take place in a more formal manner. This can be at developmental reviews, parents' evenings, Common Assessment Framework (CAF) and Team Around the Child (TAC) meetings. We must ensure that the language used in formal meeting situations is understood by everyone attending. Do avoid using jargon and acronyms; EYFS, IEP/MEP and EBD may be 'normal' language within the setting but to anyone new it can be confusing and create unnecessary barriers to the engagement of those outside of the setting. Just as active listening requires reflection, clarification and summarisation so do formal meetings. Records of the meetings should be written in ways that they are useful to the family. Where English is not the first language of the family translation may be required. Consideration should also be given to parents/carers who have low levels of literacy to ensure that information is shared in ways that are sensitive to their needs. Time to share reports and minutes before a meeting is one solution.

Knowing the needs of your community and the individuals within that community will allow for effective communication to take place where people are valued and know that their views and opinions count. The best way to develop effective communication skills is through practice; the more you engage in communication, both informal and formal, the easier it will become, thus boosting your confidence and impacting positively on your self-esteem. By developing good communication skills you will be role modelling good practice for children, young people and families. This is of particular importance when working with other professionals in a multi-agency context.

Case study

Select one of the two case studies below, deciding what you would need to do, communication wise, to manage the situation effectively.

1   Yusuf is three years old and will be starting nursery at the next intake. He lives with his mother Nadia and his father Bilal. Bilal is the main carer as Nadia is a partner in a law firm and works every day. Bilal speaks limited English but attends the local adult literacy classes to further develop his skills.
   - How will you prepare for the arrival of Yusuf?
   - How will you create the best environment for Yusuf and his parents?
   - Who will be included in the preparation?
   - How will you communicate with the family considering the initial visits and information shared on a daily basis regarding Yusuf's day in nursery?
2   Simon is 12 years old and is attending the nurture unit based in the secondary school. Simon lives with his mum Jackie and his younger sister Beth. Simon is attending the nurture unit as he has struggled to settle at the school and has appeared withdrawn and alone. He has poor communication skills with both teachers and most pupils; however, Craig, his next door neighbour, walks to and from school with him.
   - How would you communicate with Simon to assess his needs?
   - Who would support you in gaining knowledge about Simon?
   - What considerations would you make for preparing the environment for Simon?
   - How would you communicate with Jackie so that she understands the purpose of the nurture unit and the additional support that is being offered to her son?
   - How would you ensure that confidentiality is maintained in terms of the information you must share with Jackie and what Simon wants you to share with others?

Multi-agency working

Multi-agency working is about different services working in partnership in order to prevent problems from occurring in the first place. It is most effective when agencies work together with shared aims and goals. (CWDC, 2008)

Before considering the work of a multi-agency team, practitioners and those training need to be clear about their own role, the standards framework within which they work, and the roles and remits of other professionals. Oliver and Pitt (2011) highlight the range of agencies that children will experience at natural points throughout their life:

1   Midwives, health visitors, GPs and paediatricians may support the family in the early years of a child's life.

2   Social workers or community support workers may be involved to support parenting and the progression to educational professionals as the child/young person enters education environments.

3   Dentists and opticians alongside social groups, cubs, scouts, brownies and sporting groups extend the type of practitioners engaging with children and their families.

The task offered at the end of this section will allow you to explore and extend your knowledge of the roles/responsibilities of those professionals identified above.

The Lord Laming (2003) report into the death of Victoria Climbié identified a failure of communication between staff and agencies. The Green Paper *Every Child Matters* (DfES, 2003), in response to the Laming enquiry and supported by The Children Act (2004), 'constitutes one of the most radical changes to children's services planning and delivery' (Fitzgerald and Kay, 2008). The introduction of a Children's Commissioner and a duty on local authorities to make arrangements to promote cooperation between agencies and other appropriate bodies to improve the outcomes for children and their families were some of the changes identified. Local authorities were also required to adopt national strategies to be implemented and monitored by Children's Trusts.

Key changes saw the introduction of the Common Assessment Framework (CAF) allowing parents/carers and professionals to share knowledge about the child/young person, establishing a holistic view of the child/young person in the context of the family, the learning environment and the wider community. Through the CAF process lead professionals would be the key point of contact for parents/carers/children and young people, allowing early intervention and the targeting of services making them available when children, young people and families need them. Through the review of Lord Laming (2003), the ECM Green Paper (2003) consultation identified the requirement for everyone working with children and families to have a common set of skills and knowledge to support effective integrated working. Practitioners would be required to develop skills that would allow them to work effectively with other agencies.

Multi-agency working is now a well-established form of practice for many practitioners in a range of settings. Children's centres offer a range of services that are delivered by a range of professionals on a daily basis. The challenges faced by practitioners establishing multi-agency practice can be that of an agreed understanding of shared and individual professional structures and practices. An awareness of different work cultures is crucial for teams to operate effectively. An agreed understanding and approach to information sharing is important and will be discussed later on in the chapter.

For trainees and new practitioners an important aspect of multi-agency working for consideration is to familiarise yourself with local authority guidelines and learn how these are applied in policies within practice. You are encouraged to make links with practitioners who are established at multi-agency working and share practice with each other. With the sustained commitment of successive governments from the initial ECM agenda, subsequent reviews by Munro (2011) and Allen (2011) highlight the necessity for multi-agency working. Practitioners and families are faced with the challenges of working with a range of professionals with shared procedures and working methods, placing the needs of the child at the centre of decision making and agreed practices. The notion of multi-agency working will be discussed further in Chapter 12. By understanding the challenges and benefits of multi-agency working, practitioners and those training will be able to work more effectively, enhancing the opportunities that are available for children, young people and families.

Reflective task

To work effectively in multi-agency teams, practitioners and those training need to have knowledge of the professional identities of a range of practitioners working in the 0-19 workforce. Below you will see a list of some of the practitioners who work within the sector:

• Family support worker
• Social worker
• Learning mentor
• Educational psychologist
• Teaching assistant
• Health visitor
• Behaviour support worker
• Speech therapist
• Physiotherapist

• Nursery nurse/assistant
• Youth worker
• Youth offending worker
• Young adviser
• Teacher
• Police officer
• School nurse
• Child and Adolescent Mental Health (CAMHS) worker

As roles and titles of practitioners change so too will this list and your own lists of the professionals you work with. Consider the following:

- How does the work that you do link to the work of the professionals listed above?
- What skills do you have that are common? How do you know?
- What specialist skills do you have that are unique to your role? How do you know?

Child and young person development

> Children and young people grow up and develop at different speeds, emotionally, socially, physically and intellectually. It is important to understand how developmental changes can impact on a child or young person's behaviour. (CWDC, 2008)

According to the EYFS (DfE, 2012a) babies and young children develop in their own unique way at their own pace and this continues throughout adolescence and into adulthood. To enable the practitioner and those training to fully support the child, an awareness of child development is crucial. An understanding of Bowlby's (1969) attachment theory allows practitioners and those training to realise the importance of the key adult(s) in a child's life and the links that can be made to the role of the **key worker** in the early years sector (0-5), the class teacher in primary schools (5-11), and the **form tutor** in secondary (11-16) and tertiary education (16-18). To fully support the child or young person, practitioners and those training need to understand the child in the context of the family and their life away from the setting. The strong partnership links forged with parents and carers enables all those involved as key people in the child's life to share information so that a holistic approach can be taken regarding the development of the child/young person and the planning of learning experiences to meet the child's individual needs.

Practitioners and those training need to understand that families are as unique as the children and young people that they support; as a result families will develop their own **parenting style**. Baumrind (1971, cited in Hobart and Frankel, 2009a) through observations of parents' interactions with their children developed a typology of parenting styles. Maccoby and Martin (1983, cited in Hobart and Frankel, 2009a) developed this typology by suggesting a fourth parenting style: parents were classified as *Authoritarian, Authoritative, Permissive* or *Uninvolved* with the style of parenting being adopted having an impact on the child's/ young person's development. Ask yourself the following: *How do you develop an understanding of the parenting styles of the children and young people you support?* This question is an important one irrespective of the age of children/young people you work with. The relationship between the parent and the child/young person are of equal importance when the parent is caring for their child as a young baby and when the young person is in their teenage years; it can seem equally if not more challenging though! Young people are developing into autonomous beings, making choices, and developing their own identity. Peer influences will inform some of their choices and decisions. As parents are the young person's first and most enduring educator (Neaum, 2010) it is important that the relationships between the parent and child/young person are effective to enable important informed decisions to be made with regard to learning opportunities. Consider how you gather information that informs your understanding of how parents/carers and their children communicate and share information.

Reflective task

Maslow (1954) developed a theory highlighting the hierarchy of needs of the individual. The theory suggests that a person's physiological needs, safety and feelings of belonging need to be met before a child or young person can achieve and function to their optimal potential. Ask yourself: *How do you monitor that a child/young person's basic needs are met each day?*

Piaget (1896–1990; see http://tinyurl.com/cqqf3), Vygotsky (1896–1934; see http://tinyurl.com/422ae5h) and Bruner (1915–present; see http://tinyurl.com/8cb6rqb) are key theorists who inform practitioners' and trainees' understanding of child development and allow us to plan meaningful experiences for the child/young person by supporting and **scaffolding** the child's/young person's learning. Sharing this knowledge and understanding with parents and carers is crucial to enable continuity in provision and also to enable a shared awareness of the child/young person and their needs. Parents and carers who are closest to the child/ young person are most likely to see changes in a child's/young person's development and behaviour and should feel confident to share this knowledge with the setting.

As practitioners/trainees it is important to develop good observational skills and tools to support the recording of any observation undertaken of children/young people. Observations form the basis for sharing information with parents/carers and fellow practitioners. Observations are an important record of a child's/young person's development and practitioners/those training need to be aware of a range of observational recording techniques to enable recordings to be effective and information accurate – see Figure 8.1 for suggestions.

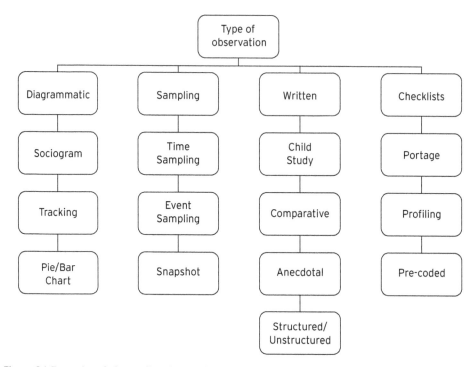

Figure 8.1 Examples of observational recording techniques

It is important that information collected through observations is recorded and shared at appropriate times with the parents/carers. Practitioners and those training should use their knowledge of child development and observational knowledge of the child/young person to identify possible developmental delay. The knowledge and understanding of the practitioner/trainee will allow the child or young person to feel supported and feel that their needs are being/will be met. It must be remembered that parents/carers and families will also require support as they come to terms with their child's changing needs. Empathy and understanding of the needs of all concerned is crucial as an aspect of understanding of being a practitioner. Knowledge of one's own professional boundaries and when to refer to other agencies is crucial to allow for effective, appropriate early intervention. Speech and language therapists, physiotherapists, behaviour intervention workers, social workers, educational psychologists, community development workers, and youth offending workers are professional people you may need to make links to with regard to improving outcomes for a child or young person you are supporting. Effective practice requires all practitioners/trainees to understand developmental norms (see http://tinyurl.com/qxlqh5y), the individual child and when a multi-agency approach is required (see Chapter 12).

Reflective task

Identify one child/young person (real/imagined) and the family home context in which they live. How do you/would you:

- Develop strategies to engage with the child/young person and their family to understand their unique needs?
- Gather information regarding the family context within which the child/young person lives?
- Share information regarding the child/young person's achievements?
- Share information regarding the child/young person's development needs?
- Share concerns regarding the child's/young person's development?
- Access specialist support?
- Record developmental progress and store personal records?

Safeguarding and promoting the welfare of children and young people

> Anyone who works with children and young people has a duty to safeguard and protect their welfare. This is a big responsibility and requires special care and attention to ensure positive outcomes for children and young people. (CWDC 2008)

The development of safeguarding practice in recent times can be linked closely to serious case reviews, the most recent reviews being those undertaken by Lord Laming following the deaths of Victoria Climbié (2003) and Peter Connolly (2008). Laming (2003) recommended the need for a shared programme of national change which included the introduction of the *Every Child Matters* (DfES, 2003) framework for practitioners working in the 0–19 sector. The ECM framework highlighted the need for practitioners to support and monitor children's development across five areas: *being healthy, staying safe, enjoying and achieving, making a positive contribution* and *achieve economic well-being*. Following the change of government in 2010 there has been a change in reference from ECM to *Helping Children Achieve More* (HCAM). The notion of child development and effective communication have already been discussed in this chapter and both serve as key skills that support the practitioner/trainee in being capable of sharing information and monitoring progress of individuals and planning for the next steps in a child's/young person's learning.

The Children Act (2004) emphasised reforms within CYPS, highlighting the need for local arrangements being developed to safeguard and promote the welfare of children, and the need for national initiatives for information sharing. Historically, a lack of information sharing has been a consistent key feature in serious case reviews. But ironically even though this was an identified feature of the Victoria Climbié case, five years later the same thing happened – how come these reforms did not save Baby P? As practitioners/trainees it is important that you are fully aware of the local and national arrangements that inform your practice with regard to safeguarding, child protection and integrated working. Individual agencies are accountable for ensuring that staff are confident and competent to carry out safeguarding duties. We strongly encourage you to investigate within your current setting/placement how safeguarding training is developed and implemented, and how practice is monitored.

There are numerous categories for safeguarding which practitioners and those training should be aware of; these are summarised in Table 8.1.

Table 8.1 The categories for safeguarding

Area of abuse	Definition	Behaviours
Physical abuse	Physical harm caused to an individual	Hitting, shaking, throwing, poisoning, burning or scalding, drowning, suffocating
Emotional abuse	The persistent emotional maltreatment of a child such as to cause severe and persistent adverse effects on the child's emotional development	Bullying, cyber bullying, deliberately silencing, making fun of the child/young person – how they speak or look
Sexual abuse	Forcing or enticing a child or young person to take part in sexual activities whether or not the child or young person is aware of what is happening	Physical contact, assault by penetration, masturbation, kissing, rubbing and touching outside of clothing. Non-contact – watching or taking part in the production of sexual images, watching sexual activity. Encouraging children to act inappropriately, grooming for sexual activity including via the internet and grooming for gangs. Child trafficking
Neglect	Persistent failure to meet a child or young person's basic physical and psychological needs likely to result in the serious impairment of a child's health or development	Inadequate food, shelter and clothing. Protecting a child from physical and emotional harm. Adequate supervision and parenting. Access to appropriate medical care and treatment

As a practitioner/trainee the information contained in Table 8.1 may raise personal feelings in relation to your own core values and your professional responsibilities. It is important that you gain support from your line manager/supervisor/mentor so that you are comfortable and confident when undertaking your professional duties and responsibilities when dealing with safeguarding issues.

Good practice requires practitioners and those training to be mindful of the signs of abuse and the importance of knowledge of developmental norms appropriate to the children and young people you support. Hobart and Frankel (2009: 65) remind us of the role of the practitioner in safeguarding: 'to record and report suspected abuse, not to investigate it'. Passing appropriate information on to your line manager/supervisor/mentor and following the procedures of the setting as set out by the safeguarding policy is crucial for an effective investigation to take place and/or support being established for the child/young person and family. Effective practice also requires practitioners and those training to understand local (regional) and national arrangements with regard to safeguarding and how to support children, young people and families through transitions to assure continuity of care and support.

Case study

Select one of the three case studies below which relate to particular age phases within an educational context.

Early Years (0–5): Lily is three years old and has recently been attending the nursery looking unkempt; her hair is unbrushed and is starting to matt together, and she smells of stale urine. Lily's mum is very quiet and prefers to push Lily through the door into nursery rather than come and meet the staff. You are Lily's key worker and have been trying to arrange a time to meet mum to review Lily's progress but this is proving difficult. Lily has been absent from nursery for one week and on her return she appears a little withdrawn. You have been playing in the water tray with Lily and she has wet the sleeves on her cardigan. You support Lily in changing her cardigan so that it can be dried and notice a large bruise on her upper arm. The shape of the bruise is that of a hand. *What would you do?*

Primary (5–11): Annika is nine years old and is a very chatty member of your class. She eagerly jumps in to do any jobs that need doing: tidying the paint pots, sharpening pencils, taking messages to other classes. It is during the lunchtime break as Annika is sharpening the pencils that she engages you in conversation and tells you that she does not like always being tired in a morning. When you ask her why she is tired she tells you that her mum and dad argue at night and it wakes her up. She tells you it is because her dad gets drunk and it makes mum cry. *What would you do?*

Secondary (11–16): Tom is 15 years old and is a potential grade A student at the start of his GCSE studies. He is very popular with his peer group and has excellent attendance and punctuation records. In previous years he has been part of the rugby and football teams but this year he has stopped all after school activities. After the Christmas holiday you notice changes in Tom's behaviour – he has been coming to school late smelling of tobacco and cannabis. *What would you do?*

Questions for reflection:

- How would you meet the needs of these children/young people? Consider the tools that you would use to gather relevant information.
- Are there policies and procedures in place in your setting/placement that would allow you to effectively support the child/young person?
- What internal and external agencies would you contact for support? Why?

Supporting transitions

Children and young people pass through a number of stages as they grow up and develop. Often they are expected to cope with huge changes such as moving from primary to secondary school or from children's to adults' services. These changes are referred to as transitions. The Common Core helps practitioners to support children and young people during these transition periods. (CWDC, 2008)

The importance of understanding the child and young person in the context of their family and wider community has been identified in the sections on effective communication, child development, safeguarding and promoting well-being. This knowledge is also of equal importance when considering transitions. Through your detailed knowledge of the child/ young person and family you will be able to establish the types of support that both the child/young person and family may require.

Dunlop and Fabian (2007) considers transition as a point at which something is left behind that constructed an identity moving into a new culture with a change in status. It is the practitioner's/trainee's role to ensure that transitions are smooth for each child, young person and their family. Knowledge of the family will allow you to identify when transitions are taking place. Children and young people will experience some transitions at the same points as their peers, these points being transition from nursery to primary school and primary to secondary schools. At these points settings can establish opportunities for group support through shared visits to the new setting and practitioner/trainee visits to see their potential new class/learning environment. It is also an opportunity for the staff to share information; this is especially important for children/young people who have additional needs or for those who struggle with transition and change.

Some of the transitions that children and young people are required to adapt to are unplanned and may only be affecting them in the setting. These sorts of transitions could be related to divorce, bereavement, family break-up or unemployment and may relate to specific kinds of children and young people, e.g. traveller children/young people, asylum seekers, refugees and children/young people in care. The Alberta Child and Youth Initiative (2006: 4) identified seven key components to support effective transitions for children and young people and these are offered for you to reflect on below:

1   Ensure basic needs are met.
2   Maintain and encourage positive relationships.
3   Provide support and resources to children and youth in their new environment and modify or adapt routines, as appropriate.
4   Provide choices and involve the child and youth in the transition process to promote and support self-advocacy.
5   Support the need for increased independence and help children and youth create their own identity.
6   Ensure that all transition plans are coordinated and integrated, and information is shared with parents [/carers] and across sectors.
7   Prepare for the transition and ensure consistency within and between environments.

You will note that the skills required for effective practice in relation to transitions require an understanding of the work context and professional environment within which practice takes place. Key to being effective in practice delivery is developing good interpersonal skills with children, young people and families so that information can be shared and a coordinated approach can be taken, keeping the child's/young person's and their family's needs central to the decisions and choices made.

Activity

Take a look at the case study below and reflect on what you would need to consider to support the transition being described.

Lydia is 15 years old and will be transferring to the secondary school that you work at next week. She lives with her mother, Ruth, her stepfather, Lee, and younger brothers Luke and Jack. Lydia has struggled to settle at her previous schools and has consequently had poor attendance. Her mother does not like to see Ruth unhappy so lets her stay at home.

- How would you prepare for Lydia's arrival?
- Who will support you in the transition? What internal and external support might be available?
- How will you ensure that Lydia has a positive successful transition?
- How would your approach differ if Ruth was attending nursery or primary school as a work experience placement?

Sharing information

Sharing information in a timely and accurate way is an essential part of helping to deliver better services. Sometimes it helps save lives. It is important to understand and respect issues and legislation surrounding the control and confidentiality of information. (CWDC, 2008)

Information sharing is a common practice for people working within the 0–19 sector. Routine information regarding operational calendars, events and general curriculum/provision advice are crucial to the effective engagement of the setting as a community. Settings that engage with children, young people and their families may also be required to share personal information specific to the child/young person and their family. The Data Protection Act (1998) gives guidance as to the legal requirements of practitioners and those training in how data should be used (see Chapter 4 for further information).

Settings need to be particularly aware of the following issues when collecting and processing personal data about children, young people and their families. Under the Data Protection Act (1998) all settings processing personal data must comply with the eight enforceable principles of good practice:

1   The data should be fairly and lawfully processed.
2   The data should be for a limited purpose.
3   The data should be adequate, relevant and accurate.
4   The data should be accurate and up to date.
5   The data should not be kept longer than is necessary and must be stored securely.
6   The data should be processed in accordance with the data subject's rights and not transferred to other countries without adequate protection.
7   The data should be secured against accidental loss, destruction or damage and against unauthorised and unlawful processing.
8   The data should not be transferred to countries outside the EEA.

For further information see http://tinyurl.com/pkebyvq.

Developing and embedding the eight key principles of good practice within data protection is important to ensure that practitioners and those training work within legal frameworks. This is particularly important when working with families where information may be needed to support a CAF or shared with other professionals. Creating an environment of trust with open transparent dialogue will allow the practitioner/trainee to gain consent from the parent/carer and child or young person to allow information to be shared with other professionals. According to Fitzgerald and Kay (2008), practitioners engaging in multi-agency working should consider how information is stored, shared and what the practitioner's/trainee's role is within the process. Where there is anxiety with regard to sharing information it usually relates to confidentiality. By following the legal frameworks contained in the Data Protection Act (1998), Children Act (2004) and the United Nations Convention on the Rights of the Child (UNCRC) (1989) practitioners and trainees will be guided to work effectively. See Chapter 4 for further information and practical advice.

When considering information sharing thought needs to be given to the reasons why successive governments continue to promote multi-agency working, which requires sharing information. Recent serious case reviews (Laming, 2003; 2009) highlighted the insular way that agencies worked, leading to disjointed working practices that allowed ineffective support being given to the child and their families. To enable agencies to work effectively, practitioners and trainees must feel confident to share information in safe ways, protecting themselves and the children and families they support. For those training in the sector it is important that you consult with your mentor/critical friend to ensure that information you use about children, young people and families for your academic submissions is suitably anonymised and that you do not share information with your peers/tutors which may be considered sensitive, confidential or inappropriate for others to be aware of.

Conclusion

This chapter has sought to raise your awareness to a range of skills and knowledge required by practitioners and those training to enable effective practice to take place when working in the 0-19 sector. While the Common Core skills underpin all practices of those working/training within the children's and young people's workforce, particular practitioners/trainees will work towards a profession specific skill set. You will have noticed as you have read through this chapter that each common core of skills and knowledge does not stand alone; each one is intrinsically linked to the others. To effectively work with other agencies you need to develop effective communication skills; safeguarding, for example, requires effective communication skills and knowledge of the work of a range of professionals in CYPS. It is important that practitioners and those training reflect on a personal and team perspective, learning from their experiences, identifying areas for development and engaging in activities that will further develop skills to improve their practice.

Areas for further consideration

There are a number of other areas for consideration which you may wish to explore as part of your own personal study. The suggestions below merely offer a select number of aspects that will help to further develop your understanding of the skills and knowledge required for effective practice:

The professional standards pertinent to one's personal working roles	The skills and knowledge required to support children, young people and families with English as an Additional Language (EAL)
The skills and knowledge required to support children, young people and families with mental health difficulties	The monitoring and assessment of practitioners' skills and knowledge base
Local and national training available to update practitioners' skills and knowledge base	The skills and knowledge required to support children, young people and families at risk

Further reading

Books

Blythe, M. and Solomon, E. (2012) *Effective Safeguarding for Children and Young People: What next after Munro?* Bristol: Policy Press.
Leading experts working in the child protection system analyse the responses to the Munro review. This book will allow you to explore recent reviews of current safeguarding practice and review personal practice in light of developing knowledge and understanding.

Cheminais, R. (2009) *Developing and Evaluating Multi-Agency Partnerships: A practical toolkit for schools and children centre managers.* London: Routledge.
This publication allows the reader to gain further knowledge of multi-agency working and also access tools that will support personal practice.

Academic publications

Harris, A. and Allen, T. (2011) Young People's Views of Multi-Agency Working. *British Education Research Journal,* 37(3), 405–419.
This journal article investigates the impact of multi-agency working on children and their families. You will be able to explore the ways in which young people experience multi-agency working and if they perceive any benefits from a coordinated approach. You will be able to see that where multi-agency working is effectively integrated and streamlined there are positive outcomes for the children and families.

Hughes, A. M. and Read, V. (2012) *Building Positive Relationships with Parents of Young Children: A guide to effective communication.* London: Routledge.
This book explores how practitioners can build warm, friendly and caring relationships with parents. The dynamics of conversation and the theory behind how relationships are formed is discussed, providing practical strategies for developing effective practice.

Website

Skills framework. For developing effective relationships with vulnerable parents to improve outcomes for children and young people. Available at: http://tinyurl.com/oacssm4
A wonderful 'visual' skills framework that has been developed to 'identif[y] the key qualities and experience, skills and knowledge that are essential to developing effective professional relationships with vulnerable parents in order to improve outcomes for children and young people' (Action for Children, n.d.).

References

Alberta Children and Youth Initiative (2006) *Guidelines for Supporting Successful Transitions for Children and Youth*. [Online]. Available at: www.child.alberta.ca/home/documents/youthprograms/Guidelines_for_Supporting_Successful_Transitions_for_Children_and_Youth.pdf (Accessed: 20 October 2012).

Allen, G. (2011) *Early Intervention: The Next Steps*. London: Cabinet Office.

Beckley, P., Elvidge, K. and Hendry, H. (2009) *Implementing the Early Years Foundation Stage: A Handbook*. Berkshire: Open University Press.

Bowlby, J. (1969) *Bowlby's Attachment Theory*. [Online]. Available at: www.simplypsychology.org/bowlby.html (Accessed: 27 October 2012).

Children Act (2004) [Online]. Available at: www.legislation.gov.uk/ukpga/2004/31/contents (Accessed: 27 October 2012).

Children's Workforce Development Council (2008) *Common Core of Skills and Knowledge*. [Online]. Available at: www.childrenmattereast.org.uk/cms/uploads/MEDIA/DOCUMENTS/Common-Core.pdf (Accessed: 30 October 2012).

Clark, A. and Marsh, P. (2011) *Listening to Children Talk: The Mosaic Approach*. London: National Children's Bureau.

Data Protection Act (1998) [Online]. Available at: www.legislation.gov.uk/ukpga/1998/29/contents (Accessed: 29 October 2012).

Department for Children, Schools and Families (2009) *United Nations Convention on the Rights of The Child: Priorities for Action*. Nottingham: DCSF Publications.

——(2010) *Working together to Safeguard Children*. Nottingham: DCSF Publications.

Department for Education (2012a) *Statutory Framework for the Early Years Foundation Stage*. [Online]. Available at: www.education.gov.uk/publications/eOrderingDownload/EYFS%20Statutory%20Framework%20March%202012.pdf (Accessed: 30 October 2012).

——(2012b) *Teacher Standards*. [Online]. Available at: www.education.gov.uk/publications/eOrderingDownload/teachers%20standards.pdf (Accessed: 25 October 2012).

Department for Education and Skills (2003) *Every Child Matters: Change for Children*. Norwich: The Stationery Office.

——(2004) *National Standards for Head teachers*. Nottingham: Department for Education and Skills.

——(2005) *Children's Workforce Strategy*. Nottingham: DfES Publications.

Dunhill, A., Elliott, B. and Shaw, A. (2010) *Effective Communication and Engagement with Children and Young People, their Families and Carers*. Exeter: Learning Matters Ltd.

Dunlop, A. W. and Fabian, H. (2007) *Informing Transitions in the Early Years: Research, policy and practice*. Berkshire: Open University Press.

Fitzgerald, D. and Kay, J. (2008) *Working together in Children's Services*. London: Routledge.

Hobart, C. and Frankel, J. (2009a) *Good Practice in Safeguarding Children*. 3rd edn. Cheltenham: Nelson Thornes.

——(2009b) *A Practical Guide to Working with Parents*. 2nd edn. Cheltenham: Nelson Thornes.

Laming, H. (2003) *The Victoria Climbie Enquiry. A Report*. [Online]. Available at: https://www.education.gov.uk/publications/eOrderingDownload/CM-5730PDF.pdf (Accessed: 1 July 2012).

——(2009) *The Protection of Children in England. A Progress Report*. [Online]. Available at: http://dera.ioe.ac.uk/8646/1/12_03_09_children.pdf (Accessed: 12 September 2012).

Maslow, A. H. (1954) *Motivation and Personality*. New York: Harper and Row.

Munro, E. (2011) *The Munro Review of Child Protection. A Child Centred System*. Norwich: The Stationery Office.

National Youth Agency (2008) *The Professional and National Occupational Standards for Youth Work.* [Online]. Available at: http://nya.org.uk/dynamic_files/Youth_Work_National_Occupational_Standards%20 2012.pdf (Accessed: 15 October 2012).

Neaum, S. (2010) *Child Development for Early Childhood Studies.* Exeter: Learning Matters Ltd.

Oliver, B. and Pitt, B. (2011) *Working with Children, Young People and Families.* Exeter: Learning Matters Ltd.

Petch, A. (2009) *Managing Transitions: Support for Individuals at Key Points of Change.* Bristol: The Policy Press.

Petrie, P. (2011) *Communication Skills for Working with Children and Young People.* 3rd edn. London: Jessica Kingsley Publishers.

Powell, J. and Uppall, E. (2012) *Safeguarding Babies and Young Children: A Guide for Early Years Professionals.* Berkshire: Open University Press.

Teaching Agency (2012) *Early Years Professional Status Standards.* [Online]. Available at: www.education. gov.uk/publications/eOrderingDownload/eyps%20standards%20from%20september%202012.pdf (Accessed: 12 October 2012).

Training and Development Agency for Schools (2010) *National Occupational Standards for Supporting Teaching and Learning.* Manchester: TDA Publications.

UNICEF (2012) *A Summary of the Rights Under the Convention of the Rights of the Child.* [Online]. Available at: www.unicef.org.uk/Documents/Publication-pdfs/betterlifeleaflet2012_press.pdf (Accessed: 30 October 2012).

9 Learning a language: How practitioners and those training to work with young people could use language learning in their practice

Mike Jackson

LEARNING OBJECTIVES

After studying this chapter, you will be able to:

✔ Identify national governance policies and relevant legislation that is pertinent to language learning.
✔ Define the principles of language learning and teaching.
✔ Evaluate the applicability of learning a language to other areas of education.
✔ Identify ways in which learning a language can benefit the learner in a wider sense.

Introduction

What is learning a language? This question is fundamental; as a languages teacher it has always been apparent that people have different views on what this means. For a secondary school teacher it may mean following a course book to get an examination result; for a primary teacher it may be getting the children to answer the register in French; for a nursery practitioner/trainee it may mean getting the children to dress up in clothing from different countries while for a youth worker it may mean organising a day trip abroad. All these activities represent equally important aspects of language learning. The main aim of this chapter is to show that while speaking a language is certainly one aspect, there is a bigger picture of learning a language and the benefits can be far-reaching. It is passionately argued that learning a language can give a young person skills and attitudes that benefit the workplace and the lives that children and young people go on to live.

Case study

Aaron has just started in a Secondary School as a teaching assistant. As he has an 'A' level in German he has been asked to support the languages department. His first Year Nine group ask why they need to learn German. What might he say to them?

Do we just learn a language to communicate?

Learning a language simply to communicate could be argued to be a very functional or basic view of its aim. Indeed, there is no doubt that this must be one of the main aims but it is hoped that reading this chapter will show practitioners and those training that there are many other aspects to language learning. These will have lasting benefits for the learner, e.g. economic benefits for the nation, helping to understand how languages work, social skills to do with talking to each other – these are all benefits that could have been listed in the case study above. Some benefits are obvious, some are more subtle. It is hoped that this chapter will offer the practitioner and those training some valuable ideas. While most language learning takes place in a school setting, it is hoped that those practitioners/trainees who do not work in educational contexts will see how learning a language can take place in many other settings associated with CYPS.

An important consideration in establishing the national picture is to know that at the time of writing the current coalition government is consulting to make Modern Foreign Languages (MFL) compulsory at Key Stage Two (7–11 years). They highlight in their executive summary that:

> Languages are vital to the social and economic well-being of the country. Studying a language helps children to understand the world in which they live and the different cultures around the globe. Being able to communicate with others in their native tongue is of intrinsic value as a starting point for building relationships in social, educational or professional life. (DfE, 2012: 1.1)

It is fortunate that the government recognises that a language can provide significant advantages for the learner. Learning a language can open many doors to a deeper understanding of other cultures (DfE, 2012). It can give the learner a wonderful *frisson* of enjoyment when the first successful conversation is made by the learner, either when a pupil receives a real letter from a Spanish pen friend, gets a text from a pupil in a partner school abroad, or defeats a French opponent when gaming online!

Before considering what language learning means in practice it is worth trying to situate ourselves in the global picture. The preponderance of European languages on the curriculum offered to children and young people is worth considering. *Does everyone speak English?*

Activity: *Which languages are spoken most?*

Take a look at the grid below and work with a colleague/peer to complete it.

Language	How many speakers?	Where is the language spoken?
Mandarin Chinese		
English		
Hindustani		
Spanish		
Russian		
Arabic		
Bengali		
Portuguese		
Malay-Indonesian		
French		

Visit http://tinyurl.com/3gjv6np as information contained within this website will offer you the answers as to how many people speak these different languages.

- Why do you feel French currently dominates in the English classroom?

An apparent influx of other nationals into this country has shown that we need to question the dominance of French; Polish may have just as much a role to play in our schools. The first part of this chapter is about coming to terms with what MFL means. It is not just having French or German as a timetabled slot on a timetable: 'Now we are going to be French!'

In terms of what happens in a school, the documents below give an overview of the main aspects of MFL.

Reflective task: *Gaining an awareness*

Download a free copy of either of the frameworks below. They can also be accessed from the National Centre for Languages (CILT): http://tinyurl.com/axqy4w2

Primary:
- The Key Stage Two Framework – available at http://tinyurl.com/anpejcc
- The QCDA schemes of work – available at http://tinyurl.com/pn4f3dd
- The TDA schemes of work – available at http://tinyurl.com/b7meood

Secondary:
- The Key Stage Three (11-16 years) Programme of study – available at http://tinyurl.com/aynsjoa

(Key Stage Four and Key Stage Five are dealt with later)

Reflect on its content, identifying *five* key pieces of information which support you in your knowledge and understanding of the guidance for learning and teaching a language.

A deeper stage of reflection can be obtained by highlighting the *differences* between the three primary schemes.

Reflect on the following:
- What does the fact that there are three possible schemes to choose from for the primary sector (not even counting the various commercial courses available) tell you about the state of language teaching in the primary sector at present?

Language teaching legislation

The only legislation that relates to the teaching of language teaching comes from the National Curriculum (NC) (DfEE/QCA, 1988) which established an entitlement to the study of a language in the maintained secondary sector. This came into force in 1988 with the Education Reform Act (ERA). Swarbrick (2002: 9) points out that 'the NC has had a profound effect on the teaching and learning of MFL'. Suddenly all secondary pupils were to learn a language and the previous split into an 'O' (Ordinary) level or a CSE (Certificate of Secondary Education – from which gaining Grade One was to equate with a pass at 'O' level) was deemed inappropriate at a time when a more egalitarian view of education prevailed, although it was apparent that a two-tier approach still continued.

Having looked at some of the documentation from the reflective task on page 142-3 it should be apparent to the reader that there does not appear to be a coherent understanding of what constitutes teaching a foreign language. There seems to exist quite a difference in their format and approaches to MFL. Imagine how confusing it can be for the language teacher to choose the 'correct' way.

This apparent disparity of approaches can be explained when factors such as age-related pedagogy and staff expertise and qualifications are included. More on this will be discussed later in the chapter.

At this point it would be beneficial to the reader to present a short historical perspective of the state of language learning. It is interesting to consider this as it highlights the changing priorities in society which had an effect on the content of guidance.

Learning a language had traditionally been seen as the preserve of a well-heeled elite with the means to travel. It was studied as an intellectual exercise that concentrated on grammatical accuracy as a means of assessment (Jones in Field, 2000: 143). The spoken language and the need to communicate were relegated at a time when English was seen as the *lingua-franca* of the world and much of the content of the 'O' level examination at the age of 16 reflected a grammatical approach to teaching (Swarbrick, 2002). A viewing of past 'O' level papers from http://tinyurl.com/cgs83y7 will quickly show the character of such examinations. With the advent of cheaper travel and the establishment of the global market, along with a move to comprehensive education during the 1970s and 1980s, a new approach was needed. This can be answered in part by considering what happens at the different age groups.

Primary French

It is of note that at present there is much discussion about the benefits to an earlier start to language learning, the current DfE consultation on Key Stage Two languages being an example. The Labour government (1997–2007) brought in the Key Stage Two Framework for Languages (DfES, 2005), which stated that learning a language allows pupils to progress through:

- oracy;
- literacy; and
- intercultural understanding

along with two 'cross-cutting' strands of:

- knowledge about language; and
- language learning strategies.

It was also becoming more accepted in schools that learning a language earlier in the primary school was an educationally sound proposal (Hood and Tobutt, 2009; Martin, 2008) despite an early attempt in the 1960s to start language learning in the primary school which failed to establish itself (Kirsch, 2008). From 2000 to 2010 there was a big push by the government to train teachers to be language specialists; PGCE students were offered a financed four-week teaching block in France, Spain, Germany or Belgium to hone language skills. Some 3,000 students had taken advantage of this by 2008 (OFSTED, 2008: 8) and would have gone to 4,600 by 2010 (DfE, 2012). It was planned by the Labour government that a language study would become statutory by law by 2010; however, the general election occurred and the Bill never got passed. According to DfE (2012: 5) £100 million had been spent on the initiative.

There was an attempt to standardise the teaching of MFL in the primary school with the then DCFS (2005) Key Stage Two Framework for languages (Martin, 2008: 21). It was realised that the secondary approach to MFL would not work in the primary context so it was linked very closely to the Primary Literacy Strategy (1998). This gave teachers guidance for a delivery of a subject that was based on primary pedagogy.

> Primary French tends and needs to be more primary than French. In other words the whole approach to languages in the primary school needs to be founded on good primary practice. (De Silva and Satchwell, 2004: 13)

The approach tended to favour a delivery based on games and songs with active learning. Driscoll *et al.* (2010: 1) highlight the enjoyment pupils derive from this approach. They state that:

> 'Children were enthusiastic about their learning experience in most case study schools and appreciated the interactive teaching, and the wide variety of game-like activities which made learning languages fun'.

Writing was relegated in importance; however, a drawback observed by Kirsch (2008) is that while pupils had developed good listening and speaking skills, their reading and writing skills were underdeveloped. This aspect was also identified by OFSTED (2005) on the Pathfinder areas. Yet there is no doubt that looking at the feedback from pupils it was a very popular aspect to their curriculum. According to the NFER (2009, cited in DfE, 2012) 92 per cent of primary schools reported that they were teaching a language in Key Stage Two which is double the number in 2002/03.

Activity: *Engaging with primary pedagogy*

Look at the suggestions below from the Key Stage Two framework – Year 4 (Oracy)

O4.2 Listen for specific words and phrases in a song, poem or story

- Count how many times they hear a particular number, word or phrase; respond with a physical movement, or by repeating the word verbally, or by piling up counters or Lego bricks, e.g. *Heads, Shoulders, Knees and Toes* in French? *Tête, Epaules, Genoux, Pieds.*
- Count how often a type of word appears, e.g. colours, animals, numbers, times, places; respond by circling pictures or numbers.
- Identify an object or picture by its description. Listen to a story and point at pictures or objects when they hear them, e.g. the little dog is walking, the big brown bear is skipping, the hungry caterpillar is not playing the guitar.
- Play and extend the word class game. Children listen to the teacher; when they hear a noun they place both hands on their head, when they hear a verb they run on the spot. This can be extended to include adjectives – wiggle one hand beside your ear; adverbs – swing your arms as if marching or walking briskly; pronouns – place only one hand on your head; conjunctions – shake hands with someone.
- Respond to poems and stories presented through PowerPoint and other multi-media texts.
- Listen to and join in with stories, songs and poems.
- Draw a picture to show understanding of an aspect of the story.

How might a Key Stage One teacher/trainee plan activities for your children as exemplified above?

OFSTED (2011) gave a positive national picture of this approach. This stated that pupils were making good progress, especially in listening and speaking. Pupils were

> 'usually very enthusiastic, looked forward to lessons, understood why it was important to learn another language and were developing a good awareness of other cultures' (OFSTED, 2011: 5).

Extending this approach to early years settings should not constitute a great deal of effort. Any of the seven areas of learning and development can be addressed with a MFL. See the case study overleaf as an example.

Case study: *Early Years*

Lisa works at a privately owned nursery. She has a GCSE in Spanish and has taken holidays in Spain. She is keen to introduce some Spanish into the routine of the nursery to try and bring a bit of intercultural 'spice' to the setting. Lisa believes that helping children to understand that there is life beyond their individual perspective is a very important lesson to learn.

Match up the five activities to one of the seven areas (two can cover other areas!):

1   Saying 'Hola!' to the children.
2   Getting the children to say 'Hola!' to each other.
3   Playing simple songs in Spanish (either bought in Spain while on holiday or downloaded from the Primary languages website – http://tinyurl.com/bj92t23).
4   Writing sand numbers in response to the Spanish word instead of English.
5   Sharing her experiences of Spanish food with the children.

Area of Learning and Development	Activity
Communication and language	
Physical development	
Personal, social and emotional development	
Literacy	
Mathematics	
Understanding the world	
Expressive arts and design	

What else might you do to give a Spanish 'feel' to Lisa's setting?

It is indeed pleasing to note that the current consultation by the coalition government to make foreign languages compulsory at KS2 have realised the importance of MFL. While there is still debate about how this can be done, the benefits of an early start are recognised:

> 'foreign language teaching improves spoken language and literacy in English and it has all-round cognitive benefits, resulting in pupils being more receptive to teaching in all subjects' (DfE, 2012: 4).

There still remain issues of transition though; even nationally only one in five secondary schools have good links with their feeder schools to provide a good transition: 'Transition arrangements to secondary schools, the joint responsibility of both phases, were generally underdeveloped' (OFSTED, 2011: 19).

A secondary school with specialist language college status is expected to work with its primary schools (according to CILT there are over 200 nationally). Out of 3,127 this leaves a lot that are not and this can only have a detrimental effect on pupils' experiences of languages. It is just as much a dilemma for a primary school that is trying to organise its Key Stage Two curriculum by incorporating a language as it is for a large secondary school that may have a large number of feeder schools.

Secondary school

Prior to 1988 MFL in the secondary school sector had been split into a grammatical approach for higher attaining pupils who would follow the 'O' Level and a more communicative based approach for pupils who would follow a 'CSE'. Following the Education Reform Act (1988) (ERA), both the 'O' level and the CSE disappeared to be replaced by the new GCSE (General Certificate of Secondary Education) examination for all. Teachers, however, had to wait until 1992 to receive the details of what to teach.

The arrival of the GCSE meant that all pupils would follow the same path. The teaching was broken down into the four Attainment Targets (AT) of Listening (AT1), Speaking (AT2), Reading (AT3) and Writing (AT4), all with 25 per cent weighting to be taught simultaneously, not exclusively. Language was taught through seven areas of experience:

- Area A: Everyday Activities;
- Area B: Personal and Social Life;
- Area C: The World Around Us;
- Area D: The World of Education, Training and Work;
- Area E: The World of Communication;
- Area F: The International World; and
- Area G: The World of Imagination and Creativity (Department of Education and Science and the Welsh Office). (DES and WO, 1991: 27)

Pupils were split into foundation and higher tiers; the former expected to gain below a grade C and the latter above a grade C. Critics might say that the two-tier approach still remains. Following shifts in thinking over the decade, the Programme of study for Key Stage Three (QCA, 2007) changed and now proposes the following key concepts and two key processes:

Key concepts:
1.1 Linguistic competence
1.2 Knowledge about language
1.3 Creativity
1.4 Intercultural understanding

Key Processes:
2.1 Developing language – learning strategies
2.2 Developing language skills

An interesting debate on this can be found in Swarbrick (2002 - see Chapter 3) that highlights the many changes to the curriculum that have bedevilled the work for teachers trying to plan for teaching MFL since the ERA. Adapting schemes of work is always a time-consuming process. However, it is of note that the current KS3 Programme of Study (as indicated in the earlier reflective task - see pages 142–43) mirrors more the primary approach by including *Intercultural Understanding* and *Knowledge about Language*. This constitutes a step in the right direction in terms of bringing the two sectors together to help their learners by presenting a more homogenous experience.

Case study: *The Key Stage Three framework*

Maria is just completing her PGCE course and one of her tasks is to show her engagement with the framework by evidencing what her Year Seven group might do under the six concepts.

By looking at the framework (available at: http://tinyurl.com/aynsjoa) can you complete the table? A few examples have been done for you.

Key concept and process	What it means in practice	A possible example in Key Stage Three
Linguistic competence	Being able to apply grammatical rules in different contexts, e.g. showing an understanding of adjective agreement.	Letting the pupils design and describe an ideal school uniform and justifying their choice.
Knowledge about language		
Creativity		
Intercultural understanding		Students research school life in France in order to produce their own PowerPoint presentation.
Developing language learning strategies		
Developing language skills		

Post 16

There have been attempts to continue the process of homogenisation at 16+. Advanced ('A') level study similarly followed a move away from the more academic type of assessment by including mixed skill testing, for instance, Listening with Writing, as well as Reading with Writing to give more importance to the content element of the new A level. Literature and current themes in society became the medium for study. The oral examination contained a prepared oral topic. Inevitably grammatical accuracy became more important. A deeper understanding of this can be made by the reader consulting the main examination boards' approach to how students are to be assessed.

Activity: *Engaging with GCSE and A level examinations*

Select any two of the following exam boards at GCSE and Advanced level:

Exam board	Web link
AQA GCSE French	http://tinyurl.com/aocdftc
EDEXCEL GCSE French	http://tinyurl.com/ajkdhzz
OCR GCSE French	http://tinyurl.com/by2o652
EDEXCEL International GCSE	http://tinyurl.com/b4e3ekh
AQA Advanced French	http://tinyurl.com/8l2q538
EDEXCEL Advanced French	http://tinyurl.com/b39ujhq
OCR Advanced French	http://tinyurl.com/bcd9vrc
OCR Vocational Qualification	http://tinyurl.com/arh68tz

This list is not exhaustive; there are many other qualifications available for languages, especially at Advanced level. Access the website and reflect on aspects of content which are of interest to you and your colleagues/peers.

When looking at post-16, do you think the Advanced level offers anything different from the Vocational qualification? Again, justify your choice.

At present, schools are not obliged to follow any one particular examination board. Departments are free to choose whichever board they feel may give the best results for their pupils. Depending on the board's individual assessment arrangements, departments decide which will suit the needs of their pupils, for example the length of examinations, the type of questions used in the comprehension papers, the variety of topics offered in the speaking examination; these all vary from board to board and can all have an effect on influencing a Head of Languages to make a choice.

Reflective task: *What do you need to know?*

Revisit the activity above. Choose either GCSE or A level and compare how the examinations are arranged. Take a piece of paper and write down as many things that *you* would want to know about each specification if you had to make a choice. Compare your list to the suggestions offered below:

The length of each examination component	*Does the length of the examination make a difference?*
The kind of linguistic skills being sought in each component	*Is it clear what the students have to learn?*
How the students will be assessed	*What support is offered by each board to the teacher in terms of exemplification of standards?* *Are you clear what each grade band represents?*

Consider the following: When looking at the specifications which of them would you have preferred? Why would you have made that choice?

Of course not all language study should be academic. Consider a youth worker who may have a group of youngsters who have never been abroad. It would be very simple, although time consuming, to organise a day trip to Boulogne. These trips do take a lot of organisation! Costings need to be worked out, e.g. the cost of a coach, staff to student ratios need to be met, permission slips need to be collected, food allergies need to be noted, CRB (now DBS) checks of accompanying adults need to be acquired, timings of ferries need to be ascertained (bearing in mind that most shops shut in Boulogne from 12-2pm!), risk assessments and contingency plans need to be formulated and put in place – these are some of the many factors that need considering. However, experience has shown that the benefits far outweigh the time taken to set a day trip up. Students going abroad on an exchange learn so much more about themselves. They learn about their own context, language and culture, and can see these so much more clearly and gain new insights. It may seem rather 'simplistic' but a visit abroad can give a profound meaning to staff and students of the purpose of education and to understanding the world community. Witness the bringing to Liverpool of groups of German students after World War Two by Eric Hawkins, an account of which can be read in his book *Listening to Lorca* (CfBT, 2012). After the bombings this city received such laudable attempts to bring reconciliation and understanding to communities, which is something that should be emulated a lot more nowadays.

Reflective task

What possible benefits might a group of teenagers gain from a day trip to France?

Consider the possible effects on their view of other people, even the fact that things will be better than they had at first thought!

Outlining the benefits for the student of learning a language is one of the stated aims of this chapter. So, what skills does the learning of MFL bring? To which other areas of learning is learning a MFL applicable? The previous activity alluded to one of the greatest advantages of learning a language, which is that of combating negative attitudes to other people. From Key Stage One to Key Stage Five, *Intercultural* or *Cultural Understanding* (IU) appears in all the schemes of work and frameworks. Its importance can become an attitude to life that will have lasting benefits to all. Raising children's awareness of linguistic and cultural diversity is an important step in the process of standing back to compare languages and create an interest in learning new languages (Datta and Pomphrey, 2004). In turn, this acceptance of other languages will have a spin-off of accepting other people. As Peiser and Jones (2012) state in the revised Programme of Study for Key Stage Three, IU is broken down into:

- appreciating the richness and diversity of other cultures; and
- recognising that there are different ways of seeing the world, and developing an international outlook.

This would translate into an affirmation of positive attitudes toward other cultures, and in developing IU pupils would develop attitudes of openness and respect for other cultures (Peiser and Jones, 2012). Their conclusion states that IU:

addresses the social cohesion agenda and the international strategy; it provides a vehicle for developing the personal, learning and thinking skills instrumental to the globalised knowledge economy of the twenty-first century; and its appearance as a curriculum strand in Key Stage 3 allows for alignment with the Key Stage 2 Framework. (Peiser and Jones, 2012: 184)

If teachers have the requisite skills to promote IU rather than use it as a tick box for the purposes of the Framework then much can be done to promote less ethno-centric attitudes in their pupils and students. For the primary practitioner/trainee the Key Stage Two framework offers a lot of advice on how to teach IU throughout.

A common problem language teachers might find is pupils struggling to accept that it is not 'daft' to have a different word order as in German or to have gender in most languages except English! The fact that Spanish can often place words that are to be emphasised at the end of the sentence, e.g. ¡Viene Mamá! (*Mum* is coming!) can cause irritation to the learner in a longer sentence. However, also consider the positive discussion that could be had when considering the differences in punctuation and the use of accents that such a short sentence offers. No language is better or worse than another; they are just different, and that acceptance on the part of the learner is just one facet of the main advantages to learning a language.

Reflective task: *Intercultural understanding*

How might the following 'differences' be used as a learning opportunity for your students?

Aspect	Explanation of why it exists	Potential to use as a learning opportunity
Eating habits of the French, e.g. are frog's legs and snails typical French foods?		
French pupils have chess as part of their timetabled lessons		
Bullfighting in Spain		
In France pupils still have to retake a school year if they do not do very well		
The German school day is 8am to 1pm and there is no school uniform		

One of the other big advantages to learning a language is the links it can create to improving literacy.

The literacy link

One of the stated aims of this chapter is to show how learning a language can have a direct link to other areas. The link to literacy is a very clear example. This is a slight move away from the original idea that one learns a language simply in order to communicate. There are certainly identifiable benefits that go beyond the need to communicate. Writers on MFL agree that helping pupils to understand their own language is a clear incentive for learners (McLachlin, 2008: 82). Pupils gain an awareness of grammatical terminology and are able to draw parallels and conclusions about other languages that enable them to reflect on language in general.

Activity: *How secure are you with grammar?*

For each term below give a definition and an example. These are all items that are taught as part of learning a language. The first is done for you by way of example.

Term	Definition	Example
Indefinite article	A or an (before a vowel)	A horse An ant
Definite article		
Noun		
Verb		
Adjective		
Adverb		
Verb		
Perfect tense		
Subordinate clause		
Transitive verb		

The list above is merely a small sample of some of the terms that pupils will come across when studying languages. Understanding the mechanics of grammar can give the freedom to manipulate language. As Pachler and Field (2003: 126) state, 'the ability to use language grammatically correctly is a key component and an integral part of effective communication'. The push to improve literacy levels under the Labour government with the National Literacy

Strategy (NLS) (introduced in 1998) created an impetus to link MFL teaching to the teaching of literacy, a fact reflected in the reworking of the MFL Framework to show more overt areas of commonality, with pupils exemplifying work at word, sentence and text levels. Morgan and Neil (2001: 40) state that from the NLS students would have learnt the meaning of 'adjective, conjunction, noun, pronoun, verb, tense, first, second and third person, adverb, clause, connectives' to mention just a few. Such terms are essential to the study of a language.

Some secondary schools created language awareness courses directly aimed at sensitising their pupils to languages and indicating any prior links such as the link between sounds and symbols learnt in early phonics teaching. These links are continued and reinforced in MFL, helping children 'to develop an awareness of sounds and words, as well as sentence structure and grammar' (Cheater and Farren, 2001: 3). It can be argued that since language sounds or phonemes are different from one language to another, teaching the alphabet too early will confuse pupils. For example, the realisation that the English letters G and J sound the other way round in French may cause considerable problems. Yet, taught at the right stage this phonetic awareness is a skill that should remain with the learner and help them to be reflective in any future language learning.

Speaking a language is clearly one of the main aims of language learning. However, it is not just in order to communicate with another person that makes it so important; the actual action of communicating partner to partner can do much to give pupils the confidence to speak calmly and politely – that must be a vital life skill. Equally, the ability to listen carefully to each other must be just as important.

The confines of the chapter means it is impossible to present a comparison of the content of the many commercial courses available to a school. However, due to the continued use of this approach, it would be an omission to not discuss this. Textbooks have always played a big part in the teaching of MFL as although they save time for the teacher in terms of planning, arguments against their use will inevitably be made as schools and society as a whole move towards a more technological age. One only has to see how iPads have begun to be used in schools. At KS3 an interesting aspect to consider is that many schools and departments still depend on a textbook approach to their planning of the following framework objectives:

- Words – teaching pupils to practice the meaning, spelling, and sound of French words together.
- Sentences – teaching pupils how to write simple grammatically correct sentences.
- Texts (reading and writing) – teaching pupils how to understand and write more complex texts using connectives, pronouns and tenses.
- Listening and speaking – linking listening and speaking to help pupils speak more accurately and authentically.
- Cultural knowledge and contact – giving pupils the opportunity to learn about France and other French-speaking countries.

These aspects clearly link with the literacy work that followed the introduction of the DfES' Primary Strategy in 2003 which established a national pattern for the teaching of literacy skills.

While learning a language can certainly help with literacy skills it is interesting to consider briefly how other cross-curricular links with other subjects can also be made. For instance, the teaching of history and geography can be strengthened by linking themes being taught in them in languages too, e.g. if the weather in Africa is being taught in Geography then why not teach weather at the same time in French? It just needs a common approach to curricular planning (Coyle in Field, 2000). Studying colours in Spanish can be applied to Art; songs in French can be learned and sung in Music. These are not just ill thought out 'bolt-ons'. At present there are schools adopting this approach called CLIL (Content and Language Integrated Learning). More can be found out about this by visiting http://tinyurl.com/32trepw.

One would hope that new technologies can provide new incentives for language learners. For instance, the ability to use SKYPE to speak to anyone in the world, the use of online gaming where video games can be played internationally, and smart phones with newly developing applications must soon give people the chance to communicate in real time. However, such wonders are still yet to be established in schools.

Conclusion

This chapter has sought to raise your awareness of an area of the curriculum that has changed from an academic elitist subject to a compulsory one in the National Curriculum to an optional one that might become compulsory in the primary sector! It also may become compulsory again in Key Stage Four under the **English Baccalaureate**. The changes in MFL delivery and teaching say as much about political interference in education as it does about the understanding any society has about the value of language study. While the chapter will only have been able to give a brief overview of some of the arguments for a language, it is hoped that you will go further and deepen your understanding of MFL.

Areas for further consideration

There are a number of other areas for consideration which you may wish to explore as part of your own personal study. The suggestions below merely offer a select number of aspects which will help to further develop your understanding of MFL:

MFL and online translation tools	Developing professional links with teachers, children/young people and schools in other countries
MFL and practical teaching resources	Learning a language through exchange programmes
MFL and adult language learning classes	Bilingualism and trilingualism in the classroom

Further reading

Books

McLachlan, A. (2008) *French in the Primary Classroom*. London: Continuum.
This book gives plenty of ideas and resources for the Non-Linguist Teacher who works in primary school or an early years setting.

Watts, C., Forder, C., Phillips, H. and Watts, C. (ed.) (2013) *Living Languages*. London: Routledge.
Living Languages is simply bursting with practical and original ideas aimed at teachers and trainee teachers of foreign languages in primary schools. Written by a team of experienced linguists, this book will inspire and motivate the foreign language classroom and the teachers who work within it. (Amazon.co.uk)

Academic publications

Tinsley, T. and Han, Y. (2011) *Language learning in secondary schools in England. Association for Language learning (ALL)*. [Online]. Available at: http://tinyurl.com/acdqogm (Accessed: 21 May 2012).
This paper covers the main issues of what is happening in MFL in schools. It gives a very well researched picture of the state of languages in the secondary school context.

Cable, C., Driscoll, P., Mitchell, R., Sing, S., Cremin T., Earl, J., Eyres, I., Holmes, B., Martin, C. with Heins, B. (2010) *Languages learning at Key Stage 2 – A longitudinal study: final report (OU)*. [Online]. Available at: http://tinyurl.com/bhatv6j (Accessed: 29 January 2012).
This qualitative study was designed to explore provision, practice and developments over three school years between 2006/07 and 2008/09 in a sample of primary schools and explore children's achievement in oracy and literacy, as well as the possible broader cross-curricular impact of languages learning.

Websites

The Primary languages website. Available at: www.primarylanguages.org.uk
This is the national gateway for advice, information and support for MFL in the primary and Early Years setting. It offers a wealth of resources and key documentation for all aspects. Sample video footage of classes in action alongside professional help make this website indispensable for anyone interested in language teaching.

References

Barton, A. (2004) *Getting the Buggers into Languages*. London: Continuum.
Bevis, R. and Gregory, A., (2005) *Mind the gap!* London: CILT.
Biriotti, L. (1999) *Grammar is fun*. London: CILT.
Cable, C., Driscoll, P., Mitchell, R., Sing, S., Cremin, T., Earl, T., Eyres, I., Holmes, B., Martin, C. with Heins, B. (2010) *Languages Learning at Key Stage 2 – A Longitudinal Study: Final Report*. Research Report No. DCSF-RR198. [Online]. Available at: http://eprints.soton.ac.uk/143157/1/DCSF-RR198.pdf (Accessed: 7 September 2013).
Cajkler, W. and Addelman, R. (2000) *The Practice of Foreign Language Teaching*. 2nd edn. London: David Fulton.
Cheater, C. (2005) *The Scheme of Work for French*. Wakefield: Teaching and Learning Publications.
Cheater, C. and Farren, A. (2001) *The Literacy Link*. London: CILT.
CILT (2004) *Piece by Piece – Languages in the Primary schools*. London: CILT.
——(2007) *Languages 2007 Digest*. London: CILT.
Datta, M. and Pomphrey, C. (2004) *A World of Languages*. London: CILT.
De Silva, J. and Satchwell, P. (2004) *A Flying Start*. London: CILT.
Department for Education (2012) *Key Stage Two consultation on Primary Languages. [Online]*. Available at: http://www.education.gov.uk/inthenews/inthenews/a00217388/overwhelming-support-for-foreign-languages-plan (Accessed: 9 December 2012).

Department for Education and Skills (2002) *Languages for all: Languages for Life.* Nottingham: DfES.

——(2005) *The Key Stage 2 Framework for Languages.* Nottingham: DfES.

——(2007) *Languages review (The Dearing Review).* Nottingham: DfES.

Evans, M. and Fisher, L. (2009) *The Impact of the Key Stage 3 Modern Foreign Languages Framework and Changes to the Curriculum on Provision and Practice.* University of Cambridge. [Online]. Available at: www.education.gov.uk/publications/standard/publicationDetail/Page1/DCSF-RR091 (Accessed: 14 January 2013).

Field, K. (ed.) (2000) *Issues in Modern Foreign Languages Teaching.* London: RoutledgeFalmer.

Hawkins, E. (1987) *Modern Languages in the Curriculum.* Bristol: The Cambridge University Press.

——(2000) *Listening to Lorca: A Journey into Language.* London: CILT.

Hood, P. and Tobutt, K. (2009) *Modern Languages in the Primary School.* London: Sage.

Kirsch, C. (2008) *Teaching Foreign Languages in the Primary School.* London: Continuum.

Martin, C. (2008) *Primary Languages.* Exeter: Learning Matters.

McLachlan, A. (2008) *French in the Primary Classroom.* London: Continuum.

Morgan, C. and Neil, P. (2001) *Teaching Modern Foreign Languages.* London: Kogan Page.

Pachler, N. and Field, K. (2003) *Learning to Teach Modern Foreign Languages in the Secondary School.* London: RoutledgeFalmer.

OFSTED (2005) *Implementing languages entitlement in primary schools. HMI 2476.* [Online]. Available at: http://dera.ioe.ac.uk/5386/1/Implementing%20languages%20entitlement%20in%20primary%20schools%20(PDF%20format).pdf (Accessed: 1 June 2013).

——(2008) *The Changing Landscape of Languages.* [Online]. Available at: http://education.staffordshire.gov.uk/NR/rdonlyres/C9799972-6C89-458C-AEF7-8E49BED8A9AD/79216/The_changing_landscape_of_languagesJuly08.pdf (Accessed: 1 June 2013).

——(2011) *Report summary Modern languages Achievement and challenge 2007–2010.* [Online]. Available at: www.ofsted.gov.uk/resources/modern-languages-achievement-and-challenge-2007-2010 (Accessed: 1 June 2013).

Peiser, G. and Jones, M. (2012) *Rhetoric or reality: intercultural understanding in the English Key Stage 3 Modern Foreign Languages curriculum.* [Online]. Available at: www.tandfonline.com/doi/abs/10.1080/09585176.2012.678499 (Accessed: 9 November 2012).

QCDA (2007) *Key Stage Two Schemes of Work.* [Online]. Available at: www.primarylanguages.org.uk/resources/qca_schemes_of_work.aspx (Accessed: 14 January 2013).

Stern, H. (1967) *Foreign Languages in the Primary School.* London: Oxford University Press.

Swarbrick, A. (ed.) (2002) *Teaching Modern Foreign Languages in Secondary Schools.* Maidenhead: Open University Press.

Wakely, C. (2010) *Take 10 en français.* Exeter: Babcock LDP.

10 *'Reflecting on reflection'*: Work-based reflective practice

Simon Brownhill

LEARNING OBJECTIVES

After studying this chapter, you will be able to:

✔ Define the terms *reflection* and *reflective practice*.
✔ Evaluate the importance of reflective practice to the service you provide/train in.
✔ Identify different cycles of reflection and reflective tools to support you in reflective activity.
✔ Evaluate practical ways in which *barriers* to reflective practice can be positively addressed.

Introduction

In all sectors across Children's and Young People's Services (CYPS) there are practitioners and those training who actively engage in work-based reflection to support their continuing/ initial professional development (CPD/IPD), inform change and improve the quality of provision and practice across the sector. From trainee teaching assistants reflecting on their ability to meet the needs of more able children in the classroom to sports practitioners using action research to evaluate their delivery of football programmes for young people with behavioural difficulties, work-based reflective practice allows people to 'consciously look at and think about [their] experiences, actions, feelings and responses and then interpret... or analys[e] them in order to learn from them' (Boud *et al.*, 1994, cited in Learning Development, 2010: 1).

As work-based reflective practice is considered to be of both personal and professional benefit (see Piaget, 1975) the last few decades have seen many academics jump on the 'reflection bandwagon' (Loughran, 2000). This resulting surge of activity has given rise to an array of perspectives, models of reflection and reflective tools being proposed to support practitioners and those training in their engagement of what many consider to be the 'key' quality that makes an individual who works/trains in CYPS effective: the ability to reflect.

Activity: *Searching for the 'key' quality*

Shakespeare (2010: 1) suggests that '[r]eflection is generally promoted in workplace learning and in many professions is specifically an aspect of professional conduct, set out by professional bodies in codes of conduct, standards, proficiencies or competencies (see for example, the UK Nursing and Midwifery Council, 200[8])'.

Consider the standards that are pertinent to your particular role in CYPS, identifying where reflection appears in these standards, for example:

- The standards of proficiency for *Social workers in England* (Health and Care Professions Council, 2012) for those who work/train in social work.
- The *Youth Work National Occupational Standards* (Learning and Skills Improvement Service, 2012) for those who work/train in the youth sector.

Alternatively, take a look at the *Common Core of Knowledge and Skills* (CWDC, 2010) which describes the knowledge and skills requirements that *all* people who work/train with children, young people and families are expected to demonstrate/develop. See the details which are available at: http://tinyurl.com/cr3kgqn.

This chapter will focus its attention on gaining clarity with regard to what reflection is, ensuring that readers recognise its importance and value at both a personal and professional level, particularly in light of changing notions of professional development and individual responsibility. While reflective cycles and reflective tools serve as key considerations within this chapter, an exploration of different types of reflection will be made, raising awareness to 'a taxonomy of reflection [that] has been developed based on Bloom's taxonomy' (Vos and Cowan, 2009: 1). The chapter begins by exploring definitions of reflection and reflective practice, relating this to academic thinking and professional practice with children, young people, families and communities.

Definitions of *reflection* and *reflective practice*

In general terms, *reflection* refers to thinking (Parker, 1997). Indeed, reflection can be considered an important basic human habit, one that serves us as an integral feature of our day-to-day lives whereby we typically ask ourselves questions: *Should I have really said 'No!' to my manager's request to work late next week?; I wonder if there is a quicker way to get to the gym?* We can thus define **reflection** as looking back at something - an event, a situation, an occasion, an incident - that may be tied to our emotions, thoughts and feelings and/or to those of others (Moon, 2005). By thinking about what happened and what was said we can ascertain whether our words/actions or the words/actions of others were apt or inappropriate. When considering the meaning of **reflective practice**, particularly that which is work-based, it is possible to think about it in very much the same way as reflection but in a more formal, structured and 'deeper' style.

Numerous definitions of the term reflective practice exist. Some are rather succinct - 'Learning from experience' (Spalding, 1998) and 'Thoughtful deliberation' (Tickle, 1994) - whereas others are more explanatory and detailed in content, examples of which include:

An active, persistent, and careful consideration of a belief or supposed form of knowledge in the light of the grounds that support it and the further conclusions to which it tends. (Dewey, 1933: 9)

A generic term for those intellectual and effective activities in which individuals engage to explore their experiences in order to lead to a new understanding and appreciation. (Boud, Keogh and Walker, 1985: 3)

For further 'prominent' definitions see Taggart and Wilson (2005: 17).

While Fook, White and Gardner (2006) argue that what is understood by reflective practice varies considerably within different disciplines and intellectual traditions, Finlay (2008: 1) highlights what are personally regarded as 'strands of consensus' between the plethora of definitions available; these have been adapted from Finlay's work and are summarised below, emphasising the importance and benefits of reflection in terms of supporting one's learning and practice:

Reflective practice is considered to be:

1   the active process of *learning through* and *from experience*;
2   about gaining *new insights* of oneself and/or of practice;
3   an *examination of assumptions* of everyday practice;
4   a *critical evaluation* of an individual's response to practice-based situations; and
5   the development of *lifelong learning* behaviours.

Activity: *The elements of reflection*

It is worthy of note that the 'strands of consensus' presented above mirror some of the *elements of reflection* presented by Learning Development (2010: 2). Visit http://tinyurl.com/ajbwyus to develop an appreciation of these elements to support your continued/developing understanding of reflection.

By reflecting on the discussion above it is possible to see how these 'strands of consensus' relate to professional practice with children, young people, families and communities:

1   *What can I learn from the way I handled that difficult situation with Jenny's mum in the outdoor play area?* (Jack, trainee early years key worker)
2   *Would some electronic visual aids have helped me to better explain the best way to bottle feed a baby to those teenage mothers?* (Halima, health worker)
3   *Are the behaviour management strategies I am actively using with my own teenage sons appropriate for the young person I have just fostered?* (Alison, foster carer)
4   *Am I responding in a professional manner to those young people who forget their manners after I have served them their school dinner?* (Jerry, secondary school cook)
5   *Am I promoting essential Library skills for children in Key Stage One in an engaging way?* (Sanjeet, trainee school library service employee).

The examples above are purposefully offered as they highlight two different *types* of reflection that practitioners and those training can actively engage in.

Types of reflection

Schön (1991) suggests that there are two types of reflection: *reflection-in-action* and *reflection-on-action*. The preposition difference between these two types of reflection is important as these help to indicate when the reflection takes place: either *during-the-event* (*-in-*) or *after-the-event* (*-on-*). Learning Development (2010: 1) suggests that reflection-in-action takes place, for example, when 'a physiotherapy student [is] working with a client on an exercise programme[,] making decisions about the suitability of particular exercises, which exercise to do next and judging the success of each exercise at the same time as they are conducting the activity'. Reflection-on-action, however, occurs 'after the activity has taken place when you [in this case the physiotherapy student] are thinking about what you... did, judging how successful you were and whether any changes to what you did could have resulted in different outcomes' (p. 1). Those readers who are currently studying (both continued and initial) will recognise that reflection-on-action is typically the type of reflection you are asked to write about as part of your professional studies.

Activity: Is it *'-in-'* or *'-on-'*?

Take another look at the five work based examples offered on page 159 that relate to the 'strands of consensus' presented on page 159 – consider whether you feel the examples describe reflection-in-action or reflection-on-action.

Answers can be found at the end of the chapter on page 171.

Griffiths and Tann (1991, cited in Cox, 2005: 463) suggest that there are five different *levels* of reflection which relate to and help to expand the 'when' element of Schön's two types of reflection:

1   *Rapid reaction*: which involves an instinctive and very immediate response.
2   *Repair*: where reflection may entail a slight pause to gather the thoughts, but action is still fairly immediate.
3   *Review*: necessitating time out to re-assess, usually some hours or days later.
4   *Research*: a systematic, sharply focused approach to reflection taking place over weeks or months.
5   *Retheorize and reformulate*: the abstract, rigorous, clearly formulated contemplation which occurs over months or years.

For those readers who are training in the 0–19 sector it is likely that levels 3 and 4 described above are pertinent to your developing capabilities; as you gain in confidence, qualify and become experienced in professional practice levels 1 and 2 become more achievable. The notion of *Retheorize and reformulate* (level 5) resonates with the **Development Plans** that settings/services are encouraged to create and review to assure continuous improvement in their provision – consider talking with your mentor/manager to ascertain how reflection is used to support the production of these Development Plans.

It is of interest that Eraut (1995) extends Schön's work by proposing a third type of reflection – *reflection-for-action* – which is considered to be anticipative in nature. This type of reflection sees practitioners and those training defining their aspirations and purposes for subsequent action, e.g. a volunteer wishes to set up a much needed breakfast club at his grandchild's primary school by the end of the school year. Wilson (2008: 183) uses different 'labels' for this third type of reflection, referring to it as both *reflection-on-the-future* and *reflection-before-action*.

Activity: *Reading and research*

There are many other types of reflection. Ruch (2002: 204–5) describes four different levels of reflection and knowledge construction, these being:

- *technical* reflection;
- *practical* reflection;
- *critical* reflection; and
- *process* reflection.

Valli (1997) describes (among others) a further two types of reflection:

- *deliberative* reflection; and
- *personalistic* reflection.

Ghaye and Lillyman (1997) identify a further five different types of reflection:

- *structured* reflection;
- *hierarchical* reflection;
- *iterative* reflection;
- *synthetic* reflection; and
- *holistic* reflection.

Select any **two** of these types of reflection (ideally from different authors) and engage in some wider reading (books, journals – professional and academic – and websites) to develop a personal understanding of these types of reflection, considering how these can be used to help to support reflective practice in your work setting/placement.

You may also wish to undertake a web search for information about *reflexive practice* which is an important component of reflection. Consider exploring materials which relate not only to your particular service but to others which make up CYPS. Alternatively, take a look at the following recommended reading:

- Cunliffe, A. L. (2009) Reflexivity, learning and reflexive practice. In: S. Armstrong and C. Fukami (eds) *Handbook in Management Learning, Education and Development*. London: Sage.

Readers may have recognised that efforts to contextualise the three types of reflection described on pages 160 and 161 purposefully relate to individuals and their solo endeavours; this helps to emphasise Alvesson and Sköldberg's (2000, p. vii) thinking that reflection is about 'one's own interpretations, looking at one's own perspectives and turning a self-critical eye onto one's own authority as interpreter and author'. This is not to say, however, that reflection is/should be a solitary undertaking; reflecting with others – referred to by Husu, Toom and Patrikainen (2006) as *guided reflection* – be they fellow colleagues, members of the senior management team (SMT), work placement mentors/critical friends or teaching tutors, can facilitate valuable opportunities for you to extract meaning from your experiences, learning from these and improve your professional practice. This can be helpful in promoting and developing the necessary attributes (qualities) that are required of practitioners/those training who engage in reflective practice such as being open, flexible, proactive and committed; see page 110 of *Reflective Practice* (available at: http://tinyurl.com/b2eu7gj) for further examples. It is worthy of note that while these listed attributes relate to those working in health and social care settings, they are easily transferable to those working/training in other sectors which make up CYPS. Having or developing these attributes, however, is not enough; to support one's own self-examination/self-evaluation and efforts at collaborative reflection the use of reflective cycles is considered to be of real value.

Reflective cycles

Reflective cycles (also referred to as models, systems or frameworks) are valuable as they serve as a useful tool to help you systematically organise your thoughts when reflecting on incidences that occur in the workplace. Many of these present reflection as a cyclical process; as a result, many cycles of reflection (as the label suggests) are presented diagrammatically using a circular pattern. These cycles are typically 'broken up' into different numbers of stages or phases; these vary between two and six:

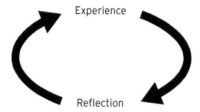

Experience

Reflection

Figure 10.1 Greenaway's (2002) reflective cycle

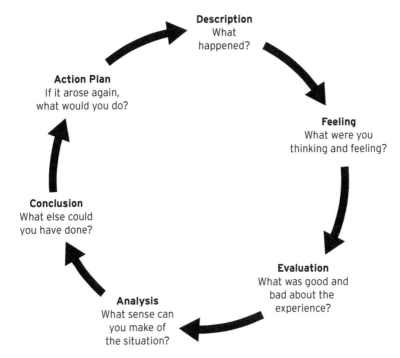

Figure 10.2 Gibbs' (1988) reflective cycle

You are encouraged to make reference to page 7 of the document *Reflection* (available at http://tinyurl.com/brosohw) for a useful set of questions to consider at each stage of Gibbs' popular cycle. These questions serve as valuable prompts or triggers to direct your thinking, many of which are based around key question stems: *Who...? What...? Where...? How...? Why...? When...?*; also see Vos and Cowan's (2009) taxonomy of reflection that is based on Bloom's taxonomy (1956). This is not to say that you cannot devise your own questions; these can be presented on cue cards, as an aide memoire list or on PowerPoint slides if you wish. Alternatives to questions are sentences starters which allow you to complete them in a way that is personal to you and your situation, examples of which include:

- *I used to think...but now I think...*
- *Next time I will remember to...*
- *I noticed that... and now I wonder...*
- *It did not help when...*

For further examples see Murphy (2009).

Activity: *Exploring other cycles of reflection*

There are many other cycles of reflection you can use to support you in your reflective endeavours:

Reflective Cycle	Web link (page reference)
Atkins and Murphy's (1994) stage model of reflection	http://tinyurl.com/b77q7bu
Johns' (1994) Model of Structured Reflection	http://tinyurl.com/aw8nqze (see page 2)
Kolb's (1984) Learning Cycle	http://tinyurl.com/5vywv8
Rolfe *et al.*'s (2001) Framework for reflexive practice	http://tinyurl.com/abwqjwy (see page 4)

Select one of the cycles listed above, making personal notes from either the web link offered or from other readings you actively engage with to demonstrate your developing understanding of your chosen cycle of reflection.

As a practitioner/trainee it is always useful to see how these cycles of reflection can be practically used to facilitate reflection. The case study below explores how a primary school teacher used the TASC (*Thinking Actively in a Social Context*) wheel approach to problem solving (Wallace, 2001 - see www.tascwheel.com/) to support him when reflecting on a rather 'awkward' issue.

Case study: *The TASC wheel and reflection*

Peter is a Newly Qualified Teacher (NQT), working in a Year 3 class in a large inner-city primary school. Behaviour in the school is considered 'problematic' by OFSTED and Peter is struggling to deal with the attention from some of the Year 6 girls who have developed a crush on him. The whole school use the *Thinking Actively in a Social Context* framework to help children develop their independent and creative thinking skills in an effort to raise attainment levels. Because the TASC wheel can also be used by adults, Peter decided to use the advocated process stages to reflect on this sensitive situation and find a way to positively deal with it. The table below presents the eight processes of the TASC wheel and Peter's personal notes.

Process	Notes
Gather/Organise *What do I know about this?*	I think some of the Year Six girls have taken a shine to me - they are blowing kisses and wolf whistling when I walk past them in school and they keep leering through the classroom window at me during playtime/lunchtime.
Identify *What is the task?*	Their behaviour is making me uncomfortable. I need them to understand that whilst their actions are flattering it is *not* appropriate for them to behave this way towards me.

Generate *How many ideas can I think of?*	• I could speak to the girls directly • Speak to the Year Six teacher • Strategically ignore it? • Discuss this with Josie, my 'critical friend' • Use assembly time to talk to the whole school about appropriate ways to behave towards teaching staff • Make the SMT [Senior Management Team] aware of the situation? • Speak to Curt [the other male teacher in the school] (Year Five) – has the same thing happened to him? What did he do about it?
Decide *Which is the best idea?*	I've decided to speak to the Year Six teacher to see if she (PB) has noted a change in the girls' behaviour (*it is not all of them*). Could something be done through PHSE+C/SEAL [Personal, Health and Social Education and Citizenship/Social and Emotional Aspects of Learning (DfES, 2006)] input at all? A 'quiet word' perhaps? Could the Head do this?
Implement *Let's do it!*	Spoke to PB during the dinner hour today. *Feel so much better!* She said she had seen some of the girls 'hovering' outside my classroom. She has already spoken to three of the girls about the wolf whistling as a parent had made a comment about this at Parents' Evening. PB said she would "nip it in the bud once and for all" with some role play and some storytelling this afternoon.
Evaluate *How well did I do?*	It's been a week now and the girls have really calmed down – no more wolf whistling! I have taken to going into the staffroom rather than staying in my classroom during lunch time/dinner time – *must remember to take my marking in there with me when it gets quiet!* I'm making sure I do not 'encourage' the girls at all – I saw one girl deliberately fluttering her eyelids at me yesterday and I told her sternly that that was inappropriate and she needed to stop it at once; her friends all looked at her and she went bright red! Didn't like doing it but I think being 'firm but fair' is necessary in the circumstances - something to talk about at my half termly review with Josie next week?
Communicate *Let's tell someone!*	Have spoken to PB – she was glad that the situation had calmed down. She said that there was 'a small gaggle of girls' who were becoming a little silly and they had not realised that their actions were making me uncomfortable. Seems the role play/storytelling has worked - wonder if I could use this to deal with the recent bout of 'stealing' that's been going on in my class?
Learn from experience *What have I learned?*	• Speak to someone – don't keep it to yourself • Try to make sure I do not put myself in situations that encourage the girls to behave inappropriately towards me • Consider the use of role play and storytelling to deal with difficult behaviours with my own class.

The case study is designed to emphasise that reflection is not a panacea and that sometimes reflection will lead practitioners to realise that the problem is not with them. Clearly the use of the TASC wheel processes above allows Peter to 'make sense' of the situation and structure his reflection with clarity. Peter's decision to record his thinking in written form supports Kerka's (1996) claim that writing is a critical aspect of knowledge processing. It is strongly advocated that you make a record of your reflections in some way – through audio, written and/or electronic means – as these can all form evidence to support the attainment of professional targets and contribute to assignments and Personal/Professional Development Portfolios (PDPs). As opposed to simply relying on self-made tables, as per Peter's example above, there are numerous *tools* that can be used to support your reflective endeavours.

Reflective tools

Gray (2006: 8) suggests that '[t]ools, by definition, help us to perform tasks more efficiently, speedily, or both'. It is important to be mindful of the fact that your memory cannot be relied on to recall all of the details relating to critical events you decide to reflect on; as such, there are a number of reflective tools available (both paper and digitally based) which can be used to put 'pen-to-paper/finger-to-keyboard' and record events and experiences; these include lesson/session/activity plans, reflective questionnaires, reflective case studies and concept mapping. The discussion in this section will focus on two key 'tools-of-the-reflective-trade': reflective diaries and reflective portfolios.

Reflective diaries

As readers will be familiar with the concept of a diary, it is deemed sufficient to explain that a reflective diary, 'as the name suggests, [is] concerned with demonstrating reflection on an experience' (Moon, 2003: 2). It is quite common for practitioners and those training to confuse these with learning journals and logs; a simple way to remember the difference is a learning journal is about recording your *learning* from what occurs while logs are simply a record of events that have happened. Reflective diaries can help you to reflect *prospectively* (before-the-event); this may include you thinking about:

● What preparations you need to make for an activity you are leading (*What resources do I need?*).
● How you are going to break down the activity into manageable stages for both you and those who are to engage in it (*What should I do first? What will the young people do in response to this? After that...?*).

Reflective diaries are typically used to help their users engage in *retrospective* reflection (after-the-event); this may include:

● descriptions of what happened;
● what was effective;
● what went wrong and why; and
● what was learned as a result of the experience.

The questions below are taken from a personal bank of reflective prompts (*start positive!*); it is hoped that these will be of some value to you when writing entries in your own reflective diary:

Figure 10.3 Reflective prompts to support reflective diary entries

You may consider purchasing an actual diary to record your reflections in but please be advised to buy a large one (A4 size) that offers a page for each day so that you have plenty of space to record your thoughts. Alternatively, you may wish to use a notebook, keep an electronic word-processed diary or an online blog, or record your thoughts verbally on a Dictaphone.

Activity: *Considering the ethical implications of using reflective diaries*

With reference to Chapter 4 ('*The Researcher and the Researched*': *Ethical research in Children's and Young People's Services*, page 45), consider the ethical implications of keeping reflective diaries with regard to issues of confidentiality, data protection and anonymity.

Compare your thinking to Bampton's (n.d.) *The Ethics of Reflective Diaries, Learning Journals and Similar Educational Tools* – available at http://tinyurl.com/btgws4b – particularly if your reflective diary forms part of an assessed submission if you are currently studying for a qualification or a degree.

Reflective portfolios

Plaza *et al.* (2007) define reflective portfolios as 'a collection of evidence that through critical reflection on its contents demonstrate achievement as well as personal and professional development'. This is not like a Work Placement Folder or a typical Record of Achievement; its very name emphasises the importance of reflective writing that appears *throughout* the entire portfolio rather than it being the final section at the end of the portfolio. Practitioners and those training typically have many questions about reflective portfolios, examples of which are offered below with a response to support your understanding of the practicalities of using these to support/evidence your reflective endeavours.

Question	Response
What can be put in a reflective portfolio? Fredrick, educational welfare officer (EWO)	Anything that might be considered a 'professional artefact' that helps to evidence that you have been reflective of your practice, for example: – activity/lesson/session plans; – appraisals/evaluations of practice and performance; – completed action plans; – reflective comments from parents and carers, mentors, practitioners, peers and service users; – critical incident accounts; – extracts from your reflective diary.
Is there a 'set way' of creating a reflective portfolio? Iris, child minder	No. Hughes and Moore (2007: 15) suggest that '[b]y their nature, these portfolios are very personal documents. They do not conform to templates, and attempts to standardise them would probably be to their detriment'. Your tutor/setting may offer you guidance, however, on possible ways to create/organise a reflective portfolio.
Can I use different media sources to help me build my reflective portfolio? Bob, trainee learning mentor	Yes. Your reflective portfolio may be solely paper-based, an e-portfolio, or a combination of the two. As such, your reflective portfolio may contain: – digital images of displays that you have created; – tape recording/sound files of reflective discussions you have had with colleagues; – scanned work produced by the children or young people you work with (remember to remove their names!); – video footage of you 'practicing' with your service users (remember to seek both verbal and written permission from all parties involved before engaging in any activity involving the taping of service users).
How can I assure 'quality' in the evidence included in my reflective portfolio? Jessica, family support worker	The following 'quality criteria' will help you to evaluate the evidence in your reflective portfolio: – Has the evidence been carefully selected? – Have you made any attempt to link the evidence to pertinent personal targets/professional standards? – Is the evidence professionally presented and annotated? – Does the evidence have personal/professional meaning and value? – Have you actually reflected on the evidence?

Reflective portfolios should not be just established and maintained by those training in the 0-19 sector; practitioners should also actively sustain production of one by way of 'portray[ing] their [continuous] higher cognitive thinking and self-reflective growth' (Whitton *et al.*, 2004: 3). It is anticipated that many practitioners, upon reading the above, may question the amount of time they have available to engage with this on top of their many professional and personal commitments. The final section of this chapter will consider practical ways to positively address select 'barriers' to ensure all those who work/train in CYPS can effectively engage in reflective activity.

Dealing with the barriers to reflection

Finlay (2008: 10) suggests that 'reflective practice is not without its "dark side"'. There are numerous issues which make reflecting on practice challenging for some professionals and trainees. Assertions such as *I'm too busy to reflect!*, *Reflection is boring!* and *Reflection makes me feel like I'm doing a bad job all the time!* are quite common, and this can result in practitioners and those training quickly becoming disengaged with reflective practice – for further barriers see Boud and Walker (1993: 79). While the suggestions below do not claim to be the definitive answer, practical strategies are offered to address four key barriers that may impact on your ability to reflect:

BARRIER 1: *I just don't seem to have time to reflect!* (Mark, youth support worker)

Strategies to try include:
- *Actively make* time – use just 10 minutes of your dinner break to engage in reflective activity; alternatively, do not leave your setting/work placement at the end of the day until you have made some attempt to reflect on your day.
- Develop *speedy* ways to record your reflections – use short hand; speak into a Dictaphone; draw pictures; write down key words and phrases to 'trigger' your memory.
- Reward yourself in some way for the time you **do** dedicate to reflection during your working week/ placement, e.g. watch TV, make a phone call, treat yourself to a chocolate.

BARRIER 2: *I can't seem to reflect on my own!* (Jenny, trainee community worker)

Strategies to try include:
- Use appraisals (for practitioners) and progress reviews (for those training) as an opportunity to reflect with mentors, colleagues and members of the SMT.
- Talk with your peers and family members where appropriate, particularly with those who work in the same service area as you.
- Consider engaging with online web forums for opportunities to reflect with practitioners/students outside of your setting/course.

BARRIER 3: *I don't know how to make my practice better after I have reflected on it!* (Harry, cultural heritage worker)

Strategies to try include:
- Access professional websites, publications and academic literature to identify different ways to develop aspects of your practice.
- Undertake observations of your mentor/colleagues, focusing on ways that they approach aspects of practice you are striving to develop.
- Willingly attend staff/team meetings, INSET training opportunities, conferences and development days that offer practical guidance with regard to key aspects of your CPD/IPD.

BARRIER 4: *I'm scared of how my setting will react to the criticisms of the management in my reflections!* (Sophie, trainee play worker)

Strategies to try include:
- Ensure that you 'balance up' the comments you make with positive observations.
- Always support your critical comments with reference to academic literature and the practices of others from professional and academic publications.
- Offer concrete strategies to address the concerns you have, e.g. draft out a continence policy if you feel the one for your setting is not effective.

Conclusion

This chapter has sought to develop your appreciation of reflection as a lifelong personal/ professional skill that can be used to raise the quality of provision you offer in CYPS. While select reflective definitions, cycles, tools and barriers have been discussed, you should be mindful that there is no *one way* of reflecting. Indeed, it is important to acknowledge that reflection can be a very personal undertaking and, as such, you should test out different cycles and tools, using those that are most appropriate and effective for you, your role and your setting/workplace. To think that reflective practice is unproblematic would be a misconception; to recognise that it takes time, practice and effort to be an effective 'reflector' shows that you have suitably reflected on the content of this chapter!

Areas for further consideration

There are a number of other areas for consideration which you may wish to explore as part of your own personal study. The suggestions below merely offer a select number of aspects which will help to further develop your understanding of reflection and reflective practice in CYPS.

Keeping reflective journals (various types)	Mentoring and coaching and reflection
Online tools for reflection e.g. blogging	Reflection, metaphors and critical thinking
Reflection and reflexiveness	The role of other adults in reflection

Further reading

Books

Moon, J. (2004) *A Handbook of Reflective and Experiential Learning: Theory and practice*. London: Routledge.
This wonderful book acts as an essential guide to understanding and using reflective and experiential learning, whether it is for personal or professional development, or as a tool for learning.

Bolton, G. (2010) *Reflective Practice: Writing and Professional Development*. 3rd edn. London: Sage.
This comprehensive book advocates that the process of reflective writing is developmental, helping to identify gaps in knowledge and adding to the journey of exploration of one's assumptions, ideas and knowledge.

Academic publications

Amulya, J. (n.d.) *What is Reflective Practice?* [Online]. Available at: http://tinyurl.com/awg64zd (Accessed: 30 December 2012).
This paper succinctly discusses reflection as 'a foundation for purposeful learning', critically considering aspects of 'the practice' of reflection, the benefits of collective and individual reflection, and what 'drives' it.

Raelin, J. A. (2002) 'I Don't Have Time to Think!' versus the Art of Reflective Practice. *Reflections*, 4(1), pp. 66-79. [Online]. Available at: http://tinyurl.com/ ac6phbz (Accessed: 30 December 2012).
This detailed 'feature' not only defines reflective practice, establishing a rationale for it and considering the practicality of reflective practice, but also offers an interesting exploration of skills needed to effectively engage in reflective discourse.

Website

Reflective Practice. Available at: http://reflectivepractice-cpd.wikispaces.com/
This wonderful resource includes a varied range of learning activities, notes, videos, downloads and more to help you to focus on key themes and topics relating to reflective practice, and provides content and examples which can be used to help practitioners and those training develop as reflective learners*.

* Please note that the website above is *education* orientated but this does not mean that materials cannot be adapted by other readers from other services.

Answers to Activity: Is it *'-in-' or '-on-'*? (page 160)

1 = On, 2 = On, 3 = In, 4 = In, 5 = In.

References

Alvesson, M. and Skölberg, K. (2000) *Reflexive Methodology: New vistas for qualitative research.* London: Sage.

Atkins, S. and Murphy, K. (1994) Reflective Practice. *Nursing Standard*, 8(39), pp. 49–56.

Bampton, K. (n.d.) *The Ethics of Reflective Diaries, Learning Journals and Similar Educational Tools.* [Online]. Available at: www.derby.ac.uk/files/the_ethics_of_reflective_diaries4.pdf (Accessed: 29 December 2012).

Bloom, B. S. and Krathwohl, D. R. (1956) *Taxonomy of educational objectives: The classification of educational goals, by a committee of college and university examiners.* Handbook 1: Cognitive domain. New York: Longmans.

Boud, D. and Walker, D. (1993) Barriers to Reflection on Experience. In Boud, D., Cohen, R. and Walker, D. (eds) (1993) *Using Experience for Learning.* Buckingham: SRHE and Open University Press.

Boud, D., Keogh, R. and Walker, D. (eds) (1985) *Reflection: Turning experience into learning.* London: Kogan Page.

Cox, E. (2005) Adult learners learning from experience: using a reflective practice model to support work-based learning. *Reflective Practice: International and Multidisciplinary Perspectives*, 6(4), pp. 459–472.

Children's Workforce Development Council (CWDC) (2010) *Common Core of Knowledge and Skills.* [Online]. Available at: www.childrensworkforcematters.org.uk/common-core (Accessed: 30 December 2012).

Department for Education and Skills (2006) *Excellence and Enjoyment: Social and emotional aspects of learning: Key stage 2 small group activities.* Nottingham: DfES Publications.

Dewey, J. (1933) *How We Think.* Buffalo, NY: Prometheus Books.

Eraut, M. (1995) Schön shock: A case for reframing reflection-in-action. *Teachers and Teaching: theory and practice*, 1(1), pp. 9–22.

Finlay, L. (2008) *Reflecting on 'Reflective practice'.* PBPL Paper 52. [Online]. Available at: www.open.ac.uk/cetl-workspace/cetlcontent/documents/4bf2b48887459.pdf (Accessed: 30 December 2012).

Fook, J., White, S. and Gardner, F. (2006) Critical reflection: a review of contemporary literature and understandings. In White, S., Fook, J. and Gardner, F. (eds) *Critical reflection in health and social care.* Maidenhead: Open University Press.

Ghaye, T. and Lillyman, S. (eds) (1997) *Learning Journals and Critical Incidents: Reflective practice for healthcare professionals.* Dinton: Quay Books.

Gibbs, G. (1988) *Learning by Doing: A Guide to Teaching and Learning Methods.* University Further Education Unit. Oxford: Oxford Brookes.

Gray, D. E. (2006) *Facilitating Management Learning – Developing Critical Reflection through Reflective Tools.* [Online]. Available at: http://epubs.surrey.ac.uk/7876/1/fulltext.pdf (Accessed: 29 December 2012).

Greenway, R. (2002) *Experiential Learning Cycles*. [Online]. Available at: http://reviewing.co.uk/research/learning.cycles.htm (Accessed: 29 December 2012).

Health and Care Professions Council (2012) *Standards of proficiency: Social workers in England*. [Online]. Available at: www.hpc-uk.org/assets/documents/10003B08Standardsofproficiency-SocialworkersinEngland.pdf (Accessed: 23 May 2013).

Hughes, J. and Moore, I. (2007) *Reflective Portfolios for Professional Development*. [Online]. Available at: www.aishe.org/readings/2007-2/chap-02.pdf (Accessed: 30 December 2012).

Husu, J., Toom, A. and Patrikainen, S. (2006) *Guided Reflection – Promoting ways to Advance Reflective Thinking in Teaching*. Paper presented at the European Conference on Educational Research, University of Geneva, 13–15 September.

Johns, C. (1994) A philosophical basis for Nursing Practice. In Johns, C. (ed) *The Burford NDU Model: Caring in Practice*. Oxford: Blackwell Scientific Publications.

Kerka, S. (1996) *Journal writing and adult learning*. ERIC Digest No. 174. [Online]. Available at: www.ericdigests.org/1997-2/journal.htm (Accessed: 29 December 2012).

Kolb, D. A. (1984) *Experiential Learning experience as a source of learning and development*. New Jersey: Prentice Hall.

Learning Development (2010) *Reflection*. [Online]. Available at: www.learningdevelopment.plymouth.ac.uk/LDstudyguides%5Cpdf/11Reflection.pdf (Accessed: 28 December 2012).

Learning and Skills Improvement Service (2012) *Youth Work National Occupational Standards*. [Online]. Available at: http://repository.excellencegateway.org.uk/fedora/objects/eg:4931/datastreams/DOC/content (Accessed: 27 December 2012).

Loughran, J. J. (2000) *Effective Reflective practice*. Paper presented at *Making a Difference through Reflective Practices: Values and Actions* conference, University College of Worcester, July.

Moon, J. (2003) *Learning journals and logs, Reflective Diaries*. [Online]. Available at: www.deakin.edu.au/itl/assets/resources/pd/tl-modules/teaching-approach/group-assignments/learning-journals.pdf (Accessed: 29 December 2012).

——(2005) *Guide for busy academics no. 4: learning through reflection*. [Online]. Available at: www.heacademy.ac.uk/assets/York/documents/resources/resourcedatabase/id69_guide_for_busy_academics_no4.doc (Accessed: 30 December 2012).

Murphy, J. (2009) *Fifty Reflective Sentence Starters*. [Online]. Available at: www.todaydocs.com/pdf/sentence+starters/ (Accessed: 30 December 2012).

Nursing and Midwifery Council (2008) *The code: Standards of conduct, performance and ethics for nurses and midwives*. [Online]. Available at: www.nmc-uk.org/Documents/Standards/The-code-A4-20100406.pdf (Accessed: 2 January 2013).

Parker, S. (1997) *Reflective teaching in the postmodern world*. Berkshire: Open University Press.

Piaget, J. (1975) *The development of thought: Equilibration of cognitive structures*. New York: Viking.

Plaza, C. M., Draugalis, J. R., Slack, M. K., Skrepnek, G. H. and Sauer, K. A. (2007) Use of Reflective Portfolios in Health Sciences Education. *American Journal of Pharmaceutical Education*, 71(2), Article 34. [Online]. Available at: www.ncbi.nlm.nih.gov/pmc/articles/PMC1858617/ (Accessed: 30 December 2012).

Rolfe, G., Freshwater, D. and Jasper, M. (2001) *Critical Reflection in Nursing and the Helping Professions: A User's Guide*. Basingstoke: Palgrave Macmillan.

Ruch, G. (2002) From triangle to spiral: Reflective practice in social work education, practice and research. *Social Work Education: The International Journal*, 21(2), pp. 199–216.

Schön, D. (1991) *The Reflective Practitioner*. Aldershot: Ashgate Publishing Ltd.

Shakespeare, P. (2010) *Reflection, Practice learning and documentation*. The Open University. [Online]. Available at: www.open.ac.uk/opencetl/files/opencetl/file/ecms/web-content/Shakespeare-P-(2010)-Reflection-Practice-learning-and-documentation.pdf (Accessed: 27 December 2012).

Spalding, N. J. (1998) Reflection in Professional Development: A Personal Experience. *British Journal of Therapy and Rehabilitation*, 5(7), pp. 379–382.

Taggart, G. L. and Wilson, A. P. (2005) *Promoting Reflective Thinking in Teachers*. 2nd edn. Thousand Oaks, California: Corwin Press.

Tickle, L. (1994) *The Induction of New Teachers*. London: Castell.

Valli, L. (1997) Listening to other voices: A description of teacher reflection in the United States. *Peabody Journal of Education*, 72 (1), pp. 67–88.

Vos, H. and Cowan, J. (2009) *Reflection and teaching: a taxonomy*. [Online]. Available at: http://doc.utwente.nl/67980/1/Refl%2BTeachTaxonomyDocPi.doc (Accessed: 30 December 2012).

Wallace, B. (ed) (2001) *Teaching Thinking Skills Across the Primary Curriculum*. London: NACE/David Fulton.

Whitton, D., Sinclair, C., Barker, K., Nanlohy, P. and Nosworthy, M. (2004) *Learning for Teaching: Teaching for Learning*. Southbank, Victoria: Thomson Learning.

Wilson, J. P. (2008) Reflecting-on-the-future: a chronological consideration of reflective practice. *Reflective Practice: International and Multidisciplinary Perspectives*, 9(2), pp. 177–184.

Section 4

The Community

11 Parents, carers and the community: The collaborative relationship

Debrah Turner

LEARNING OBJECTIVES

After studying this chapter, you will be able to:

✔ Identify research, policy, legislation and initiatives which have informed this area of practice.
✔ Define the role of the parents, carers and the community in a child's or young person's life.
✔ Evaluate types of parental involvement and how these can be developed to create effective parental partnerships.
✔ Identify ways in which working in partnership informs quality practice.

Introduction

Within the Children's and Young People's workforce (CYPS) there is an expectation that practitioners and those training for a career in the sector recognise the importance of working in **partnership** with parents, carers and the wider community. This chapter will explore the concept of working with parents and carers from a practitioner and setting perspective by putting the theory into practice. Consideration will be given to the notion of relationships and how to build and develop these with parents, carers and the community that will allow collaborative working to support the needs of children, young people and families.

This chapter will also facilitate a critical understanding of the role of the parent/carer, models of parenting, and the concept of partnership. The barriers which may undermine the relationship between parent/carer/child and practitioner will also be highlighted as this is seen as being crucial in terms of being able to support and develop relationships that foster mutual trust and understanding, allowing children and young people to be viewed and supported in a holistic way. Families can engage with and be supported by many different agencies; this is a notion which will be discussed through reflective case studies and activities in the chapter.

Reflective task: *Gaining an awareness*

Depending on your work context or area of interest download a copy of either:

- Teachers' Standards (Early Years) – available at: http://tinyurl.com/om6ot5a.
- The Common Core of Skills and Knowledge – available at: http://tinyurl.com/8nq7kv2.
- National Occupational Standards in Youth work – available at: http://tinyurl.com/bqka7sf.

Reflect on the key standards/statements in the document and identify the key standards designed to develop partnerships with parents/carers and the community.

Discuss these standards with a colleague/tutor/mentor and explore the advantages and disadvantages of each relevant standard to your current practice.

This chapter will focus its attention on ways in which you can enhance your skills and understanding while working with parents, carers and the community. It is important for you to recognise that settings should strive to create an atmosphere where parents, carers and members of the local community are welcomed, accepted and valued (Fitzgerald, 2004; Boult, 2006), with an emphasis on knowing one's local community in terms of ethnic, religious and socio-economic mix.

Legislation which has shaped working with parents, carers and the community

Historically there has been a plethora of legislation and guidance produced by both national and local governments aimed at creating a co-ordinated framework of services to address the care and educational needs of children and young people. This section explores a number of government policies and research documents which have contributed to the way that partnership working has developed, and although partnership with parents is strongly encouraged by both the former and current government (DCSF, 2008; DfE, 2012) the initiative only gained momentum during the 1960s. Indeed as Alexander (2010: 73) states, school gates still displayed 'No parents beyond this point' signs up to 20 years after the end of World War Two. This supports the notion that at that time parents, the home, the community and schools were seen as completely separate entities and did not encroach on each other's perceived roles or responsibilities.

Primary Education was influenced by the Plowden Report (1967), which instigated change after identifying a link between educational achievement and parental attitudes to learning. Subsequently, the Warnock Report (1978) emphasised the vital role of parents and the importance of parental involvement. In the early years sector, the Effective Provision of Preschool Education (EPPE) study in 2003 also reinforced that parental partnerships have a positive impact on children's achievements. The Children's Plan (2007) reiterated that the government is not responsible for bringing up children and young people and highlighted the importance of a partnership that supports children and young people in their learning. While it is not essential that you acquire extensive knowledge of the above, it is strongly recommended that you demonstrate an awareness of the current research, national policy and legislation which is influencing the workforce in relation to working collaboratively with parents, carers and the community.

Activity: Engaging with national research, policy and legislation

Select any two of the documents listed below which are pertinent to the service you work/train in, making notes to demonstrate your awareness and engagement with the documentation:

Document	Web Link
The Field Report (2010) - *Independent Review of Poverty and Life Chances.* The report focuses on early intervention as a way to tackle child poverty.	http://tinyurl.com/brxlmvg
The Allen Report (2011) - *Early Intervention: The Next Steps.* This report concludes that early intervention for vulnerable children will break the cycle of dysfunction in families.	http://tinyurl.com/6g8dtg2
The Effective Provision of Pre-school Education (EPPE) Project (2004)	http://tinyurl.com/9c5x2l4
The Impact of Parental Involvement, Parental Support and Family Education on Pupil Achievements and Adjustment (2003)	http://tinyurl.com/9lgyxsa
The Impact of Parental Involvement on Children's Education (2007)	http://tinyurl.com/8mjbjcq

---

Furthermore, the guidance to the Early Years Foundation Stage (EYFS) (DfE, 2012) also recognises the importance of involving parents and carers in their child's learning by acknowledging them as 'children's first and most enduring educators'; also this is supported by Wheeler and Connor (2009: 2.2) who suggest that 'parents and practitioners working together has a positive impact on children's development and learning'. The EYFS also acknowledges that positive relationships for the child should involve the wider community, not just the immediate family circle; similar sentiments are mirrored in the health sector and the youth sector.

The role of the parent

NOTE: *For the purpose of clarity the term 'parent' will be used to encapsulate both the biological adult and the carer in this chapter.*

It is conceivable that practitioners/trainees and parents hold different views as to what constitutes working in partnership. To fully understand the concept of parent partnership there needs to be some clarity regarding what constitutes a partnership. Regardless of the age of the child/young person a partnership results when two parties support each other's roles and co-operate with each other (Driessen, Smitt and Sleegers, 2005; Hodge and Runswick, 2008). There should be a common goal and the relationship should be founded on the mutual respect of views and opinions (Marrow and Malin, 2004; Dunlop and Fabian, 2007; Argent, 2007; O'Connor, 2008).

Promoting and working in partnership is often seen as one of the most important and influential roles in a child/young person's life. It is only through a successful partnership between the practitioner, the parent/carer and the community that the full development potential of the child/young person can be fully realised. This starts in the early years where the EYFS promotes learning and teaching to ensure children are prepared for school life. It provides a broad range of knowledge and skills to support the right foundation for future progress through school and into adult life.

Research from Stern (2003) suggests that parent partnerships can enhance the way in which primary schools promote learning. There are two key findings from Desforges' and Abouchaar's (2003) research into the impact of parental involvement in children's education; firstly, parent involvement in early years (birth to five years) could have a significant impact on cognitive development, and secondly, parents involved in a child's school life from ages 7–16 years is one of the strongest influences on the child's future achievement.

If indeed a partnership is based on the definition of common goals and mutual respect then the rights of the parent must be recognised by practitioners (Everett, 1999). It is argued that parent partnerships tend to be on the setting's terms and are all too often 'tokenistic' (Austin, 2007: 108). This can lead to marginalising the role of the parent and treating them more as a resource to support the practitioner/teacher rather than an equal partner in the decision-making process of the setting (Caroline, 2010).

 Activity: *Exploring the role of the parent*

Consider the different family structures and environmental factors within your local community and what impact these changes have had on children/young people in the community. Think about **nuclear families**, **extended families**, working parents, child care and environmental factors such as poverty, housing, and employment.

Discuss with a colleague/tutor/mentor and explore the potential impact of each factor on the child/young person.

Models of parenting

The structure of families has changed dramatically over the centuries and this has had a significant impact in the work of practitioners. Belsky (1984) researched the factors affecting parental behaviour and how such factors affect child-rearing, which in turn influences child development. At the family level, Belsky's interest is primarily on interpersonal interactions between parent and child. The model presumes that parenting is directly influenced by forces emanating from within the individual parent (*personality*), within the individual child (*child characteristics of individuality*), and from the broader social context in which the parent–child relationship is embedded. Specifically, marital relations, social networks, and jobs influence individual personality and general psychological well-being of parents and thereby parental functioning and, in turn, child development.

Maccoby and Martin (1983) described different parenting styles as detailed below, extending on an original model by Baumrind (1971). Children who were exposed to each individual style were categorised as follows:

- **Authoritarian parents** = children/young people are less happy, more anxious and withdrawn, possibly more hostile and aggressive with peers.
- **Authoritative parents** = children/young people are more confident and independent, socialise more effectively with peers and conform more readily to controls and disciplinary measures, less anxious and achieve better in school.
- **Permissive parents** = children/young people are less able to regulate their own responses and therefore have poorer impulse control. Social relationships/their ability to get on with peers may be affected. The child/young person may be less persistent in tasks and more likely to give up, thus having a negative impact on learning and achievement.
- **Uninvolved parents** = the child/young person is insecurely attached, may do less well in school and be socially isolated.

Case studies: *Thinking about parenting styles*

Select one of the case studies below which is most applicable to your own work/training context:

Case Study 1. A 3-year-old child has bitten another child and the wound has started bleeding. Although the child who was bitten is clearly distressed the child who is responsible for the biting thinks that this is funny. How would you handle this situation?

Case Study 2. A 13-year-old girl has just confided to you that she is pregnant but has asked you to keep this confidential and not tell her parents. How would you respond in this situation?

Case Study 3. A 16-year-old student comes into college and is clearly under the influence of drugs. The student is incoherent, behaving aggressively and not responding to staff members' requests. How would you handle this situation?

- Consider your responsibility, the child/young person's rights, confidentiality and issues, and how parents/carers might respond in each situation.
- What strategies would you use to discuss this issue with parents/carers who display each of the four parenting styles described above?
- What are the implications for you in terms of working in partnership with the parent, in relation to policy making and day-to-day practice?

Family structures and community identities have and continue to evolve. It is more common to find children and young people spending more time in the community away from their families/carers. This could be as a result of extended family members taking additional responsibilities in sharing the care of younger children or young people attending organised clubs/groups in the community which offer out-of-school activities such as sports clubs, dance groups and computer clubs. Research results shown in *The Good Childhood Inquiry* (Layard and Dunn, 2009) highlight the long-term effects of these changes to family structures and community identities:

- Highest rates of 'harming behaviour' – rates of emotional and behavioural difficulties in 15/16-year-olds have risen considerably over the last 30 years.
- Twenty eight per cent of children have no contact with their biological fathers.
- Mental health – one in ten 16-year-olds have mental health difficulties, e.g. ADHD, eating disorders, depression and anxiety.
- Family disruption – 70 per cent of mothers of babies aged 9-12 months do some paid work.
- Unstable living conditions – relative poverty has risen in the last 50 years.

Take a moment to reflect on the points above – *how do they make you feel? Do you agree with them? Do you think that there are any changes that are not mentioned above which may be positive in nature?*

Potential barriers to partnership

There are potential barriers which hinder working with parents, carers and the community; these barriers could include parents'/carers' prior experiences of education, family values, work commitments, and language barriers which may hinder them from participating fully in the work and ethos of the setting. Peters *et al.* (2007) cited that 44 per cent of parents acknowledged their working hours as the main obstacle to becoming more involved in their child's learning. However, a study of children under five years of age, conducted by practitioners at the Penn Green Centre in 2007, concluded that when parents were presented with a variety of ways to become involved in their child's learning, 84 per cent of them were able to engage. The amount of involvement may not be as important as the *quality* of involvement as Peters (2007) found 37 per cent of parents who had minimal involvement in their child's education still felt involved.

Other reasons why parents/carers may not feel comfortable to become involved could include confusion regarding roles within a partnership which can cause barriers to be built up. Indeed, parents/carers are still viewed by a number of practitioners as *helpers* rather than *partners* who are actively contributing to their child's learning and education (Whalley, 1997). Parents have a wealth of knowledge and skills to offer but they are sometimes reluctant to become 'involved' in their son's/daughter's education because of the following:

- time constraints, if working or studying;
- a lack of confidence in their skills;
- fear of admitting they may not know everything;

- fear of being judged;
- cultural, religious reasons or special needs;
- disaffection by the education system as a response to their own experiences as a child.

It is important to break this cycle as parents who feel this way could have a learned behaviour that is passed to their own children (Whalley, 2004). Bear in mind that you will also work with parents who could feel under pressure to be involved in their child's/young person's education when in fact they would be more than happy to let the setting make the decisions (Blasi, 2001).

Activity: *Why is parent partnership important?*

Make a list to illustrate different ways you could help parents/carers to get 'through the door', i.e. into the setting. Compare and contrast your own thoughts to the ideas offered below:

- Parent volunteer rotas;
- Parent/child reading sessions;
- Parents' evenings;
- Workshops;
- Information sessions;
- Guest speakers;
- Parent governors; and
- Committee members.

How many of your ideas do you use in practice? How effective are they?

You may have noticed during your practice or training that some staff members may see parents as a threat on their professional territory; however, when practitioners share information about child development and the curriculum with parents then both parents and children benefit (Athey, 1990). Practitioners need to address their own attitudes towards the partnership role and not just assume that they are the experts on the subject of educating children (Austin, 2007; Souto-Manning and Swick, 2006).

Settings need to explore and implement ways of working where the role of the parent, the community and the practitioner complement each other (Todd and Higgins, 1998). Parents' perceptions of the education system can also be a significant factor in the level of parental involvement in their children's education. Indeed, Johnson (2010) discussed how parental beliefs and expectations impact on the aspirations of the child/young person and indeed what the child/young person sees as worthwhile.

The concept of partnership

Henderson *et al.* (1986, cited in Leuder, 2005: 13) identifies five basic parent involvement roles, which include:

- Parents as partners responsible for their child's education and social development;
- Parents as collaborators and problem solvers, reinforcing the school's/setting's efforts with their child;
- Parents as an audience attending and appreciating the school's/setting's (and their child's) performance and productions;
- Parents as supporters providing voluntary assistance to practitioners/teachers and members of the governing board; and
- Parents as advisers and/or decision makers providing input on policy making.

In your settings you should strive to create an atmosphere where parents are welcomed, accepted and valued. Although researchers have noted the importance of parent partnership (Williams, 2004; Berk, 2004) there are different perspectives as to how settings implement systems to encourage parental partnership. Brooker (2002) and Mayall (2002) noted ways in which parents are effectively socialised into the ethos of a setting and suggest that conformity to that ethos is what has underpinned many models of parental involvement. Nevertheless, Brooker (2002) argues that a setting which allows parents/carers to regularly observe practice and speak to staff does not necessarily lead to genuine collaboration regarding their child's education and development. Brooker's research focused primarily on early years cultures and has provided insights into the way settings perceive their relationship with parents and, conversely, how parents perceive the experience of settings. It was found that practitioners' attitudes to parents were strongly influenced by both the amount of involvement that the parent had in the child's learning and the expression of interest from the parent regarding their child's education and learning. Brooker (2002) suggests that in some settings practitioners welcome the involvement of the parents who do not question policy and procedure and who do not undermine their authority.

Reflective task

Consider your work/training specialism and, using websites and online local authority links, research the community and surroundings where you work to identify any agencies or groups which could offer links to community partnership in each of the following settings:

a) Nursery   b) Primary School   c) Secondary School   d) Tertiary College

Reflect upon the services and support that could be provided in the areas of health services, community police support, and child and youth community groups for sport.

Discuss with colleagues/peers the advantages and disadvantages of each agency you have identified in your own community.

Ways of working in partnership to inform quality practice

It is strongly advocated that parents' views need to be heard and considered in more depth (Siraj-Blatchford *et al.*, 2002; Desforges and Abouchaar, 2003). Parents should receive necessary support to enable them to take on the role of co-educator of the child. As a result of findings in the EPPE project, Sylva *et al.* (2004) concluded that home learning can, by the age of three years, give the child social and intellectual benefits. Raffaele and Knoff (1999: 452) claim that work on home–school collaboration should build on a foundation of core beliefs: 'collaboration should be pro-active rather than reactive' and 'collaboration recognises and values the contributions parents have to make'. If parents are motivated to come into settings purely through guilt at leaving their child or because it is 'their turn', then they will not fully engage with the process. Parents should be allowed to engage in their child's learning in a way which suits their personal circumstances, while acknowledging that 'parents and early childhood educators can form a powerful partnership helping children develop and learn' (Bruce, 1994: 21).

Beveridge (2004) conducted research in primary schools and concluded that teachers' attitudes can often be negative and stereotypical regarding parental motivation and their competences and skills within the educational domain, and that parents are aware of these attitudes and can react adversely to them as a result. It is suggested that if parents 'feel respected in their own right as parents' and 'perceive that their child is a valued member of the school' (p. 63) then relationships will be enhanced and more productive for both the parent and the child. As highlighted by DfES (2006), settings need to consider a range of opportunities which they can provide to enable parents to become fully involved in their child's education. Examples can include parents supporting literacy by listening to children read, supporting children with extra-curricular activities, helping to run creative workshops or story-telling sessions. Parents can be unsure of what is expected of them in terms of sharing information, which is why the process can indeed be difficult due to a lack of understanding about each other's roles (both parent and practitioner).

Practitioners should share information with parents but also they must give parents an opportunity to share information in return so that mutual trust can develop. It is not merely the issue of working with parents, as Whalley (2004) claims, but it is also that parents are genuinely unsure what is expected of them in their co-educator role within a setting, alongside practitioners. An important point to highlight is research conducted by Bastiani (1997) who concluded that while parents expressed a need for information about the child's progress and attainment, they also wanted reassurance that staff understood their child's social and personal needs. By sharing information between both parties this reassurance can be met as parents can cascade important information to others.

Case study

The local community centre has invited parents to attend an information session/workshop to receive advice on internet safety. There are 20 parents in attendance whose children range between the ages of seven and fifteen years. The trainer allocated a time slot of one hour to complete the workshop, after which time the room is booked by another group.

A presentation was given by the trainer, followed by a practical demonstration by the trainer; there was a five-minute question and answer session and then the workshop ended.

When parents were asked for feedback from the workshop they were quite negative. The parents felt this was a good idea as it is an area where they needed support in order to try and keep their children safe online but they did not feel as if their concerns had been listened to or their questions answered. They also still felt unsure how to practically protect their children.

Consider the response from the parents – how could you address their concerns if you were to organise a workshop on the topic of internet safety in your own setting?

Developing collaborative working between the setting and the community

Why is it important to recognise community in partnership working?

Bronfenbrenner's Ecological Environment Model (1979) explored the link between all environmental factors that a child is exposed to. The child is at the centre of the Ecological Environment Model and there is a ripple effect of environmental and community factors which influence the child:

- **First circle** = Microsystem: this explores the influence of the child's direct contacts; mainly family, early years setting, school.
- **Second circle** = Mesosystem: this explores the relationship between the elements within the microsystem, e.g. relationship between home and school.
- **Third circle** = Exosystem: this explores indirect influential factors, e.g. parents' work, social contacts, income, local environment.
- **Fourth circle** = Macrosystem: the wider culture in which family exists, e.g. political context, community.

This model emphasises that there are a number of significant factors which impact on a child's development from birth onwards and sees community experiences as a significant part of the child's enrichment and development.

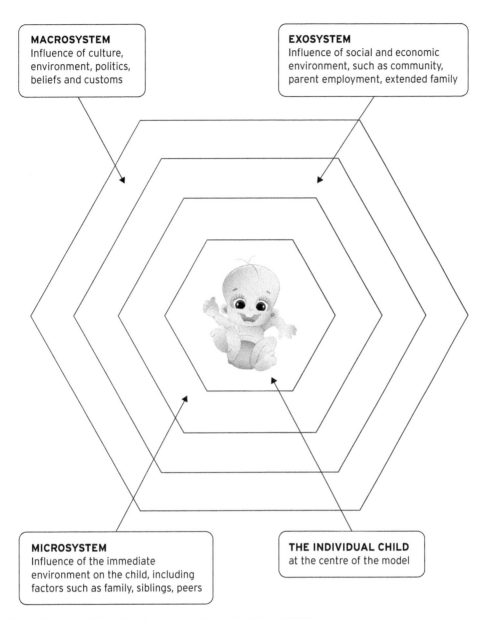

MACROSYSTEM
Influence of culture,
environment, politics,
beliefs and customs

EXOSYSTEM
Influence of social and economic
environment, such as community,
parent employment, extended family

MICROSYSTEM
Influence of the immediate
environment on the child, including
factors such as family, siblings, peers

THE INDIVIDUAL CHILD
at the centre of the model

Figure 11.1 Adapted from Bronfenbrenner's Ecological Model (1979)

Activity

Discuss with colleagues/peers how you feel that the community can become involved in partnership with your setting. Ideas you may wish to consider may include:

- Local initiatives;
- Youth clubs;
- Volunteers to run sessions, e.g. gardening, music, art, drama, sport, computers;
- Community policing; and
- Organise advice sessions on drugs, alcohol, contraception, teenage pregnancy.

Create a directory of local contacts within the community who could support you with these initiatives.

According to Harkin, Turner and Dawn (2001) there are a number of issues which can affect children and young people in today's society; these include:

- Acquired Immune Deficiency Syndrome (AIDS) and Human Immuno-deficiency Virus (HIV);
- Early exposure to adult issues through the media, e.g. pornography, chat rooms;
- Lack of clear moral framework;
- Sexual abuse;
- Dysfunctional family life;
- Lack of parental authority;
- Inner city problems, e.g. poor housing conditions, overcrowding, unemployment, homelessness;
- Drugs.

Within the community there are organisations which parents and young people can access; these include:

Table 11.1 Community support and the potential help they offer

Community support	Potential help
Careers Advisers http://tinyurl.com/6mo7wm9	Further Education advice Careers advice
Mental Health Service http://tinyurl.com/7habwtx	This agency offers advice about mental health issues which can be anything from depression, suicidal tendencies, self-harming, or counselling for abuse
Counselling http://tinyurl.com/9eg5bs2	Offers personal advice to young students

Other support agencies which may be located in your local community could include:

- Citizen's Advice Bureau;
- NHS services (sexual issues, drugs, alcohol, medical conditions);
- Social Services;

- Teenage Pregnancy Advisory Unit; and
- Educational psychologists, speech and language therapists, behaviour specialists (through local authority referrals).

These services tend to be dependent on government or local authority funding and in the current climate of cutbacks and service mergers these services may be very different, in terms of availability, within your local community.

Conclusion

Engaging parents and the community in the child's learning, from the outset, will help each stage of their child's development, which should ultimately help raise the achievement levels of their children (Desforges and Abouchaar, 2003). Research has consistently indicated that parental involvement is integral to children's development; the Plowden Report (1967) recognised the contribution that parents can make provided there is a close partnership between the setting and parents.

Mills (1996) recorded that while settings have established strong school/home links there has been less success with families with English as an Additional Language. As she suggests, 'schools have found that cultural and linguistic differences have created barriers to collaboration' (Mills, 1996: 84). Practitioners need to ensure that they are creating opportunities for *all* parents to be involved, irrespective of race, creed, gender or ability. This can be facilitated by displaying dual language signs, interpreters, positive discrimination, signers and ease of access.

In relation to the community, Croll (2002) confirms the clear links between parental socio-economic status and social, emotional and behavioural difficulties. Parents experience high levels of stress, perhaps in 'run-down', poorer neighbourhoods; this can adversely affect not only the interactions with their child but also their involvement in the community and with education services (Beveridge, 2004).

Areas for further consideration

There are a number of other areas of consideration which you may wish to explore as part of your own personal study. The suggestions below merely offer a number of aspects which may support your understanding of working with parents, carers and the community.

Dealing with issues of confidentiality	Working with parents from culturally diverse backgrounds
Developing communication skills	Preparing parents for parenting
The learning partnership	Understanding conflict resolution

Further reading

Books

Porter, L. (2008) *Teacher-Parent Collaboration – Early Years to Adolescence.* Victoria: Acer Press.

Whalley, M. (2008) *Involving Parents in their Child's Learning.* London: Paul Chapman Publishing.
The above texts explore in further detail the relationships between parents, practitioners, children and the community. The books identify a variety of ways to engage parents in their child's education and the benefits of parental involvement on educational achievement.

Academic publications

Argent, K. (2007) Every Child Matters: Change for parents/carers and families? *Education*, 35 (3), 295–303.

Bruce, T. (1994) Seeing Play for what it is; Parents and Professional Workers Together. *International Journal of Early Years Education*, 12 (1), 17–22.

Legace-Seguin, D. and D'entremont, M. (2006) The Role of Child Negative Effect in the Relations between Parenting Styles and Play. *Early Child Development and Care*, 176 (5), 461–477.
The above papers research the importance of early education and each highlights the important role of parents in supporting their child's educational achievement.

Websites

Carry, B. (2011) *Working Together: Parents and Early Years Practitioners.* Available at: http://parenting-portal.com/blog/parenting-working-together-parents-early-years-practitioners/

Fatherhood Institute (2010) *Fatherhood Institute Research Summary: Fathers and their Children's Education.* Available at: www.fatherhoodinstitute.org/ index.php?id=12&cID=583.
The above websites look at issues that might affect partnership working and how these barriers might be overcome. The final website identifies the importance of engaging fathers in their child's learning journey.

References

Alexander, R. (2010) *Children, their world, their education.* Oxon: Routledge.

Argent, K. (2007) Every Child Matters: Change for parents/carers and families? *Education*, 35 (3), 295–303.

Athey, C. (1990) *Extending Thought in Young Children.* London: Paul Chapman Publishing.

Austin, R. (2007) *Letting the Outside in, Developing teaching and learning. Beyond the Early Years Classroom.* Stoke on Trent: Trentham Books Ltd.

Bastiani, J. (1997) *Working with Parents: a whole school approach.* Windsor: NFER-Nelson.

Baumrind, D. (1971) Current Patterns of Parental Authority. *Developmental Psychology Monographs*, 4, 1–103.

Belsky, J. (1984) The determinants of parenting: A process model. *Child Development*, 55 (1), 83–96.

Berk, L. (2004) *Awakening Children's Minds: How parents and teachers can make a difference.* Oxford: Oxford University Press.

Beveridge, S. (2004) *Developing Partnerships for Inclusive Education.* London: Routledge-Falmer.

Blasi, M. J. (2001) Rethinking Family-School Relations: A critique of parental involvement in schooling, *Childhood Education*, 78 (1), 537–542.

Boult, B. (2006) *176 Ways to Involve Parents.* 2nd edn. London: Sage.

Bronfenbrenner, U. (1979) *Ecology of Human Development.* Cambridge, MA: Harvard University Press.

Brooker, L. (2002) *Starting School-Young Children Learning Cultures.* Buckingham: Open University Press.

Bruce, T. (1994) Seeing Play for what it is; Parents and Professional Workers Together. *International Journal of Early Years Education*, 12 (1), 17–22.

——(2003) *Developing Learning in Early Childhood.* London: Sage.

Caroline, S. (2010) *Encyclopaedia of Cross Cultural School Psychology.* [Online]. Available at: http://books.google.com/books?ID=F9F7NOZGJMOC&pg=researchandvalidity (Accessed: 10 October 2012).

Carry, B. (2011) *Working Together: Parents and Early Years Practitioners.* [Online]. Available at: http://parenting-portal.com/blog/parenting-working-together-parents-early-years-practitioners/ (Accessed: 13 September 2012).

Croll, P. (2002) Social deprivation, school level achievement and special educational needs. *British Journal of Special Education*, 44 (1), 43–53.

Department for Children, Schools and Families (2003) *Every Child Matters Working with Parents, Carers and Families.* [Online]. Available at: www.dcsf.gov.uk/everychildmatters/strategy/parent/workingwithparentscarersandfamilies (Accessed: 16 February 2012).

——(2007) *The Children's Plan, Building Brighter Futures.* Norwich: Crown Publications.

——(2008) *Early Learning Partnership Project (ELPP).* [Online]. Available at: www.familyandparenting.org/Filestore/Documents/ publications/ELPP_summary-8web_FINAL.pdf (Accessed: 1 April 2012).

——(2008) *Parents as Partners in Early Learning Project (PPEL).* [Online]. Available at: http://nationalstrategies.standards.dcsf.gov.uk/node/ 84956 (Accessed: 3 April 2012).

Department for Education (2012) *Practice Guidance for the Early Years Foundation Stage.* London: Crown.

Department for Education and Skills (2006) *Parents, Early Years and Learning.* Nottingham: DfE Publications.

Desforges, C. and Abouchaar, A. (2003) The Impact Of Parental Involvement, Parental Support and Family Education on Pupil Achievements and Adjustment: A Literature Review, *Research Report 433.* London: DfES Publications.

Dreissen, G., Smitt, F. and Sleegers, P. (2005) Parental Involvement and Educational Achievement. *British Education Research Journal*, 31 (4), 509–532. [Online]. Available at: http://ejournals.ebsco.com/direct.asp?ArticleID=4e7f8a8f75d931af443f (Accessed: 16 October 2012).

Dunlop, A. W. and Fabian, H. (2007) *Informing Transitions in the Early Years: Research, Policy and Practice.* Maidenhead: Open University Press.

Everett, G. H. (1999) The Business of Learning: Parents as Full, Un-willing or Sleeping Partners. *International Studies of Sociology of Education*, 9 (3), 267–278. [Online]. Available at: http://ejournals.ebsco.com/direct.asp?Article ID=4B778BCOC1F4E21B615E (Accessed: 1 May 2012).

Fitzgerald, D. (2004) *Parent Partnership in the Early Years.* London: Continuum.

Harkin, J., Turner, G. and Dawn, T. (2001) *Teaching Young Adults: A handbook for teachers in post-compulsory education.* London: Routledge.

Hodge, N. and Runswick-Cole, K. (2008) Problematising Parent-Professional Partnerships in Education. *Disability and Society*, 23 (6), 637–647. [Online]. Available at: http://ejournals.ebsco.com/direct.asp?ArticleID=4746a5ec41cb8d58bf79 (Accessed: 6 August 2012).

Johnson, J. (2010) *Positive Trusting Relationships with Children in Early Years Settings.* Exeter: Learning Matters.

Layard, R. and Dunn, J. (2009) *A Good Childhood.* London: Penguin.

Leuder, D. (2005) *Creating Relationships with Parents.* Oxford: Rowman and Littlefield.

Maccoby, E. E. and Martin, J. A. (1983) Socialization in the context of the family: Parent–child interaction. In: P. H. Mussen and E. M. Hetherington (eds) *Handbook of child psychology: Vol. 4. Socialization, personality, and social development.* 4th edn. New York: Wiley.

Marrow, G. and Malin, N. (2004) Parents and Professionals Working Together: Turning Rhetoric into Reality. *Early Years*, 35 (3), 295–303. [Online]. Available at: http://ejournals.ebsco.com/direct.asp?Article (Accessed: 4 April 2012).

Mayall, B. (2002) *Towards a Sociology for Childhood*. Buckingham: Open University Press.

Melhuish, E., Sylva, K., Sammons, P., Siraj-Blatchford, I. and Taggart, B. (2001) *The Effective Provision of Pre-school Education (EPPE) Project*. London: DfEE.

Mills, J. (1996) *Partnership in Primary School*. London: Routledge.

O'Connor, U. (2008) Meeting in the Middle: A Study of Parent-Professional Partnerships, *European Journal of Special Needs*, 22 (3), 253–268. [Online]. Available at: http://ejournals.ebsco.com/direct.as p?ArticleID=4F3D974D88430E70D7A67 (Accessed: 2 October 2012).

Peters, M., Seeds, K., Goldstein, A. and Coleman, N. (2007) *Parental Involvement in Children's Education*. DCSF Research Report RR034. London: Department for Children, Schools and Families.

Plowden Report, The (1967) [Online]. Available at: www.educationengland.org.uk/documents/Plowden (Accessed: 3 April 2012).

Raffaele, L. M. and Knoff, H. M. (1999) Improving Home-School Collaboration with Disadvantaged Families: Organisational Principles, perspectives and approaches. *School Psychology Review*, 28, (3), 448–466.

Rex, J. (1974) *Sociology and the Demystification of the Modern World*. London: Routledge.

Siraj-Blatchford, I., Sylva, K., Muttock, S., Guildon, R. and Bell, D. (2002) *Researching Effective Pedagogy in the Early Years*. (REPEY). Research Report RR356. Department for Education Studies. Oxford: DfES Publications.

Souto-Manning, M. and Swick, K. J. (2006) Teachers' Beliefs about Parent and Family Involvement: Rethinking our family involvement paradigm. *Early Childhood Education Journal*, 34 (2), 187–193. [Online]. Available at: http://ejournals.ebsco.com/direct.asp?Article ID=4FD699C24A1DA75807AA (Accessed: 6 April 2012).

Stern, J. (2003) *Involving Parents*. London: Continuum.

Sylva, K., Melhuish, E., Sammons, P., Siraj-Blatchford, I. and Taggart, B. (2004) *The Effective Provision of Pre-school Education (EPPE) Project*. London: DfES Publications.

Todd, E. and Higgins, S. (1998) Powerlessness in Professional and Parent Partnerships. *British Journal of Sociology of Education*, 19 (2), 227–236. [Online]. Available at: http://ejournals.ebsco.com/direct.asp?A rticleID=439FBB7AC5A4B0B58F1F (Accessed: 11 October 2012).

Warnock Report, The (1978) [Online]. Available at: www.educationengland.org.uk/documents/Warnock (Accessed: 20 June 2012).

Whalley, M. (1997) *Involving Parents in their Children's Learning*. London: Paul Chapman Publishing.

——(2004) *Working with Parents*. London: Hodder and Stoughton.

Wheeler, H. and Connor, J. (2009) *Parents, early years and learning: Parents as Partners in the Early Years Foundation Stage – Principles into Practice*. London: National Children's Bureau.

Williams, F. (2004) Commentary on Every Child Matters, DfES Green Paper. *Critical Society Policy*, 24 (3), 406–427.

12 Integrated working: From the theory to the practice

Deborah Hussain and Simon Brownhill

LEARNING OBJECTIVES

After studying this chapter, you will be able to:

✔ Define the terms *integrated working, multi-agency panel, multi-agency team* and *team around the child.*

✔ Recognise the historical context of integrated working and the prominent themes that emerge from serious case reviews.

✔ Identify the role of the lead professional and agencies working together to meet the needs of a child or young person through the Common Assessment Framework (CAF) process.

✔ Recognise practical ways in which barriers to integrated working can be overcome.

Introduction

Integrated working continues to be high on the agenda of successive UK governments who acknowledge that well planned, organised strategic service delivery positively affects the lives of children, young people and families (DfE, 2013b). This chapter explores how **integrated services** have developed working practices in the 0-19 sector by considering the impact of this on service users and professionals. The notion of integrated working, while possibly being an unfamiliar idea to those training to work in CYPS, is not a new concept (World Health Organisation [WHO], 2008); however, it seems that reviewing how agencies work together usually occurs following serious case reviews which are the result of *ineffective* integrated working. Those serious case reviews undertaken by Lord Laming into the deaths of Victoria Climbié (Laming, 2003) and 'Baby P' (Laming, 2009) not only highlight the real need for agencies and services to work together but also the challenges that are faced at a local and national level to ensure practitioners and those training effectively meet the diverse needs of children and young people. This chapter will explore legislation that has informed policies and working practices within the 0-19 sector including the Children Act

(2004) and *Every Child Matters* agenda (DfES, 2004); the chapter will also explore tools that support quality integrated working practices in the sector including the Common Assessment Framework (CAF) (see CWDC, 2009a) and the role of the lead professional.

Activity: *A review of current practice relating to integrated working*

Use the grid below to review different areas of practice in your work setting/placement. If other professionals are involved in supporting provision in your work setting/placement please identify these individuals/services and evaluate the quality of the integrated working currently taking place. If you do not have additional support in your work setting/placement, consider the areas of practice below, acknowledging those who may be able to support the practice that you currently offer/support.

Area of practice	Who is/who could be involved?	Positives	Challenges	Areas for development
Attendance				
Health issues				
Behaviour management				
Fitness and sport				
Support for children/young people with SEND				
Staff training and development				
Family support/ family learning				
Community engagement				
Extended provision, e.g. breakfast club/ afterschool club				

This chapter will initially consider some of the key definitions and terminology that are associated with integrated working.

Integrated working: understanding terminology and definitions

When developing an understanding of integrated working confusion can arise when you come across new terminology and definitions which serve to explain how agencies in the 0–19 sector work together. The key terms and definitions offered in this detailed first section are considered to be the most important ones for readers to be aware of and to understand, irrespective of their role or service that they provide. As you engage with these terms consider discussing your personal understanding of these different terms with colleagues/ peers *before* reading the definitions offered – how does your knowledge compare?

Universal services

Universal services are the services that children, young people and families access without special referral. Examples of universal services include GPs, dentists, opticians, nurseries, schools, colleges and hospitals. Every child and young person living in the UK has a right to access these services.

Targeted services

Targeted services provide support aimed at particular groups of children and young people; these are often accessed from within universal services. Targeted services include Sure Start children's centres that offer services which are available to all as well as services provided directly to individual children, young people and their families such as parenting support and those services provided by social services.

Specialist services

Specialist services are those that are required when universal services cannot meet the needs of the child, the young person or the family. Specialist services include family support workers, speech and language therapists, behaviour support workers, physiotherapists, youth offending workers, dieticians, and child and adolescent mental health workers.

Activity: *Which service?*

For each of the case studies below consider which service – *universal, targeted* or *specialist* – would be appropriate to meet the needs of those described below. Talk with your colleagues/peers about which *specific* professional(s)/service(s) would be the most suitable, e.g. *a key person in a nursery setting.*

Case Study A: Will and his partner Ben have begun caring for a baby girl who was born with congenital heart defects and vertebral abnormalities. The baby's mother, Will's step sister, is suffering from severe depression and has begun to drink heavily. Will and Ben are unsure as to which service is able to support them.

Case Study B: Denise and Joggy have recently become the proud parents of a beautiful healthy baby girl. They have begun to consider which services they should approach to support the educational needs of their daughter when Denise returns to work full time.

Case Study C: Chloe is struggling to breastfeed her baby boy effectively. Her friends have suggested that she seek help but Chloe is unsure as to which service she should approach.

Answers can be found at the end of the chapter (page 207).

Core agencies

Professionals working in CYPS belong to a specific **core agency**. The core agencies cover all services that are available to children and young people (0-19); these services are available beyond the age of 19 for those young people who are looked after or have one or more special educational need or disability. The core agencies are health, education and social services. Partnership Boards were established in response to the Children Act (2004), which provides the legal guidance for the development of children's services. These Boards work to improve the way that services in CYPS are planned, commissioned, delivered and evaluated.

Integrated working

> Integrated working is where everyone supporting children and young people works together effectively to put the child at the centre, meet their needs and improve their lives. (Children's Workforce Development Council, 2008: 2)

The crucial part of this definition is that the agencies work together *effectively*. To work in this way would indicate that agencies would work together as a team (see Anning *et al.*, 2006) in a formal, planned way. This highlights the need for strategic planning to take place within the services offered by local authorities to ensure effective service delivery. Integrated working cannot happen if core agencies within the local authority do not establish service level agreements and protocols that allow for effective sharing of information (see Davis, 2011 for further information).

Multi-agency panel

The NSPCC (2011) defines a **multi-agency panel** as:

> a group of people from different agencies that meet regularly for short periods of time to discuss children and young people with additional needs who may require multi-agency support. Panels are often used to allocate resources to new cases and to review progress across existing cases. Members remain employed by their home agency.

An example of a multi-agency panel would be the youth inclusion and support panel (YISP). The youth inclusion and support panel would meet to discuss cases where children and young people (8-13+ year olds) have needs (e.g. are considered to be at high risk of offending and exhibiting anti-social behaviour) that are not being met by universal services. The casework arising from the multi-agency panel may be undertaken by panel members or may be undertaken by key workers (see http://tinyurl.com/c3ve22v for some interesting case studies and downloadable material).

Multi-agency team (MAT)

> A multi-agency team is a more formal arrangement when practitioners are seconded or recruited into a team, share a team identity and tend to be managed by one team leader.

Multi-agency team members may maintain links with their home agencies through supervision and training. (NSPCC, 2011)

Alternative references to MAT include multi-agency support teams (MAST) and multi-agency support hubs (MASH). An example of a multi-agency team model includes Behaviour Education Support Teams (BEST). BEST were established to pilot the *Every Child Matters* agenda (DfES, 2004) where practitioners from key core agencies were seconded to form multi-agency teams that worked in partnership with children, young people, families and universal services to remove barriers to a child or young person's learning and development. Alternative references to BESTs include Behaviour Support Service (BSS), Behaviour Support Team (BST), and Behaviour Improvement Team (BIT). BEST members included police officers, youth offending workers, speech and language therapists, school nurses, child and adolescent mental health workers, family support workers and senior learning mentors. Team members kept strong links with their core agencies, sharing learning and understanding from the range of professionals within the teams.

Activity: *Engaging with research reports*

Consider downloading the research report by Halsey *et al.* (2005) from the DfE website (available at: http://tinyurl.com/c36qktv) for an evaluation of the impact of Behaviour and Education Support Teams on children's and young people's lives.

While these teams continue to exist in many local authorities (Derbyshire, Hampshire, and Wigan) many BEST teams in other areas are either being superseded by Targeted Youth Support Teams (TYSTs) or are being disbanded due to government cuts.

Team around the child (TAC)

The Children's Workforce Development Council (2009b: 10) defines the **team around the child** (TAC) as:

> a model of multi-agency service provision. The TAC brings together a range of different practitioners from across the children and young people's workforce to support an individual child or young person and their family. The members of the TAC develop and deliver a package of solution-focused support to meet the needs identified through the common assessment.

The TAC model of working does not rely on professionals being co-located and working together all the time; it is a flexible arrangement that allows appropriate professionals to work together to meet the needs of the child or young person. Each professional in the TAC is accountable to their own line manager but will have accountability for developing and delivering the plan of support for the child or young person. An interesting example of a TAC model, proposed by Shropshire Council, can be found on page 2 of the document *Integrated services and the Team Around the Child* (available at: http://tinyurl.com/crxbrsm). Also see Siraj-Blatchford *et al.* (2007); CWDC (2009b) and DfE (2012a) for further information about TAC.

Activity: *Developing a local perspective on integrated working*

Thus far a selection of the most important terms and definitions associated with integrated working has been offered to you. For effective practice to take place it is important that you have knowledge of how integrated working is established and operates at a local level within your local authority. By developing a good local perspective you will be able to understand how agencies and services are best placed to support the children and young people you work with. Ask yourself the following:

- What do I need to know?
- Who is responsible for leading integrated working in the local authority?
- How do I contact these people?
- What links does the setting/placement have with these agencies?
- Who is the lead within the setting for co-ordinating integrated working?

While it is important for practitioners and those training to have a sound knowledge and understanding of the key terms associated with integrated working, we believe it to be very important that you understand *why* this way of working is so passionately advocated in the 0–19 sector.

Integrated working: a historical context

In the introduction to this chapter we stated that working together in CYPS is not a new concept; however, the effectiveness (or *in*effectiveness) of integrated working is often highlighted when serious case reviews relating to child protection issues are undertaken. One of the first serious case reviews was the inquiry into the death of Maria Colwell (DHSS, 1974). The inquiry identified three main factors that contributed to Maria's death:

1   the lack of communication between the agencies who were aware of her vulnerable situation;
2   inadequate training for social workers assigned to at-risk children; and
3   changes in the make-up of society.

From this inquiry Area Child Protection Committees (ACPCs) were set up to co-ordinate child protection cases at a local level. Child Protection registers were established to ensure that all children at risk were identified and their details were kept locally in the register. These changes were made to ensure that children would be protected and agencies would be able to work together, sharing information more easily (see page 204–205 for further information relating to this).

The next major changes to policy and practice came from the recommendations in the Jasmine Beckford inquiry (see Hawkes, n.d.) which saw the development of the Children Act 1989 (see http://tinyurl.com/bngoq7b). The main aims of the Act, in relation to integrated working, were to achieve a better balance between protecting children and enabling parents to challenge state intervention, while encouraging greater partnership between statutory authorities and parents. The notion of parental responsibility was introduced with the welfare of the child being of paramount importance. The Children Act 1989 strengthened the rights of children and families and made it clear that social services were supported by health and education services. One may question why the welfare of children was not of paramount importance *before* the Act was introduced; however, as with all inquiries, where weaknesses to existing practice are found action is identified that helps to reduce the risk of similar situations arising again. Indeed, when we reflect on the two inquiries outlined above we can see that each inquiry reviewed existing practice and developed new legislation from the 'lessons learned' to ensure that similar failings would not happen again. The Laming inquiry into the death of Victoria Climbié (Laming, 2003) unfortunately compounded both public and media opinion that lessons were *not* being learned by front-line professionals working with children, young people and families. The review highlighted a lack of good practice; the Assistant Commissioner of the Metropolitan Police William Griffiths acknowledged that despite the Children Act 1989 being in place for almost a decade the same rigour was not given to investigations against children as there was to similar crimes against adults.

> Victoria was known to no less than two further housing departments, four social services departments, two child protection teams of the Metropolitan Police Service, a specialist centre managed by the NSPCC, and she was admitted to two different hospitals because of suspected deliberate harm. (Laming, 2003: 3)

Many people have asked the question: 'So what went wrong?' (see Parton, 2004). We have considered this ourselves, and with reference to inquiry reports we have collated together some conclusions:

- there was repetition of the practice breakdown evident throughout the 1970s and 1980s;
- there was a lack of co-ordination, co-operation and disconnected communication between services;
- there was a breakdown in working relations between practitioners;
- there was a failure to intervene early enough;
- safeguarding was not considered to be a collective responsibility;
- there was poor co-ordination of services;
- there was a failure to share information;
- there was an absence of an accountable figure; and
- **front-line workers** were dealing with staff vacancies, poor management and lack of effective training.

The Laming Report (2003) was pivotal in highlighting the need to restructure the way agencies work together, highlighting 108 recommendations which included:

1   The establishment of a ministerial Children and Families board chaired by a cabinet minister.
2   The establishment of a National Agency for Children and Families.
3   The appointment of a Children's Commissioner for England.
4   The Green Paper *Every Child Matters* (2004).
5   The Children Act (2004) (see http://tinyurl.com/2errq2b).

The recommendations and restructure of children's services were undertaken to prevent children at risk moving between services with limited joined up working. See Lord *et al.* (2008) for an evaluation of the early impact of integrated children's services. Unfortunately in 2009 Lord Laming was asked to undertake a review of the progress made with regard to the protection of children in England as a result of yet another serious case review. Peter Connelly (known as 'Baby P') was 17 months old when he died suffering more than 50 injuries despite being on the at-risk register and receiving 60 visits from social workers, police and health professionals in the eight-month period before his death in 2007. In light of the review and recommendations from the Laming Review (2003) similarities can be drawn between Victoria Climbié and Peter Connelly and earlier serious case reviews. These, rather surprisingly, mirror those offered in the list on page 199.

Activity: *Reading*

Consider reading the executive summary of the *Serious Case Review: Baby Peter* by Haringey LSBC (2009) which is available at http://tinyurl.com/pfklbs. While we recognise that this might be considered by some practitioners/trainees to be a slightly unsettling read we merely wish to raise awareness as to what *can* happen when professionals and services do not work together in an integrated and effective manner.

Lord Laming was asked to undertake a progress report into the protection of children in England in 2009, in which he made further recommendations with regard to practice (see http://tinyurl.com/cbr7m5b). Notably the legal framework and restructuring of services were seen to need no further restructure; however, development still needed to take place in areas of effective leadership and staff training, the development of front-line workers and the development of effective practice in working across organisational boundaries and cultures (pp. 83–92). The current coalition government (DfE, 2013b) still recognise the need for the children's workforce to work collaboratively and acknowledge the challenges faced in developing and promoting effective ways of working; see *Working Together to Safeguard Children* – available at http://tinyurl.com/d979vyp – for further information.

Activity: *Reading and reflection*

Select *one* of the two readings below:

- Munro, E. (2012) *The Munro Review of Child Protection. Progress report: Moving towards a child centred system.* [Online]. Available at: http://tinyurl.com/cc6ykcw (Accessed: 12 May 2013).
- Stuart, K. (2012) Leading multi-professional teams in the children's workforce: an action research project. *International Journal of Integrated Care*, 12 (Jan–March). [Online]. Available at: http://tinyurl.com/cl8q84g (Accessed: 12 May 2013).

Make personal notes as you actively engage with this reading to demonstrate your continued/developing understanding of either the progress being made to 'create a work environment that will better support professionals in giving children and young people the help they need' (Munro, 2012: 3) or the importance of trust as being 'central to [the] effective leadership of multi-professional teams' (Stuart, 2012).

Integrated working and *Every Child Matters* (Helping Children Achieve More)

The *Every Child Matters* (ECM) initiative (DfES, 2004) was developed as a response to the Laming Inquiry (2003) aimed at promoting workforce reform while improving outcomes for children, young people and families. Following the death of Victoria Climbié, government legislation was developed to ensure that similar failings within the children's workforce would be reduced through the development of integrated working practices (Davis and Smith, 2012). This legislation was developed by listening to the voices of children and young people; it was found that they wanted to *be healthy, stay safe, enjoy and achieve, make a positive contribution* and *achieve economic well-being* (see Argent, 2007). These five outcomes were developed as part of the Children Act (2004), which provides the legislative framework for the *Every Child Matters* initiative. The changes that have been discussed in this chapter outline a radical change in the whole children's services structure. The focus of these changes was on prevention and early intervention with services working more closely and effectively together. Laming's recommendations outlined that child protection should not be seen separate from policies to improve children's lives as a whole. The link was made to focus on universal services as well as specialist services for children with additional needs. *Every Child Matters* aims to ensure that every child has the chance to fulfil their potential (Field, 2010). The Every Child Matters Outcomes Framework (DCSF, 2008b) explicitly links the Children's Plan 2020 (DCSF, 2008a), the Every Child Matters outcomes and the aims of National Public Service Agreements (PSAs) and Departmental Strategic Objectives (DSOs). It is important for practitioners and those training to appreciate how the ECM outcomes relate to integrated practice. In this section we will consider two of these in detail - *being healthy* and *staying safe*.

Integrated working and *being healthy*

This broad outcome includes aims which serve to promote a child or young person's physical, mental, emotional and sexual health including promoting healthy lifestyles and the right to choose not to take illegal drugs. Professionals support the health and wellbeing of a child pre-conception and throughout pregnancy. Health visitors, midwives and GPs offer parents/carers support and guidance with regard to their own health and that of the unborn child. Throughout a child or young person's life opportunities arise to support healthy lifestyles. Within both the primary and secondary school context healthy eating is promoted at breakfast clubs, during the school day and at afterschool clubs. Recent initiatives to support children's mental and emotional health have included the initiative *Social and Emotional Aspects of Learning* (SEAL) (DCSF, 2007). The Allen Review (2011) highlights early intervention as being the key to enable children from the ages of birth to three years old to build the essential social and emotional bedrock needed so that they grow up to become more effective parents/carers. It is imperative that people working with children, young people and families understand the holistic background of each child and family, thus enabling them to support the child/young person's health and wellbeing appropriately. If parents/carers choose to make unhealthy life choices then this can have a negative impact on their child's health. By working in partnership with parents/carers a family approach to healthy living can be adopted, allowing practitioners and those training to fully understand the child/young person in a family context. Practitioners would also be able to assess how children and young people are kept safe by parents/carers and whether they are providing them with safe homes and stability.

Integrated working and *staying safe*

The outcome *staying safe* encompasses the areas of staying safe from maltreatment, neglect and sexual exploitation, accidental injury and death, bullying and discrimination, crime and anti-social behaviour in and out of school, ensuring that children and young people have security, stability and are cared for. It is clear that some elements of staying safe are linked to child protection and safeguarding. Early intervention strategies are not all aimed at children in the early years but are aimed at addressing an issue before it becomes serious. Anti-bullying strategies would be one area where early intervention is adopted. Once seen as an incident that took place between one or more individuals in a physical proximity, technological developments allow bullying to take place through internet chat rooms and social networking sites, via text messages and mobile phone calls. Consider the strategies that are in place in your practice/setting to promote anti-bullying behaviours. In the early years discussions take place around being friends, sharing and caring. This continues in the primary and secondary settings with further developments taking place regarding online safety and cyber bullying. Some settings adopt a restorative justice approach to incidents of bullying (see http://restorativejustice4schools.co.uk/) whereby the two people involved are allowed to come together to repair the relationship, fostering a sense of social responsibility and shared accountability. By supporting children and young people to stay safe by fostering secure stable environments they will be better placed to enjoy and achieve.

For an interesting critique of restorative justice within the content of children's residential care see Willmott (2007).

 Activity: *Exploring the other ECM outcomes*

As a practitioner/trainee consider how you support/could support children and young people to *enjoy and achieve, make a positive contribution* and *achieve economic wellbeing*.

- How do you monitor each individual child's/young person's progress in these areas?
- How do you share the information with the child/young person and parents/carers?
- If you decide that a child or young person requires specialist support in relation to one or more of these outcomes how do you gather information and access additional services?

Also consider reading Frost and Stein (2009).

The Common Assessment Framework

One of the key elements of integrated working is assessment. This normally revolves around the consent-based **Common Assessment Framework** (CAF), which is described by DfE (2013a) as 'a standardised process to enable practitioners to undertake an early and initial assessment of a child's or young person's needs for extra services and to act on'. The CAF is a four-step process whereby practitioners can:

1   identify a child's or young person's needs early on;
2   assess those needs holistically;
3   deliver co-ordinated services; and
4   review progress made.

The CAF is designed to be used when:

●   a practitioner is worried about how well a child or young person is progressing (e.g. they have concerns about the child's/young person's health, development, welfare, behaviour, progress in learning or any other aspect of their wellbeing);
●   a child or young person, or their parent/carer, raises a concern with a practitioner; or
●   a child's or young person's needs are unclear, or are broader than the practitioner's service can address.

It is important that you recognise that the CAF process is entirely voluntary and informed consent is mandatory (see Chapter 4, page 50–52 for further details); individuals and families do not have to engage with the process if they do not want to. If they do choose to they can select what information they want to share. It is also important that the CAF process is not seen as a 'referral' process but more as a 'request for services'.

Activity: *Exploring the CAF at a national and local level*

Visit http://tinyurl.com/ausvckq which offers up-to-date information from the DfE about the CAF process, the pre-CAF and full CAF forms, and the decommissioned national eCAF (the electronically enabled version of the CAF form and process). Compare the practices being advocated on these web pages to those of your local authority.

Lead professional

We believe that those children and young people who require integrated support from more than one practitioner should experience a service which is effectively 'seamless'. This is delivered most effectively when one practitioner, known as a **lead professional**, takes a primary role to ensure that front-line services are well co-ordinated, coherent and are achieving their intended outcomes in relation to supporting children/young people. The lead professional is usually agreed upon by representatives from the various agencies involved in consultation with the child/young person/family based on who they think is the best-placed person to take on this role. 'The lead professional may be based in any sector of the children, young people or family workforce, depending on the issues involved and the individual relationship with the child' (DfE, 2012b). It is important to remember that the lead professional is not a new role, but more a set of core functions to help deliver effective, integrated support; these include:

- acting as a single point of contact for the child, young person or family;
- co-ordinating the delivery of the actions agreed by the practitioners involved; and
- reducing any overlap and inconsistency in the services that are offered to families.

There are many questions that practitioners and those training have about the lead professional with regard to the tasks that they carry out, their 'skills set', how they are supervised and trained to undertake their 'core functions' and what administrative support is available to assist lead professionals; you are actively encouraged to visit http://tinyurl.com/coo9hrl and explore the *Connected to this* downloads that are available on this webpage, paying particular attention to the *Frequently asked questions about the lead professional* PDF.

Information sharing

The DfE (2011) state that '[f]ront-line practitioners who provide services to children, young people and families often have to make decisions on sharing information with other practitioners about those they are involved with. This calls for professional judgement on a case-by-case basis.' Because practitioners and those training are sometimes uncertain about the legal framework relating to information sharing this can sometimes hamper effective information sharing. Materials and 'How to' guides have been produced by the DfE to provide practitioners and their managers with guidance on when and how to share information both legally and professionally. We strongly encourage you to visit http://tinyurl.com/7rvhdsv and download/actively engage with the materials that are on offer on this website. To support quality practice in this aspect of integrated working, we present the seven golden rules for information sharing (DCSF, 2008c: 4–5) which resonate with our own recommendations that are based on our extensive professional practice across in the 0–19 sector:

1 Remember that the Data Protection Act is not a barrier to sharing information but provides a framework to ensure that personal information about living persons is shared appropriately.
2 Be open and honest with the person (and/or their family where appropriate) from the outset about why, what, how and with whom information will, or could be shared, and seek their agreement, unless it is unsafe or inappropriate to do so.
3 Seek advice if you are in any doubt, without disclosing the identity of the person/s where possible.
4 Share with consent where appropriate and, where possible, respect the wishes of those who do not consent to share confidential information. You may still share information without consent if, in your judgement, that lack of consent can be overridden in the public interest. You will need to base your judgement on the facts of the case.
5 Consider safety and wellbeing – base your information sharing decisions on considerations of the safety and wellbeing of the person and others who may be affected by their actions.
6 *Necessary, proportionate, relevant, accurate, timely* and *secure* – ensure that the information you share is necessary for the purpose for which you are sharing it, is shared only with those people who need to have it, is accurate and up-to-date, is shared in a timely fashion, and is shared securely.

7   Keep a record of your decision and the reasons for it – whether it is to share information or not. If you decide to share, then record what you have shared, with whom and for what purpose.

Case studies

Visit http://tinyurl.com/c2n3cbx for an interesting selection of case studies based on the practices of Leicestershire County Council who have worked with its partners to improve service delivery by safely and effectively sharing appropriate information about families. Select the most relevant case study to your own setting/placement, considering any implications for your own professional practice.

Conclusion

This chapter has sought to highlight the importance of integrated working so that services positively impact on the lives of those they are designed to support (see Harris and Allen, 2011). It is hoped that you recognise that there are many benefits to integrated working (see Cheminais, 2009: 26-27 for examples), the most notable being able to provide children, young people and families with 'swift and easy access' to skilled and knowledgeable professionals, high quality information and effective services. It must be recognised, however, that there are many barriers or *challenges* to this way of working, the most notable relating to financial uncertainties, differences in professional cultures, blurred professional boundaries (see Rushmer and Pallis, 2002; Robinson, Anning and Frost, 2006; Hymans, 2008) and a lack of clarity around roles and responsibilities (see Cheminais, 2009: 27-28). While Brown and White (2006: 19-20) acknowledge what they describe as 'key success factors' in assuring quality integrated working, we conclude this chapter by offering you the five top tips from the Leeds Challenge (IDeA, 2009: 5) which encapsulate the very best practice in not only 'meeting the challenge' but overcoming the barriers to integrated working:

1   Keep bringing people back to the focus on outcomes. This holds integrated services together.
2   Make use of common processes such as the Common Assessment Framework used in Children's [and Young People's] Services.
3   Recognise that everyone has a leadership role in integrated working.
4   Develop a common language between the different professions and groups of staff. Allow time to explore differences in language and culture.
5   Encourage staff on the ground to innovate and develop local solutions.

Areas for further consideration

There are a number of other areas of consideration which you may wish to explore as part of your own personal study. The suggestions below merely offer a number of aspects which may support your continued understanding of integrated working:

Integrated working and safeguarding	Integrated working and managing change
Integrated working and SWOT analysis	Building professional relationships between services
Integrated working and leadership styles	Integrated working and transitions of children and young people

Further reading

Books

Edmond, N. and Price, M. (eds) (2012) *Integrated Working with Children and Young People: Supporting development from birth to nineteen.* London: Sage.
This interdisciplinary text looks at learning and development from birth to 19 years, providing an accessible introduction to the common areas of study across the many integrated roles that support learning and development in the 0–19 workforce.

Kellett, M. (2011) *Children's Perspectives on Integrated Services: Every Child Matters in Policy and Practice (Interagency Working in Health and Social Care).* London: Palgrave Macmillan.
This book offers a helpful, constructive and timely appraisal of the value of integrated services. It covers a range of issues linked to the topics of health, social care and education. Weaving the voice of the child throughout, this book provides a cutting-edge overview of children's services as they have developed under the New Labour government and a reflective assessment of the legacy of ECM.

Academic journal articles

Canavan, J., Coen, L., Dolan, P. and Whyte, L. (2009) Privileging Practice: Facing the Challenge of Integrated Working for Outcomes for Children. *Children & Society*, 23, 377–388. [Online]. Available at: http://tinyurl.com/bszwwrb (Accessed: 12 May 2013).
This article advocates the value of reflective practice in helping practitioners to engage with the 'theoretical and practical challenges of integrated working' and 'achieve the balance between policy and services blueprints and the realities of practice' which is considered to be 'a necessity in achieving better outcomes for children' (p. 377).

Maslin-Prothero, S. E. and Bennion, A. E. (2010) Integrated team working: a literature review. *International Journal of Integrated Care*, 10, 1–11. [Online]. Available at: http://tinyurl.com/dxsb4cr (Accessed: 12 May 2013).
This article reports on a systematic literature review which was undertaken to provide a background understanding of the literature around integrated health and social care. Identified recommendations for integrated working are considered 'valuable for practitioners who are establishing services or want to improve integrated care in their own practice'.

Website

Integrated working. Available at: http://tinyurl.com/d8fde6q
This is a UK government website (DfE) which contains the most up-to-date information about integrated working, the lead professional, multi-agency working, TAC, and information sharing.

Answers to Activity: Which service? (page 195)

Case Study A = *specialist*; Case Study B = *universal*; Case Study C = *targeted*

Reference list

Allen, G. (2011) *Early Intervention: The Next Steps*. [Online]. Available at: http://tinyurl.com/6g8dtg2 (Accessed: 10 January 2013).

Anning, A., Cottrell, D., Frost, N., Green, J. and Robinson, M. (2006) *Developing Multi-professional Teamwork for Integrated Children's Services*. Maidenhead: Open University Press.

Argent, K. (2007) Every Child Matters: Change for parents/carers and families? Can schools work with families to promote knowledge and understanding of government expectations? *Education, 3-13*, 35 (3), 295-303.

Brown, K. and White, K. (2006) *Exploring the evidence base for Integrated Children's Services*. [Online]. Available at: http://tinyurl.com/bb64amj (Accessed: 8 January 2013).

Cheminais, R. (2009) The Benefits and Challenges of Collaborative Multi-Agency Working (Chapter 2). In *Effective Multi-Agency Partnerships: Putting Every Child Matters into Practice*. London: Sage. pp. 23-44. [Online]. Available at: www.sagepub.com/upm-data/25241_02_Cheminais_Ch_02.pdf (Accessed: 13 May 2013).

Children Act (2004). [Online]. Available at: www.legislation.gov.uk/ukpga/2004/31/pdfs/ukpga_20040031_en.pdf (Accessed: 16 May 2013).

Children's Workforce Development Council (2008) *Integrated working explained*. [Online]. Available at: www.hascaltd.co.uk/resources/intergratedworking.pdf (Accessed: 18 May 2013).

——(2009a) *The Common Assessment Framework for Children and Young People: A Guide for Managers*. Leeds: Children's Workforce Development Council.

——(2009b) *The Team Around the Child and the Lead Professional. A Guide for Practitioners*. [Online]. Available at: http://tinyurl.com/ch5ssne (Accessed: 14 January 2013).

Davis, J. M. (2011) *Integrated Children's Services*. London: Sage.

Davis, J. M. and Smith, M. (2012) *Working in Multi-Professional Contexts*. London: Sage.

Department for Children, Schools and Families (2007) *Social and emotional aspects of learning for secondary schools*. Nottingham: DCSF Publications.

——(2008a) *2020 Children and Young People's Workforce Strategy*. [Online]. Available at: http://tinyurl.com/a7ofdx6 (Accessed: 23 January 2013).

——(2008b) *Every Child Matters Outcomes Framework*. [Online]. Available at: http://tinyurl.com/brd4pay (Accessed: 28 February 2013).

——(2008c) *Information Sharing: Pocket guide*. [Online]. Available at: www.unison.org.uk/file/A8157.pdf (Accessed: 13 May 2013).

Department for Education (2011) *Information Sharing*. [Online]. Available at: www.education.gov.uk/childrenandyoungpeople/strategy/integratedworking/a0072915/information-sharing (Accessed: 18 May 2013).

——(2012a) *Team Around the Child*. [Online]. Available at: http://tinyurl.com/ab24raj (Accessed: 14 January 2013).

——(2012b) *The lead professional*. [Online]. Available at: www.education.gov.uk/childrenandyoungpeople/strategy/integratedworking/a0068961/the-lead-professional (Accessed: 18 May 2013).

——(2013a) *The CAF process*. [Online]. Available at: www.education.gov.uk/childrenandyoungpeople/strategy/integratedworking/caf/a0068957/the-caf-process (Accessed: 13 May 2013).

——(2013b) *Working Together to Safeguard Children*. [Online]. Available at: http://tinyurl.com/d979vyp (Accessed: 18 May 2013).

Department for Education and Schools (DfES) (2004) *Every Child Matters Change for Children*. [Online]. Available at: http://tinyurl.com/bcnpwv5 (Accessed: 23 January 2013).

Department for Health and Social Security (DHSS) (1974) *Report of the Committee of Inquiry into the care and supervision provided by local authorities and other agencies in relation to Maria Colwell and the co-ordination between them*. London: Her Majesty's Stationery Office.

Field, F. (2010) *The Foundation Years: preventing poor children becoming poor adults*. [Online]. Available at: http://tinyurl.com/bnba97j (Accessed: 10 January 2013).

Frost, N. and Stein, M. (2009) Outcomes of Integrated Working with Children and Young People. *Children and Society*, 23 (5), 315–319.

Halsey, K., Gulliver, C., Johnson, A., Martin, K. and Kinder, K. (2005) *Evaluation of Behaviour and Education Support Teams*. Research Report No. 706. Nottingham: DfES Publications.

Haringey Local Safeguarding Children's Board (2009) *Serious Case Review Baby Peter*. [Online]. Available at: http://tinyurl.com/pfklbs (Accessed: 24 January 2013).

Harris, A. and Allen, T. (2011) Young People's Views of Multi-Agency Working. *British Educational Research Journal*, 37(3), 405–419.

Hawkes, S. (n.d.) *The Assessment of Need and the Assessment of Risk: The Challenges for Child Protection*. [Online]. Available at: http://tinyurl.com/c7sm96b (Accessed: 18 May 2013).

Hymans, M. (2008) How constructs about "Professional Identities" might act as a barrier to multi-agency working. *Educational Psychology in Practice: theory, research and practice in educational psychology*, 24(4), 175–191.

IDeA (Improvement and Development Agency) (2009) *Integrated working: learning from the Leeds Leadership Challenge*. [Online]. Available at: www.idea.gov.uk/idk/aio/21571108 (Accessed: 13 May 2013).

Laming, W. H. (2003) *The Victoria Climbié Inquiry. Summary and Recommendations*. [Online]. Available at: http://tinyurl.com/bf63et5 (Accessed: 10 January 2013).

——(2009) *The Protection of Children in England: A Progress Report*. [Online]. Available at: http://webarchive.nationalarchives.gov.uk/20130401151715/https://www.education.gov.uk/publications/eOrderingDownload/HC-330.pdf (Accessed: 12 January 2013).

Lord, P., Kinder, K., Wilkin, A., Atkinson, M. and Harland, J. (2008) *Evaluating the Early Impact of Integrated Children's Services Round 1. Final Report*. Slough: NFER.

Munro, E. (2012) *The Munro Review of Child Protection. Progress report: Moving towards a child centred system*. [Online]. Available at: http://tinyurl.com/cc6ykcw (Accessed: 12 May 2013).

National Society for the Prevention of Cruelty to Children (NSPCC) (2011) *Safe Activities for Everyone Network*. [Online]. Available at: http://tinyurl.com/bz4fvee (Accessed: 23 January 2013).

Parton, N. (2004) From Maria Colwell to Victoria Climbié: Reflections on a generation of public inquiries into child abuse. *Child Abuse Review*, 13 (2), 80–94.

Robinson, M., Anning, A. and Frost, N. (2006) 'When is a teacher not a teacher?' Knowledge creation and the professional identity of teachers within multi-agency teams. *Studies in Continuing Education*, 27(2), 175–191.

Rushmer, R. and Pallis, G. (2002) Inter-Professional Working: The Wisdom of Integrated Working and the Disaster of Blurred Boundaries. *Public Money and Management*, 23 (1), 59–66.

Siraj-Blatchford, I., Clarke, K. and Needham, M. (2007) *The Team Around the Child*. Stoke on Trent: Trentham Books.

Stuart, K. (2012) Leading multi-professional teams in the children's workforce: an action research project. *International Journal of Integrated Care*, 12 (Jan–March). [Online]. Available at: http://tinyurl.com/cl8q84g (Accessed: 12 May 2013).

Willmott, N. (2007) *A review of the use of restorative justice in children's residential care*. London: National Children's Bureau. [Online]. Available at: http://www.judgesandmagistrates.org/RJ_in_rcc_review%20Natasha%20Wilmott.pdf (Accessed: 22 June 2013).

World Health Organisation (WHO) (2008) *Integrated Health Services – what and why?* Technical Brief No.1. [Online]. Available at: www.who.int/healthsystems/service_delivery_techbrief1.pdf (Accessed: 11 May 2013).

13 The learning community: International lessons

Mabel Ann Brown

LEARNING OBJECTIVES

After studying this chapter, you will be able to:

✔ Argue and evaluate the reasoning behind school starting ages for children in different countries.
✔ Identify and define differences in early years and primary curriculums from different countries.
✔ Evaluate comparisons in educational and early years care provision on an international scale.
✔ Evaluate and argue the benefits of growing up in certain communities.

Introduction

This chapter will consider some of the different practices such as school starting age and curriculum requirements that may influence achievement by the time children are 15 years of age. It will focus its attention on evaluating early years care and provision on an international scale, debating the benefits of growing up in certain communities. The chapter will also investigate how growing up in certain communities influences child and youth development as considered by Bronfenbrenner in the 1970s. The term 'community' can be interpreted in different ways but for the purpose of this chapter it refers to the community of practice within the wider physical community. Bronfenbrenner (1994) envisaged the child at the centre was influenced by the systems which surrounded them, thus children are influenced by the systems they experience.

The focus of the chapter will be comparisons that will be made between Finland, Belgium, Germany and England with further links being made to the US, Japan and New Zealand. Although this chapter is routed in the early years and primary context, the complexity of this has significant implications for the secondary and post-16 age range in a variety of contexts.

Activity

For those working with young people post-16 please consider reading the following:

- Burkhard, M. (2006) Similarities and links between early childhood education and informal education in youth work for adolescents. *European Early Childhood Education Research Journal*, 14 (2), 21-33.
- Bottrell, D. and Armstrong, D. (2007) Changes and Exchanges in Marginal Youth Transitions. *Journal of Youth Studies*, 10 (3), 353-371.

The modern world has enabled people to explore far shores with the advent of mobile phones in 1973 and SKYPE in 2003 but it has also brought greater realisation of what people in other countries are achieving. No longer are children and young people being prepared for a life in one country but rather for a life that involves trade, travel and communication on a global scale. Many national decisions are partly influenced by discussions in Brussels and in terms of education the Organisation for Economic Cooperation and Development (OECD) collates education statistics and encompasses information from 34 OECD member countries and 41 partner countries and economies through the PISA survey.

International comparisons are being made on every aspect of life including educational opportunities. In 2009 the OECD PISA published data that pointed to the fact that by the age of 15, children in the UK were underperforming in reading, mathematics and science when assessed against their European counterparts; as underperformance can have a significant impact on long-term employability there has been cause for concern. However, whether these performance tables are an accurate indication is debatable as discussed by Burdett (2013) but they certainly seemed to indicate a need for possible change.

Table 13.1 A sample from the OECD PISA 2009 Database

A sample from the OECD PISA 2009 Database								
	On the overall reading scale	Access and retrieve	Integrate and interpret	Reflect and evaluate	Continuous texts	Non-continuous texts	On the mathematics scale	On the science scale
Finland	536	532	538	536	535	535	541	554
Belgium	506	513	504	505	504	511	515	507
Germany	497	501	501	491	496	497	513	520
UK	494	491	491	503	492	506	492	514
Japan	520	530	520	521	520	518	529	539
New Zealand	521	521	517	531	518	532	519	532
USA	500	492	495	512	500	503	487	502

Adapted from OECD (2009) PISA 2009 Database. Available at: http://tinyurl.com/988cuhy

Reflective Task

Explore and reflect on the OECD PISA 2009 results and consider their implications for practice. These are available at http://tinyurl.com/2ax2f7n. Readers may wish to compare these results with those from 2012 (see http://www.oecd.org/pisa/).

For the purpose of this chapter the international comparisons will be made with England but further information on Scotland and Wales can be located on the following websites:

- www.educationscotland.gov.uk/
- http://wales.gov.uk/topics/educationandskills/?lang=en

School starting ages

A significant difference in international practice is the school starting age which could potentially be a reason for the differing PISA statistics. The school starting age in England is the term before a child is five years old while in Finland the school starting age is seven, although many children in Finland (96 per cent approximately) do attend a pre-school year. Penn (2011: 10) claims 'the school starting age of 5 in the UK as an accident of history (a footnote to legislation passed in 1870), rather than a considered pedagogic choice'. Children growing up in Finland will therefore experience a very different start in terms of education to a child growing up in England; however, there is, as Penn (2011: 209) points out, frequently no rationale for the way in which services, particularly in the early years, are presented in different countries. Frequently the early years, primary and secondary systems are a mixture of ambiguities based on policies, finance, politics and society that have evolved over time. The case study below demonstrates the kind of day a Finnish child might experience before the age of seven.

Case study: *A typical pre-school day in a Day Nursery in Finland*

- breakfast;
- outside play for one hour;
- share books while children change out of outdoor clothes which are dried if necessary for the afternoon play;
- music/story/number/play/board games/construction kits/painting/writing (the children can choose which activity they wish to engage in for the most part);
- lunch (children in turn are encouraged to set the table or help with preparations);
- free drawing or play;
- sleep opportunity for those children that require this/quiet activities;
- mid-afternoon snack; and
- outside play (one hour).

The table below shares some of the different practices that take place in other countries in relation to pre-school funding, ethos and progress and choice of primary and staffing.

Table 13.2 Comparative practice in the early years (adapted from Brown, 2010)

A sample from the OECD PISA 2009 Database				
	Pre-school funding	**Parental choice**	**Assessment of children**	**Staffing**
Flanders, Belgium			Each pre-primary school in Flanders must monitor their own children's developmental progress but there are no national tests.	
Germany	In Germany the last pre-school year is funded.	In Germany parents have some choice in the primary school for their child. Within Germany some choice with cluster schools is being introduced for children who are sufficiently able and if the school is willing to accept them.		In Germany schools cannot choose their own staff.
Finland	In Finland the Pre-schools receive some money and parents pay a contribution based on their income.	In Finland children frequently attend a local school.	A development portfolio is maintained but there are no tests.	
England	In England there is some pre-school funding dependent on the child's age.	In England parents to some extent can choose a school for their child, in reality not all children receive the school of their choice.	The EYFS Profile monitors children's progress and is completed by the staff.	In England schools and governors select their own staff.
New Zealand	A range of settings with an emphasis on diversity and community government funded initiatives.		*Te Whariki*, a non-prescriptive approach with four principles giving rise to five strands.	
Japan	Privately operated pre-schools are available.		An emphasis on group rules and behaviour.	
USA	Pre-school/nursery for (2–4) and Kindergartens (5–6) – parents pay for these.	State control over facilities.	Each state determines the requirements that a student should meet. Emphasis is placed on individuality.	

Finnish children do have a pre-school opportunity when they are six but school attendance is not compulsory until they are seven. Stakes (2003: 3) in the *National Curriculum Guidelines on Early Childhood Education and Care In Finland* (2004) (cited in Brown, 2009) states that care, education and teaching have 'different emphasis in different situations' and that the care element is a stronger feature in the early years; in Finland the practitioners 'share the day to day education and care of the young child with the parents... for the child's well-being'.

This emphasis on care is also emphasised in the Steiner (1861–1925) approach. Children at home with their parents or carers might receive a more Steiner approach with warm, sensitive relationships as Penn (2011: 58) refers to studies of mothering that suggest that children at home with their mothers would receive a 'focus on the material and emotional welfare' as opposed to a more distant relationship created by a teacher or professional who might focus further on education matters. In order to address this, Germany adopts the Kindergarten approach for children below the age of six which is broadly influenced by Froebel (1782–1852) (see http://tinyurl.com/c8btmfk). The educational system post six years old in Germany is four years of primary followed by secondary schools for academics (Gymnasium) or vocational education for those less-academic (Hauptschule).

An early school starting age such as England should be beneficial in that children are in a setting for a longer period of time but not all data appears to reflect this, for instance the OECD PISA (2009) as this example below demonstrates.

Consider this!

John in Australia can start school when he is six and Jari in Finland can start school when he is seven, but Harry in England has to start school when he is nearly five. These children will complete the OECD PISA, a series of tests, when they are fifteen; if current trends prevail Jari will be the most successful at age fifteen.

Reflect on this and consider the potential value or potential harm in this for the children and young people concerned.

Meanwhile, if you grow up in Belgium educational pre-school provision is available for children but children attend compulsory school between the ages of six and eighteen. Pre-school is fundamentally taken up by many parents in Belgium as there are three separate language communities (Flanders, Wallonia and Brussels) thus many children need to master or become familiar with a second language prior to attending school.

Evidence from the OECD PISA (2009) would appear to suggest that a later starting age is more beneficial for children or it could be the type of experience rather than the child's age that is significant. This also agrees with the philosophy of Steiner (1861–1925), who placed a significant emphasis on play up until the age of seven (Gray and MacBlain, 2012). Steiner believed that there needed to be an opportunity to draw and explore the natural world with the more formal learning best left until children are more mature.

Unfortunately children's needs are not the only significant factor in countries' choices as there are 'sociopolitical and economic factors, power structures and values within communities and societies' (Moss, 2008 cited in Papatheodorou and Moyles, 2012: 2) that impact on child development. Each country is different and the systems within it are different, thus children are influenced in many different ways.

In Saxony in Germany the State minister for Education and Cultural Affairs Steffen Flath (2006) claimed the 'educational environment is versatile and multi-faceted as are the educational requirements'. The theme in Saxony Germany is that 'Everyone Counts', a theme that resonates in policy making in England to *Every Child Matters* (DfES, 2003) or as it is now referred to since 2010 as *Helping Children Achieve More* (DfE, 2010). How this is demonstrated in practice will impact on children's outcomes. In Saxony the Kindergarten (a preparatory year) and Grundschule (primary school) work closely together with lessons focused on children's individual knowledge and experience, giving children an opportunity to share what they can do, thus developing the child's self-image (Saxony State Ministry, 2006). The focus is then on language, reading and writing, sciences, mathematics, foreign languages, religion and ethics. In Finland the emphasis would be on mark making/writing and then reading with other subjects such as Maths being introduced through physical practical activities initially. The broader subject areas would be introduced after children are seven in Finland.

In some ways the Finns and Saxons are similar in that children have the support for a 'second chance' or an opportunity to repeat a year if it is necessary or thought to be beneficial (see http://tinyurl.com/c8btmfk for further information). In England this can happen too but it is the exception rather than the rule and applies to very few cases.

Early years provision in Finland is designed to support parents and carers who are working, but in England it is also provided for children who are recognised as having a need for family reasons, particularly in cases where parenting is considered deficient for some reason. If the pre-school provision is effective then the pre-school experience can 'enhance the all-round development of children' as recognised in the EPPE (Sylva *et al.*, 2004). If the pre-school makes a difference to children's life chances then it is important that the best systems are available in preparation for compulsory education.

Once in compulsory education the community then impacts on children's development further by imposing a curriculum upon the children either as guidance (Finland) or as a requirement (England). The Finnish Curriculum – *The National Curriculum Guidelines on Early Childhood Education and Care In Finland* (2004) – was not mandatory. An emphasis was placed on the professionalism of the staff who encouraged children and used the guidance with professional discretion. The focus in Finland was to encourage independent learning and promote children's personal and social development initially. Academic learning is encouraged when children are ready. This very much supports the Steiner theory of responding to the changing needs of children, as highlighted in Gray and MacBlain (2012: 23). This challenges the idea of young children being *taught* and emphasises the notion of children learning *for themselves* when they are ready.

Early years and primary curriculums

Any curriculum is devised to implement what the decision makers believe to be important. One of the main purposes of education is to provide the next generation with the skills and knowledge that may be necessary to survive an unknown future and adapt to new technologies and understanding. Education attempts to provide children and young people with the skills to facilitate future changes. However, we actually prepare them in the present times with little conception of what might be the future. Each country in the world is continually attempting to meet this challenge via their curriculum and institutional practices. Some countries try to clarify what children need to know while others approach learning differently and focus more on social, physical and moral skills.

Te Whariki was developed in New Zealand in 1996 as the first early childhood care and education curriculum for children from birth to school entry (Ministry of Education, 1996 cited in Duhn, 2006); the Early Years Foundation Stage (EYFS) (DfE, 2012: 3) replicates elements of this with its areas of learning and development and learning goals. *Te Whariki* aimed to produce a certain kind of child based on a vision of the ideal child (Duhn, 2006). It was also 'part of an international trend to strengthen connections between the economic success of the nation and education' (May, 2001: 244, cited in Duhn, 2006: 193); this can also be observed in England in the *Every Child Matters* (DfES, 2003) 'making a positive contribution' and 'achieving economic well-being' components (see *Helping Children Achieve More*, DfE, 2010).

The *Te Whariki* 'good child' had the principles of 'empowerment, holistic development, family and community and relationships at the centre of the curriculum' (Duhn, 2006: 196). Bronfenbrenner (cited in Penn, 2005: 44) saw this as children being influenced by the microsystem, the mesosystem or the neighbourhood and the exosystem or government (see Chapter 11, page 187).

The term *Te Whariki* means 'woven mat' and the implication was that children are shaped by the community at a local, national and international level into becoming lifelong learners and problem solvers who can contribute to society (Duhn, 2006: 199). However, much of what they become is shaped by politics, policies and the facilities in existence at any given time.

Plowden (CACE, 1967: para 505, cited in Alexander, 2010: 177) claimed that: 'A school is not merely a teaching shop. It is a *community* in which children learn to live first and foremost as children and not as adults… Knowledge does not fall into neatly separate compartments.'

Access to this community for many children in England begins in the early years childcare settings where the children meet other families and practitioners outside their family circle. In England these settings follow the Early Years Foundation Stage (DfE, 2012).

The EYFS framework aimed to reduce bureaucracy, provide learning and development requirements, while promoting communication and language, physical development and personal, social and emotional development. There are progress checks for children aged two enabling early intervention and close parent partnership is encouraged (DfE, 2013). In reality more settings are taking in two year olds and struggling to provide qualified staff in a difficult economic climate who follow a career path that continues to pay low wages. One proposed way to address this is to increase the ratio of children to one adult but this is controversial for health and safety reasons. An example from the EYFS (DfE, 2012) can be explored through the case study below.

Case study

'We welcomed the introduction of the new EYFS, particularly the focus on the three prime areas. We have a strong focus on language development, using listening groups, signs and symbols and songs to promote listening and understanding, an approach which is particularly pertinent to the new curriculum. We had followed the proposals from the Tickell Review (2011) and have found the new *Development Matters* to be helpful and informative. The new Learning Journeys that have been implemented in Nottinghamshire in response to the new EYFS require practitioners to have a sound knowledge and understanding of child development to effectively assess a child's age and stage of development; our staff team are beginning to appreciate the benefits as they get used to the new framework. The Tickell Review recommended less bureaucracy but that does not seem to be the case, and we continue to explore ways of streamlining our processes to ensure that staff can prioritise children's learning and development. Having implemented the changes in practice in terms of observing, assessing and recording children's learning, our focus is now on the development of new systems to track progress and to assess children's starting points. We have also used the characteristics of effective learning to ensure that our team continue to plan opportunities for children to explore, to learn through their play and above all, to have fun!'

Director, Private Day Nursery, UK

Reflect on the above, considering your personal and professional response to the case study.

At the age of five, children in England experience the statutory National Curriculum. The National Curriculum (DfEE/QCA, 1987) was split into phases: Key Stage One for 5-7 year olds, Key Stage Two for 7-11 year olds, Key Stage Three for 11-14 year olds and Key Stage Four for 14-16 year olds which was linked to Piaget's stages of development (Bruce, 2010: 96). In England a new National Curriculum has been proposed. Below is an adapted table demonstrating the much debated proposed new National Curriculum (DfE, 2013).

Table 13.3 Proposed structure of the new National Curriculum (DfE, 2013)

	Key Stage 1	Key Stage 2	Key Stage 3
Age	5-7	7-11	11-14
Core Subjects			
English	√	√	√
Mathematics	√	√	√
Science	√	√	√
Foundation Subjects			
Art and Design	√	√	√
Citizenship			√
Computing	√	√	√
Design and technology	√	√	√
Foreign Languages		√	√ Referred to as modern foreign languages (MFL)
Geography	√	√	√
History	√	√	√
Music	√	√	√
Physical education	√	√	√

Pollard (1996: 133 cited in Thornton, 1998) made the comment that all curricula reflects the values and priorities of those who construct it and Rousseau claimed in 1991 that it is essential that what is implemented is fit for purpose and enables 'the full actualization of man's potential' (p. 3). Thus 'central prescription' (Thornton, 1998) of the National Curriculum in England remained unchallenged to some extent until 2010 when Alexander published his findings after a four-year study. This was even more significant as many teachers in England were voicing a need for change.

Voices of concern had been raised even in 2003 when Hargreaves (2003) remarked that teaching had been reduced to a 'job to maintain order, teach to the test and follow standardized curriculum scripts... the drones and clones of policy makers' anaemic ambitions' (Hargreaves, 2003 cited in Thomas, 2012: 4). The current situation in England in 2013 is an attempt to reduce the 'central prescription' and enable a more creative approach encouraging industries and businesses to get involved in children's education.

Table 13.4 demonstrates some of the comparative international differences in practice relating to pre-school and school provision.

Table 13.4 International comparisons of pre-school and school provision

	Pre-school	Primary	Secondary	Post-16
England	0–5 years	5–11 years	11–16 years	Further Education/ Vocational
Germany	0–6 years (Froebel approach)	6–11	11–14/14–16	Further Education/ Vocational
Belgium	0–6 years (Montessori and Steiner approach) Belgium has had state funded nurseries for 3–5 year olds since 1900	6–12	12–18 (some part time study is allowed post-16)	
Finland	0–6 years	7–16 (Nine years of basic education)		Vocational/Higher Education
USA	Pre-school/nursery (age 2–4) Kindergartens age 5–6 all private institutions	6–16 Compulsory schooling in most states		Some states require students to attend until 18
Japan	Public and Private Pre-school and nursery (0–5) years – focus on health and well-being)	Elementary – Primary (6–12 years old Middle (12–15 year olds + some private schools) High School 15–18 years		4 years University/ Graduate school/ technical college
New Zealand	Teacher led or parent led services	Create and innovate – the overarching theme Years 1–8 children commence age 5 or 6 years old (Primary and Intermediate) Year 9 (aged 12/13) children move on to High School or secondary or College		

Activity: *International comparisons*

A further diagram of international comparisons can be located on page 48 of Penn, H. (2011) *Quality in Early Childhood Services: An international perspective*. Maidenhead: Open University Press.

Penn (2011) explores the idea of quality and the range of systems that have evolved internationally. Compare this diagram with any practice that you have observed or experienced recently.

The curriculum for statutory age children is a requirement and mandatory in many countries but this control can be by central government or more locally by the state. Within the context of Germany, schooling is mandatory in Germany between the ages of six and fourteen. The curriculum is the responsibility of the states or provinces with much less state or federal educational control (see http://tinyurl.com/c8btmfk for further details). The school curriculum in Germany focuses on mainly academic subjects commencing at 7.30am or 8am until 1pm but there is some afternoon time given over to homework, sports and physical activity as observed personally in a German school. In England the school day is longer, commencing about 9am and finishing at approximately 3.15pm to 3.30pm. The children in England undertake their homework at home after this time or at after-school homework clubs.

Learning a second language is important in both Germany and Finland. In Germany the children start learning English in Grade 3 (aged eight approximately) with two lessons being dedicated to this each week. In Finland the children learn to speak Finnish, English and Swedish; they are given visual access to this from an early age in the pre-schools. An example of this is calendars with the day and date displayed in more than one language.

Hall and Ozerk (2010, cited in Alexander, 2010: 211) claim that:

> England differs from many other countries in not as yet making PSHE, citizenship and a modern foreign language compulsory at the primary stage. There is also a grey area where matters like global awareness are concerned. They are increasingly encouraged but not obligatory.

As the English language is spoken throughout a large part of the world it has become difficult to determine which other language our schools in England should offer, particularly as there are over 200 languages spoken within the country (Alexander, 2010: 113). Children in England do get the chance to study a foreign language in the latter part of Key Stage Two and they can pursue a language between the ages of 11–14.

While languages are seen as essential in some countries, for example Finland, others consider the health of the child as significantly important. Japan is more concerned with the whole child's development than whether a child can achieve in a test at the age of 15. This is passionately explored by Iguchi in Brown and White (2014). This emphasis on the whole child and well-being can also be observed in recent thinking in England.

The Cambridge Primary Review in England (Alexander, 2009) proposed 12 aims for the twenty-first century; this included 'well-being and empowerment' thus sharing this idea of healthier children. It also proposed eight domains of knowledge at the centre of which was 'language, oracy and literacy'. There was a suggestion for a 'community curriculum' as opposed to a National Curriculum to allow for and meet local needs. The curriculum debate in England 2013 continues following considerable consultation and discussion. The only thing that can be certain is that the curriculum needs to continue to change in order to remain current.

Comparisons in educational and early years care provision internationally

All countries' economic success depends on the skills and attributes of the next generation, thus the DfES (2004) spoke of children and young people *making a positive contribution* and *achieving economic well-being*. Economic recovery is important for the whole of society, both nationally and internationally, but although it is necessary, it is not easy to achieve.

Activity

Engage with the following two readings and discuss these with colleagues/peers:

- DCSF (2008) *2020 Children and Young People's Workforce Strategy*. Nottingham: DCSF.
- Thomas, L. (2012) *Re-thinking the Importance of Teaching: Curriculum and Collaboration in an era of Localism*. London: RSA Projects.

Ask yourself the following:

1   Should directives come from the EU or from national governments? Why?
2   Would a more generic European system be more effective? Why/not?

In the same way that communities and individual countries consider centralising practice, voices have been raised about complete international curriculum parity. However, advocates of the European Commission 2020 have been criticised in Erixon's (2010) policy brief as one central strategy can become a restriction: 'the belief that one central strategy can fit the entire European Union – 27 economies with different reform needs and priorities – borders on a central planning mentality that can only do damage to economic growth'. One central strategy would dismiss alternative practices and this could be detrimental to creativity and the use of personal initiative. Research also points to personal initiative positively impacting on work innovativeness over a period of time (see http://tinyurl.com/8ntnbup for further details).

Current thinking is moving towards more autonomy in England but with accountability in relation to professionalism. The Thomas RSA project (2012) devolves central government power to the schools and attempts to return some autonomy to the professionals in the education sector in England. Schools can elect to become academies and new schools can be set up but in Sweden these actions have led to more choice but also to some schools failing to recruit and therefore closing. However, it is suggested that 'parents with children who attend independent schools in Sweden are more satisfied than those with children in municipal schools' (Swedish Institute, 2012).

A significant feature of Finland is the requirement for all staff who work with children to be well qualified. According to eurydice (2008: 65) all types of pre-primary establishment catering for children from a very early age must employ staff with qualifications in education in Denmark, Finland and Norway. Since *Every Child Matters* (DfES, 2003) and the Children's Workforce Strategy (DfES, 2005) there has been a move towards raising the standards of those working with children in England.

The standards of attainment children achieve are reliant on many factors, one of which is the standard of the workforce, as identified in EPPE (Sylva *et al.*, 2004), but there are other factors as suggested in a study between America and Japan that was undertaken by Knipprath (2005). It was observed that the success of Japanese children in comparison to American children was higher and she concludes that the teachers' learning and teaching styles, cultural beliefs and the organisation of the schooling, plus parental input, all influence academic achievement.

Alexander (2010: 15) suggests that we are living in the 'era of globalisation' but what is unclear is how much of the world's tensions, values and issues (moral, political and economic) should be considered in the classroom for fear of being accused of indoctrination. This is approached in Germany by having ethics classes built into the timetable for those children who do not participate in religious education. The *Helping Children Achieve More* agenda (formerly ECM [DFES, 2003]) encourages making a positive contribution to society and 'forming their own views with a right to express those views' (UNCRC, 1989, cited in Alexander, 2010: 144). Children cannot do this without some knowledge of existing world issues. Thus there is a definite requirement for children to gain personal experiences that they can then build upon. Where possible, the schools in Germany provide new experiences; for example, the circus visits the school and children have opportunities to try out new skills, e.g. riding a unicycle or juggling. In England, visitors such as the police or animal wardens are invited into school or the children are taken out to see new things such as the fire station or a museum. In recent times children in Loughborough have used social networking systems in the form of SKYPE to share knowledge and experiences with children in Dresden, Germany (Brown, 2011).

The most common method internationally for success, according to Alexander (2010: 294), is a combination of high expectations and interactive whole class teaching with well-structured textbooks and less work sheets. However, quality is somewhat difficult to define yet that is what each country strives for. Quality also raises issues of analysis, measurement and accountability covering a range of assumptions about childhood (Penn, 2011: 5). Constantly working towards tests in England as part of accountability may have actually narrowed the curriculum as schools struggled to achieve these levels of attainment. It certainly made some children question the value of some subjects as during a recent visit to a local primary school one child observed that 'If we are tested in maths, English and science, don't the other subjects matter?'

The National Curriculum in England is packaged into subject labels such as English, Maths or History but these are quite vague with regards to content or how it is delivered, thus knowing what subjects we or another country delivers is only a portion of the whole picture. However, it is interesting to note that some countries focus more time on some subjects initially.

Table 13.5 European comparison of curriculum time allocation (adapted from Brown, 2008)

Finland (per week, per subject, Year 1) (age 7)	England (per week, per subject) (age 7)	Germany Primary Level Grundschule
7 hours reading and writing 3 hours Maths 2 hours + 2 hours Art and Craft 2 hours music 2 hours Gymnastics/sports 1 hour religion 1 hour combined Biology/the Environment/Geography	A comparatively equal allowance of Maths and English on a daily basis, primarily in the mornings The afternoons given over to other subjects	Reading and writing Sciences (Our world, human coexistence and the interaction with plants and animals) Mathematics Foreign Languages Religion/Ethics
Finland **Year 2 (age 8)**	**England** **Year 3 (age 8)**	
6 hours reading and writing 4 hours maths	A comparatively equal allowance of Maths and English on a daily basis The afternoons given over to other subjects	

Reflection task

In Finland children participate in seven hours of reading and writing per week when aged seven and six hours per week when aged eight. The children in Finland also learn to write first and then read in agreement with the Steiner philosophy (Carnie, 2003).

Consider what you have observed in practice: what proportion of their time do children spend on reading and writing each week in the setting you work/train in? In what ways could this be significant?

Currently we live in an information age with children for the most part having access to books, televisions, videos, computers and radios. Children can no longer be a vessel to fill but rather they need the skills to access all these media tools. A designated closed curriculum could be too restrictive as the future is always an uncertain commodity with the skills needed today not necessarily being those required by tomorrow. Collaborative research undertaken in the UK (Brown *et al.*, 2011) sought to investigate the use of SKYPE in primary education. The research indicated that this social tool could have a significant role in bringing children together nationally and internationally in the future.

Parents, teachers and children have voiced concerns about the impact of an ICT world but children cannot be deprived access to this feature of society. The ICT curriculum for schools is changing with an emphasis less on mastering Word and PowerPoint and more on being creative with the introduction of the Raspberry Pi, a small computer that plugs into a TV and a keyboard having programming potential (see www.raspberrypi.org/faqs for further details). However, as a colleague reflected, 'Only a few children will potentially go on to develop programmes!' so perhaps this is a strategy for the few rather than the majority. Nevertheless, until everyone has access to computers and to faster internet connections there will always be some children who are disadvantaged. There is an assumption that everyone has it but many children cannot engage with their homework electronically due to limited access at home. Yet again the community is either limiting or extending opportunities for children.

The benefits of growing up in certain communities

Policy makers focus on improving education but they rely heavily on how they believe education systems are succeeding. However, national standards are no longer believed to be entirely relevant or sufficient; the emphasis is much more on an international comparison. The OECD PISA evaluates the efficiency of 70 countries (see http://tinyurl.com/2ax2f7n for further details).

The difficulty with such a comparison is that each international community is very diverse in much the same way that communities differ throughout Britain, thus it is difficult to compare like with like. PISA 2009 revealed wide differences but could potentially offer opportunities for improvement such as the 'importation' of 'pre-school models in Scandinavia and Reggio Emilia' to 'enrich children's development in Western societies' (Jones, Holmes and Powell, 2005: 186).

The BBC (2012) stated that the population in England and Wales had increased by 7 per cent between the 2001 and 2011 census. Fifty-five per cent of this increase is linked to immigration. The population was 56.1 million in 2011 and one in six of this number was aged 65 or over. The demography of Britain has and is continually changing. If Steiner is correct and the sense of belonging is important then somehow we need to continue to develop a sense of unity, collective identity and shared culture. Yet in 2008 over 240 languages were spoken in Britain (Alexander, 2010). One in seven primary pupils had English as a second language (EAL) compared with one in ten in 2004 and 23.3 per cent of pupils aged over five were from minority ethnic groups. As Carnie (2003: 14) states: '[t]he emphasis needs to be on the community - on creating schools where all people have a sense of belonging and can actively contribute so that education is a dynamic, meaningful and relevant process'. However, it must also be remembered that children are not just there to be filled with information; we are not just 'lighting a fire or filling a bucket' (Carnie, 2003: 1). Each child is an individual with varying needs and abilities and it is up to the professional/those training to enable these children to develop and, with the Steiner approach in mind, allow these children to grow into who they are to be.

The age at which children commence school is seemingly irrelevant; it is the quality of the experiences that children receive that is most important, whether this is in the home or in a setting. If we follow the Finnish perspective social and emotional opportunities are critical, but if we consider the New Zealand *Te Whariki* we are aiming for an 'ideal child' and perceptions of this can vary within communities. Lessons can be learnt from other countries but the system that evolves needs to reflect the people in the country and the communities that it represents. There needs to be space within the curriculum for future developments and opportunities to trial and evaluate new ideas. Young children need to be nurtured and their self-image promoted, but as an African proverb says 'it takes a whole village to educate a child'. Education thus does not just happen in a nursery or a school; it happens within the community.

Layard and Dunn (2009: 162) claim that '[i]n Denmark, Sweden and the Netherlands around two thirds of people believe that most people can be trusted'. These are also countries where child well-being is highest. Politicians, parents and communities need to trust the professionals and work together to enhance child well-being. As Layard and Dunn (2009: 9) state: 'children flourish when they have a sense of meaning in their lives, which comes both from social engagement and from enthusiastic development of their own interests and talents'. The learning community is therefore essential for all children to achieve.

Conclusion

This chapter has sought to consider how growing up in different communities can impact on children's overall development. You should reflect that there is no one clear answer in terms of what helps children to succeed. The starting age may be pertinent but the experiences within the community and family are likely to be more significant. The curriculum that children are exposed to may also impact on their development and life chances. The early years and primary curriculums in each country are different and are defined by the culture in which they have been developed. You should now be able to reflect on these differences and evaluate provision on a national and international level, thus enabling you to argue the benefits of growing up in certain communities!

Areas for further consideration

There are a number of other areas that you may wish to explore for your own personal study. These suggestions will further your reflection on the impact of growing up in certain communities.

Men who work in settings	Outdoor provision
The role of 'rest' in different settings	Provision, pay and status
Creativity and the curriculums	Catering for the needs of boys in settings

Further reading

Books

Brown, M. A. and White, J. (eds) (2014) *Exploring Childhood in a Comparative Context: An introductory guide for students.* London: Routledge.
This book considers childhood in a number of different countries, offering the reader an opportunity to hear the voice of the children and people within these countries.

Penn, H. (2011) *Quality in Early Childhood Services: An international perspective.* Maidenhead: Open University Press.
This book considers quality across a range of countries and considers some of the complexities of what children should be learning and the needs of parents for childcare.

Academic publications

Duhn, I. (2006) The Making of Global Citizens: Traces of cosmopolitanism in the New Zealand early childhood curriculum, Te Whariki. *Contemporary Issues in Early Childhood,* 7 (3) 191-202.
This Early Childhood article explores Te Whariki *and the concepts behind this approach.*

Wickrama, K. A. S. and Noh, S. (2009) The Long Arm of Community: The influence of childhood community contexts across the early life course. *Journal of Youth Adolescence,* 39, 894-910.
This study considers the long-term impact of community on childhood and academic attainment.

Website

UNICEF (2013) Available at: www.unicef.org/media/files/RC11-ENG-embargo.pdf
This document undertakes a comparison of child development in different countries.

References

Alexander, R. (1984) *Primary Teaching.* Sussex: Holt, Rinehart & Winston.

——(2009) Towards a New Primary Curriculum: a report from the Cambridge Primary Review. Part 2: The Future. Cambridge: University of Cambridge Faculty of Education. [Online]. Available at: www.primaryreview. org.uk/Downloads/Curriculum_report/CPR_Curric_rep_Pt2_Future.pdf (Accessed: 2 September 2013).

——(2010) *Children, their World, their Education. Final report and recommendations of the Cambridge Primary Review.* Oxon: Routledge.

Bottrell, D. and Armstrong, D. (2007) Changes and Exchanges in Marginal Youth Transitions. *Journal of Youth Studies,* 10 (3), 353–371.

Bronfenbrenner, U. (1994) Ecological models of human development. In: *International Encyclopaedia of Education,* Vol. 3, 2nd edn. Oxford: Elsevier. Reprinted in: Gauvain, M. and Cole, M. (eds) *Readings on the development of children,* 2nd edn. (pp. 37–43). NY: Freeman.

Brown, M. A. (2009) *To consider ways of improving the UK's early year's education systems through a comparative study of the Finnish Education system (reading and language development) and the approaches to its delivery.* A paper presented at BESA Conference 2009, Staffordshire University, 3 July.

Brown, M. A. and White, J. (eds) (2014) *Exploring Childhood in a Comparative Context: An introductory guide for students.* London: Routledge.

Brown, M. A., Davis, C. and Hewitt, D. (2011) *How can Skype be used as a cost-effective tool for developing awareness in staff and students of international and inter-cultural dimensions in education?* Teaching Informed Research Project, University of Derby.

Bruce, T. (2010) *Early Childhood: A guide for students.* 2nd edn. London: Sage.

Burdett, N. (2013) *The misuse of international studies in UK education.* NFER. [Online]. Available at: http://tinyurl.com/d72th6l (Accessed: 25 February 2013).

Burkhard, M. (2006) Similarities and links between early childhood education and informal education in youth work for adolescents. *European Early Childhood Education Research Journal,* 14 (2), 21–33.

Carnie, F. (2003) *Alternative Approaches to Education: A guide for parents and teachers.* Oxon: RoutledgeFalmer.

DCSF (2008) *Children and Young People's Workforce Strategy 2020.* Nottingham: DCSF.

DfE (2011) *Inspiring Communities, Changing Behaviour* [Online]. Available at: www.gov.uk/government/ uploads/system/uploads/attachment_data/file/6003/19234911.pdf (Accessed: 20 February 2013).

——(2012) *Statutory Framework for the Early Years Foundation Stage* [Online]. Available at: www.education. gov.uk/publications/standard/AllPublications/Page1/DFE-00023-2012 (Accessed: 2 September 2013).

——(2013a) *Early Years Foundation Stage.* [Online]. Available at: www.education.gov.uk/childrenandyoung people/earlylearningandchildcare/delivery/education/a0068102/early-years-foundation-stage-eyfs (Accessed: 1 February 2013).

——(2013b) *Primary National Curriculum until 2014.* [Online]. Available at: www.education.gov.uk/ schools/teachingandlearning/curriculum/primary (Accessed: 1 February 2013).

DfES (2003) *Every Child Matters: Change for Children.* London: Crown.

——(2005) *Common Core of Skills and Knowledge for the Children's Workforce Every Child Matters: Change for Children.* Nottingham: DfES.

Dowling, M. (2007) *Young Children's Personal, Social and Emotional Development.* 2nd edn. London: Paul Chapman.

Duhn, I. (2006) The Making of Global Citizens: Traces of cosmopolitanism in the New Zealand early childhood curriculum, *Te Whariki. Contemporary Issues in Early Childhood,* 7 (3) 191-202.

Education in Japan. (n.d.) [Online]. Available at: www.education-in-japan.info/sub1.html (Accessed: 5 February 2013).

Erixon, F. (2010) *The Case against Europe's 2020 Agenda*. European Centre for International Political Economy Policy Briefs, 01/2010. [Online]. Available at: http://tinyurl.com/cusbxum (Accessed: 1 February 2013).

European Commission (2012) *Europe 2020 - Top Billing For Education and Youth*. [Online]. Available at: http://ec.europa.eu/commission2010-2014/vassiliou/headlines/news/2010/03/20100308_en.htm (Accessed: 9 October 2012).

ExpatFocus (2012) *Belgium – Education and Schools*. [Online]. Available at: www.expatfocus.com/expatriate-belgium-education-schools?gclid=CKO6zOvLirICFc93fAod7kUATQ (Accessed: 9 October 2012).

Flath, S. (2006) *Many Roads to Success: The Saxon School System*. Freistaat Sachsen State Ministry of Education and Cultural Affairs. [Online]. Available at: www.sachsen-macht-schule.de (Accessed: 28 July 2012).

Flippo, H. (2012) *The German Way and More: Language and Culture in Germany, Austria and Switzerland*. [Online]. Available at: www.german-way.com/educ.html (Accessed: 28 July 2012).

Gray, C. and MacBlain, S. (2012) *Learning Theories in Childhood*. London: Sage.

Hakanen, J. (2008) Positive Gain Spirals at Work: From job resources to work engagement, personal initiative and work-unit innovativeness. *Journal of Vocational Behaviour*, 73 (1), 78–91.

Jones, L., Holmes, R. and Powell, J. (2005) *Early Childhood Studies: A Multi-professional Perspective*. Maidenhead: Open University Press.

Knipprath, H. (2005) The Role of Parents and Community in the Education of the Japanese Child. *Educational Research for Policy and Practice*, 3, 95–107.

Layard, R. and Dunn, J. (2009) *A Good Childhood*. London: Penguin.

Lifelong Learning Programme (2010) *Welcome to the Lifelong Learning Programme*. [Online]. Available at: www.lifelonglearningprogramme.org.uk/ (Accessed: 28 July 2012).

Ministry of Education (2013a) *New Zealand Education System Overview*. [Online]. Available at: www.minedu.govt.nz/NZEducation/EducationPolicies/InternationalEducation/ForInternationalStudentsAndParents/NZEdOverview/Education_in_New_Zealand.aspx (Accessed: 5 February 2013).

——(2013b) *Welcome to Early Childhood Education*. [Online]. Available at: www.educate.ece.govt.nz/learning/curriculumAndLearning/TeWhariki.aspx (Accessed: 5 February 2013).

Nationmaster (2012) *Education in Belgium: International Educational Statistics*. [Online]. Available at: www.nationmaster.com/country/be-belgium/edu-education (Accessed: 28 August 2012).

OECD (2009) *Pisa 2009 Results: Executive Summary*. [Online]. Available at: www.oecd.org/pisa/pisaproducts/46619703.pdf (Accessed: 28 August 2012).

Oliver, B. and Pitt, P. (2011) *Working with Children, Young People and Families: A course for Foundation Degrees*. Exeter: Learning Matters.

Papatheodorou, T. and Moyles, J. (2012) *Cross-Cultural Perspectives on Early Childhood*. London: Sage.

Penn, H. (2005) *Understanding Early Childhood Issues and Controversies*. Maidenhead: Open University Press.

——(2011) *Quality in Early Childhood Services: An international perspective*. Maidenhead: Open University Press.

Rose, J. (2008) *Independent Review of the Primary Curriculum: Final Report*. Nottingham: DCSF Publications.

Rousseau, J. J. (1991) *Emile or On Education*. London: Penguin.

Sharp, J., Ward, S. and Hankin, L. (2009) *Education Studies: An issues-based approach*. Exeter: Learning Matters.

Stakes (2003) *The National Curriculum Guidelines on Early Childhood Education and Care In Finland*. Ministry of Social Affairs and Health.

Swedish Institute (2012) *Facts about Sweden: Education*. [Online]. Available at: www.sweden.se (Accessed: 10 October 2012).

Sylva K., Melhuish, E., Sammons, P., Siraj-Blatchford, I. and Taggart, B. (2004) *The Effective Provision of Pre-School Education (EPPE) Project: Findings from Pre-school to end of Key Stage 1.* [Online]. Available at: http://eppe.ioe.ac.uk/eppe/eppepdfs/RBTec1223sept0412.pdf (Accessed: 2 September 2013)

The American School System (2013) [Online]. Available at: www.rzuser.uni-heidelberg.de/~el6/presentations/pres_c2_uss/TheAmericanSchoolSystem.htm (Accessed: 5 February 2013).

Thomas, L. (2012) *Rethinking the importance of teaching: Curriculum and Collaboration in an era of Localism.* London: RSA Projects.

Thornton, M. (1998) *Subject Specialists – Primary Schools.* Occasional Paper No. 10, September. [Online]. Available at: www.ucet.ac.uk/op10.html (Accessed: 28 July 2012).

Viewing the Japanese School System through the Prism of PISA. (n.d.) [Online]. Available at: www.oecd.org/japan/46623994.pdf (Accessed: 6 May 2013).

Wickrama, K. A. S. and Noh, S. (2009) The Long Arm of Community: The influence of childhood community contexts across the Early Life Course. *Journal of Youth Adolescence*, 39 (8), 894–910.

Looking back, looking forward

Simon Brownhill

The notion of empowerment, as emphasised by the title of this book, has served as an underlying 'driving force' for the content of this book. While reference to it may have not been explicit, it is hoped that you will recognise how the numerous authors of this book have been careful to include information, research, ideas, practical strategies, viewpoints, thinking and activities which will empower you following your active engagement with them. As this chapter is designed to 'close' the book, it is hoped that you will keep this notion of empowerment in mind as we look back on the book's content and look forward, beyond the book, to the future.

In the Introduction (page 5) it was made clear that we recognised that the book could not possibly address all aspects of practice in the 0-19 workforce due to its wordage limitations, nor could it consider in depth every setting type or practitioner who has the good fortune of working in CYPS. Looking back, we feel we have discussed a range of current issues and important considerations which directly impact on active practitioners and those training in the 0-19 sector; many of these issues and considerations are pertinent to the whole workforce whereas others have a greater relevance to particular contexts and age groups. We are certain that there are points we have made which you are in full agreement with whereas there are others which you may have questioned or disagreed with. We welcome those readers who not only embrace the ideas and thinking explored in this book but also those who challenge advocated policy, provision and practice. It is important to recognise that there is no 'one answer' when it comes to working with children and young people; there will always be variations in practitioners'/trainees' thinking, perspectives and provision in the 0-19 sector. Looking forward, as long as the best interests of children, young people and families remain in the forefront of the minds of all practitioners and those training in CYPS then we will feel that this book has made some impact on quality provision.

Looking back, the complexity of some of the topics of discussion in this book means that at times we have only been able to 'scratch the surface' of the knowledge and understanding which currently exists - again, we make no apology for this; if you wish to know more about particular topics then you will be able to find entire texts solely dedicated to the likes of ethical research and work-based reflective practice to help enrich your knowledge and understanding. Looking back, we have strived to offer you cohesive chapters to 'fire your interest' and, looking forward, we actively encourage you to seek other sources of information, be they in the form of books (academic/professional), journals (academic/professional) and/or quality websites (academic/professional) to support your growing interest and understanding of, for example, international practices, the roles and responsibilities of practitioners in the workforce, and work-based learning. While each chapter has offered you a 'digestible diet' of information, activities, case studies, reflective tasks and links to wider readings, we actively encourage you to supplement your reading with the work of others to strengthen your understanding, compare viewpoints and gain a deeper appreciation of the ideas and the content presented in this book.

As provision and practice in the 0–19 sector continues to evolve and develop, so too does our knowledge and understanding of theory and pedagogy. This book thus serves as a timely 'snapshot' of how CYPS looks and operates. As new academic thinking helps to shape new policies and procedures, we hope that, looking forward, your appreciation of quality provision continues to drive standards in your settings. We recognise that the current climate in which CYPS finds itself is particularly volatile and it is very difficult to know how policy making will continue to impact on the services offered for children, young people and their families, be they positive or not so positive. We sincerely hope that financial cutbacks do not continue to reduce the quantity and quality of the services already available, but that you maintain strength in your capabilities and self-belief while continuing to invest your time and efforts in supporting the children and young people you work with who may, one day, be leading our country to a bright and better future.

We sincerely hope that this book has made you think about you as a person, you as a professional working/training in the sector, and, most importantly, the children/young people you have the good fortune of working with. Looking forward, we hope that you continue to evolve as a professional in the 0–19 workforce, striving to 'better yourself' by continuing your academic studies, attending conferences, courses and workshops, building and maintaining links with quality providers and professionals, mentoring others (as and where appropriate), and engaging with documentation which describes up-to-date thinking and cutting edge practice which you can embrace as your own in your settings/placements. We recognise that working/training in the 0–19 sector is complex, demanding and extremely hard work; however, there is no job that we know of that is constantly varied, always interesting and really does make a difference to the lives of children, young people and families. It is hoped that this book has helped, and *continues* to help, you positively influence those you come into contact with as part of your professional duties. Children and young people only have one life; let us empower each and every single one of them to live a wonderful and fulfilling one.

Glossary

The following terms/abbreviations are used throughout this book:

Andragogy   The process of helping adults to learn themselves

Anonymity   An ethical principle of ensuring that research participants or organisations are not identified by name in research findings

Asperger's Syndrome   A developmental disorder related to autism and characterised by higher than average intellectual ability coupled with impaired social skills and restrictive, repetitive patterns of interest and activities

At risk   A term used to describe individuals who are more likely to experience problems than others

Attention Deficit Hyperactivity Disorder   A condition in which a child exhibits signs of developmentally inappropriate hyperactivity, impulsivity, and inattention

Autism   A mental condition, present from early childhood, characterised by great difficulty in communicating and forming relationships with other people and in using language and abstract concepts

Beneficence   An ethical principle that imposes a duty to benefit others and maximise net benefits. Refers to the notion of 'doing good'

Bibliography   A list of all of the works which have been *consulted* and all of the works which have been *referred to* in a piece of writing

Case study   An examination of a real or simulated problem structured so that learning can take place

Child protection   An activity undertaken to protect specific children who are suffering, or are likely to suffer, significant harm

Coaching   A process that involves an individual enabling another individual to learn and develop, and their performance and potential to improve

Code   See *Pseudonym*

Common Assessment Framework   A standardised four-step process to enable practitioners to undertake an early and initial assessment of a child's or young person's needs for extra services and to act on these

Confidentiality   A set of rules or a promise that limits access or places restrictions on certain types of information held by an individual/a setting/service

Core agency   The term used to describe the services that are available to children and young people. There are three core agencies: health, education and social services

Critical thinking   The ability to think in an analytical and evaluative manner

Deep learning   Learning that connects with other skills or knowledge that have been previously learned

Development Plan   A document which allows settings to identify areas of development which serve as target areas for improvement within a particular timeframe

Differentiation   An adjustment to provision and practice in response to the needs of the individual

Disability   A condition that affects an individual's mental, sensory or mobility functions to undertake or perform a task

Discussion   A conversation or debate about a certain topic with others

Dyslexia   A term for disorders that involve difficulty in learning to read or interpret words, letters, and other symbols

Dyspraxia   A motor learning difficulty that can affect planning of movements and co-ordination as a result of brain messages not being accurately transmitted to the body

Emotional health   The degree to which an individual feels emotionally secure and relaxed in everyday life

Emotional intelligence   The ability to monitor one's own and others' feelings and emotions and to use this information to guide one's thinking and actions

English Baccalaureate   A performance measure which recognises where pupils have secured a C grade or better at GCSE level across a core of academic subjects – English, mathematics, history or geography, the sciences and a language. It is not a qualification in itself

Epilepsy   A chronic neurological condition characterised by recurrent unprovoked seizures

Extended family   The term used to define a family that extends beyond the *nuclear family* consisting of grandparents, aunts, uncles, and cousins who all live nearby or in the same household

Extrinsic motivation   Motivation that comes from outside an individual. Motivating factors are external through the use of rewards such as money or grades

Flexible learning   Learning which takes place through a flexible choice of programmes, models of delivery, content and timeframes

Form tutor   A teacher whose job involves looking after a particular class of students, supporting their pastoral needs and monitoring their progress both academically and socially

Front-line worker   A professional/practitioner who is the first point of contact with service users

Gifted   The term used to describe individuals whose actual/natural potential is distinctly above average in areas of human ability

Holistic   Meaning 'whole'. In the context of the *holistic development* of children and young people this refers to their physical, intellectual, linguistic, emotional and social development

Incentive   Something that motivates an individual to perform an action

Inclusion   The act of enabling all individuals to participate fully in the life and work of settings irrespective of their needs

Informal education   The term used to describe education outside of a standard school setting (not necessarily physically outside)

Informed consent   A process for getting permission before conducting a research involving practitioners, service users and settings

Integrated services   The term used to describe services that work effectively together in an integrated manner to support children and young people, putting CYP at the centre to meet their needs and improve their lives

Integration   The education of children and young people with SEND in mainstream settings

Inter-professional working   Term used to describe members of different professions and/or agencies working together to provide integrated provision for the benefit of service users. Also known as *integrated working*

Integrated working   See *Inter-professional working*

Intrinsic motivation   Motivation that is driven by an interest or enjoyment in the task itself, and exists within the individual rather than relying on external pressures or a desire for reward

Key worker   A named member of staff who has close personal interaction day to day with a child; one who has more contact with them than other adults in the setting

Kinaesthetic   A learning style in which learning takes place by the individual carrying out a physical activity. Also known as *tactile learning*

Lead professional   An individual who acts as a single point of contact that the child or young person and their family can trust when a child or young person is receiving multiple services

Learning pain barrier   A term used to describe feelings that are associated with the difficulties of studying/learning something new

Learning style   An individual's natural pattern of acquiring and processing information in learning situations

Legislation   The laws or the process by which laws are enacted

Literacy   Reading and writing

Mentoring   A system of semi-structured guidance where one person shares their knowledge, skills and experience to assist others to progress in their own lives and careers

Multi-agency panel   A group of people from different agencies that meet regularly for short periods of time to discuss children and young people with additional needs who may require multi-agency support

Multi-agency team   A group of professions and practitioners who come from different sectors in the 0–19 sector who work collaboratively as a team

Multi-agency working   The bringing together of practitioners from different sectors and professions to provide an integrated way of working to support children, young people and families

Multi-sensory learning   Learning which takes place when more than one of the senses is used to acquire and retain information

Non-maleficence   An ethical principle that holds that researchers must not make matters worse. Refers to the notion of 'not doing harm'

Nuclear family   A family group consisting of a pair of adults (mother and father) and their children

Oracy   Speaking and listening

Parent/carer   An adult who raises a child or young person

Parenting style   The way that parents/carers rear their child/ren

Partnership   An arrangement where individuals agree to cooperate together to advance their mutual interests

Pedagogy   The art or science of being a teacher

Physical health   Anything that has to do with our bodies as a physical entity

Policy   A principle or rule to guide decisions and achieve rational outcomes

Practitioner   A term used to describe anyone who works (paid/voluntary) in CYPS

Professional   See *Practitioner*

Pseudonym   A fictitious name, digit or alphabet letter which is used to describe/identify a research participant

Reference list   A list of works which have been cited (referred to) in a piece of writing

Reflection   Looking back and thinking about an event, a situation, an occasion or an incident

Reflective practice   An active process of learning through and learning from experience

Resilience   The capacity to withstand, adapt and overcome risk and adversity

Risk   The threat of damage, injury, liability, loss, or any other negative occurrence that is caused by external or internal vulnerabilities

Role model   An individual who is looked up to and revered by someone else

Role play   An activity where Individuals 'work in role' (act) as another individual, real or imagined

Safeguarding   The protection of children and young people from maltreatment

Scaffolding   A term used to describe the ongoing support provided to a learner (e.g. a child or young person) by an expert (e.g. a practitioner)

Self-regulation   The ability to independently plan, monitor and assess one's own learning

Setting   Any location where children, young people, families and communities can access services

Shower mapping   A method of generating a variety of ideas or solutions to problems in a short period of time. Also known as *thought shower*

Simulation   A replication of a real or possible situation

Skill   The ability to do something well

Skill mix   The altering of the skill component of jobs within a setting or a service and moving work between different groups of staff

Social pedagogy   An academic discipline concerned with the theory and practice of holistic education and care

Socratic Seminar   Collaborative, intellectual dialogue that is facilitated with a range of dialogic learning and teaching methods including open questions, discussions and role-play

Special educational need   A term which describes the needs or disabilities that affect an individual's ability to learn

Specialist services   Services that are required when universal services cannot meet the needs of the child, young person or the family. Examples include family support workers, speech and language therapists and behaviour support workers

Surface learning   The ability to recall significant pieces of information, e.g. key dates or theories

Support staff   Individuals who work for a service to keep it running and to support those who are involved in the main service being offered

Synaptic connection   Information that is passed between nerve cells in the brain

Talented   A term used to describe individuals whose developed *skills* are distinctly above average in areas of human performance

Targeted services   Services aimed at supporting groups of children and young people. Examples include SureStart children's centres, parenting support and services provided by social services

Targeted support   Additional support that is tailored to the circumstances of the individual

Team around the child   A model of multi-agency service provision which brings together a range of different practitioners from across the CYP workforce to support an individual child or young person and their family, developing and delivering a package of solution-focused support to meet identified needs

Trainee   Anyone who is studying/training to work in CYPS

Transition   A term used to describe a period of change in a child or young person's life, e.g. a location move, a physical change or a change in the family make up

Universal services   Services that children, young people and families access without special referral. Examples include GPs, dentists, opticians, nurseries, schools, colleges and hospitals

Work-based learning   Learning which takes place within a work-based context

Workforce   A term used to describe all individuals who work/train in CYPS

Writer's block   An inability to begin or continue writing for reasons other than a basic level of skill or commitment

Index

Figures are shown by a page reference in *italics*, tables are in **bold** and a glossary term is in ***bold and italics.***

Abbott, L. 83-4
Abott-Chapman, J. and Denholm, C. 104-5
abuse, signs of 132
academic lists 21
academic reading 19-21
academic writing 23-6
Adair, J. 113
Ainscow, M. *et al* (2006) 90
Alberta Child and Youth Initiative 134
Alexander, R. 220
Allen Report (2011) 179, 201
Alvesson, M. and Sköldberg, K. 162
andragogy 38-9, ***230***
anonymity 52-3, ***230***
Area Child Protection Committees (ACPCs) 198
Asperger's Syndrome 93, 96, ***230***
assignments: '12 Grid' method **24**; essay structure 25-6; feedback, importance of 26; mind mapping method 24; PEET rule 25; planning 23-4; rules for academic writing 24-5
Attention Deficit Hyperactivity Disorder (ADHD) 85, 96, ***230***
autism 85, 94, 96, ***230***
Avramidis, E. *et al* (2002) 89

Babbie, E. 53
Baby P 1, 131, 200

Bastiani, J. 185
Batsleer, J. and Davies, B. 111
Baurimnd, D. 181
Behaviour Education Support Teams (BEST) 197
Behaviour Improvement Team (BIT) 197
Behaviour Support Services (BSS) 197
Behaviour Support Team (BST) 197
Belgium **211**, **213**, 214, **218**
Bell, N.J. and Bell, R.W. 105, 108, 112
Belsky, J. 180-1
beneficence (research) 47-8, ***230***
Betts, G. and Niehart, M. 71, **72-4**
Beveridge, S. 185
bibliographies 21, ***230***
Bloom, Benjamin 39, 78, 163
Boud, D. *et al* (1985) 159
Boud, D. *et al* (1994) 157
Bowlby, J. 128-9
British Dyslexia Association 83
Brofenbrenner, U. 186, *187*, 216
Brooker, L. 184
Bruce, T. 185
Bruner, Jerome 129
bullying 202

Cambridge Primary Review 219-20
carers *see* parents/carers
Carnie, F. 223

case studies **230**

Centre for British Practitioners (CfBT) Education Trust 1, 68

Centre for Studies in Inclusive Education (2002) 90

Cheater, C. and Farren, A. 153

child protection **230** see also risk

Child Protection registers 198

children: research and informed consent 51; sense of risk 101, 102

Children Act (1989) 198-9

Children Act (2004) 30, **88**, 127, 131, 136, 201

Children's and Young People's Services (CYPS): and funding 2-3; importance of 1-2

Children's Plan 178

Children's Workforce Strategy (DfES, 2005) 30, 31, 220

Clark, A. and Marsh, P. 125

Clarke, J. and Nicholson, J. 106

Climbié, Victoria 1, 127, 131, 199, 201

coaching 77-8, **230**

Common Assessment Framework (CAF) 127, 202-3, **230**

Common Core of Skills and Knowledge (CWDC, 2010): adoption by local authorities 122; child/young person development 128-31; effective communication 124-6; incorporation in profession-specific standards 123-4; information, sharing 135-6; multi-agency working 126-8; observational recording techniques **130**; observational skills 129-30; overview 121-3; safeguarding and promoting welfare 131-3, **132**; supporting transitions 133-5; work-based learning 32-3; and work-based reflection 158

communication: with families/communities 125-6, 134, 201-2; inter-agency 127, 131

communities: and child education 215-16, 223; collaboration with the setting 186-9, *187*, **188**; and effective communication 125-6, 134, 201-2; structure of 182

communities of practice 39-40

confidentiality **230**

Connelly, Peter (Baby P.) 200

Connolly, P. 48

Content and Language Integrated Learning 154

continuing professional development (CPD) 32 see also work-based reflection

core agency **231**

core services 196

Council of Curriculum, Examinations and Assessment (CCEA) 94

critical thinking 21-3, *22*, **231**

Croll, P. 189

curriculum: differentiation of 78, 80, **231**; early years and primary 215-20; English Baccalaureate 154, **231**; European comparison of curriculum time allocation **222**; international parity 220; National Curriculum (England) 68, 143, 214, 217-18, **217**, 221-2

Daniel, B. and Wassell, S. 110

Data Protection Act (1998) 54, 135-6, 204

De Silva, J. and Satchwell, P. 144

Declaration of Helsinki (WMA) 51, 56

deep learning 13, 15, 20, **231**

development plans 160-1, **231**

Dewey, J. 159

differentiation (curriculum) 78, 80, **231**

disability **231** see also special educational need or disability (SEND)

discussion **231**

Dittrich, W. and Tutt, R. 94

Doel, M. and Sawdon, C. 111

Driscoll, P. *et al* (2010) 144

Dunlop, A.W. and Fabian, H. 134

Dux award scheme 68

dyslexia 85, 94, 95, 96, **231**

dyspraxia 85, 94, 96, **231**

Early Years Foundation Stage (EYFS) 123, 128-31, 216-17
Early Years Initial Teacher Training 30
Early Years Professional Status (EYPS) 30, 31-2
early years settings: comparative practice (international) **213**; curriculum 215-20; international comparisons **218**; modern foreign language learning 145-6; professional standards 31-2; school starting ages (international) 212-15
Education Reform Act 147
educational settings: access to SEND support systems 84-6; parent partnerships 178-9; research ethical guidelines 49; strategies to manage SEND 95-6
Effective Provision of Pre-school Education (EPPE) Project 30, 178, 179
emotional health 14, 201, **231**
emotional intelligence 101, **231**
employers: involvement in flexible work-based learning 37; research and informed consent 51
empowerment, notion of 228
England **213**, **218**, **222**
English Baccalaureate 154, **231**
environment, physical 125
epilepsy 94, **231**
Eraut, M. 161
ethics: beneficence and non-maleficence 47-8; confidentiality 53-4, 135-6, 204-5, **230**; Data Protection Act (1998) 54, 135-6, 204; ethical approval 49-50; guidelines 49-50; informed consent (research) 50-2; participant incentives (research) 54-6; and reflective diaries 167; respondent anonymity 52-3, **230**; work-based research 46-7
Every Child Matters (ECM): *and Common Core of Skills and Knowledge* 104, 121, 122; impact of 1, 127, 131, 221;

integrated working 201; legislation 30, 31
Excellence in Cities (EiC) (DfES, 2003) 67, 68
Excellence in Schools 68
extended family **231**
extrinsic motivation **231**
Eyre, D. 70

family: context 134; structure of 180-1, 182, 201-2 *see also* parents/carers
Family Intervention Programmes (FIPs) 30
Farrell, M. 91
Field Report (2010) 179
Finland: curriculum time allocations **222**; early years settings 212, **213**, 214, 215; modern foreign language learning 219; OECD PISA (2009) **211**; pre-school and school provision **218**; staff qualifications 221
Finlay, L. 169
Fitzgerald, D. and Kay, J. 136
Flath, Steffen 215
flexible work-based learning: assessment methods *41*; basic approaches 34-5; case studies 36-7; employer involvement 37; foundation degrees 33-4; higher apprenticeships 34; individual learning paths (ILPs) 35-6; student attributes 35; teaching methods 38-9; term **231**; time management 35
form tutors 128-9, **231**
foundation degrees 33-4
Foundations for Quality (DfE, 2013) 30, 31
front-line workers **231**
Furlong, A. and Cartmel, F. 101

Gagne, F. 66-7
Germany: curriculum 221, **222**; early years settings **213**, 214; educational policies 215, 219; OECD PISA (2009) **211**; pre-school and school provision **218**
Ghaye, T. and Lillyman, S. 161

gifted and talented children: definitions
66-7, **231**; differentiation (curriculum)
78, 80, **231**; and disabilities 94-5;
government initiatives **69**; home/
school environment 75, 79; identifying
70-1; learning needs 75-6, 78-9, 80;
legislation 68, **69**; mentoring/
coaching 77; six types **72-4**; social
and emotional needs 76-7
Gilligan, R. 106
Good Childhood Inquiry 182
Graduate Leader Fund (GLF) 30
Greig, A. *et al* (2007) 50
Griffiths and Tann 160

Haight, A. 47
Hall, K. and Ozerk, K. 219
Hannell, G. 93
Harkin, J. *et al* (2001) 188
health, physical and mental 14-15
health and social care, research ethical
guidelines 49
Helping Children Achieve More 30, 122, 201
Hepburn, L. and White, R. 103
Hersey, P. and Blanchard, K.H. 77
High Learning Potential (HLP) 67, 71
higher apprenticeships 34
Higher Level Teaching Assistants (HLTA) 30,
32
Hobart, C. and Frankel, J. 132
holistic **231**

Impact of Parental Involvement on
Children's Education (2007) 179
Impact of Parental Involvement, Parental
Support and Family Education on
Pupil Achievements and Adjustments
(2003) 179
incentives for research participation 54-6,
231
inclusion **231**
inclusive practice: defining 89-91; ensuring
inclusive practice 91; from integration
to inclusion, SEND 86-9, **88**

Individual Learning Plans (ILPs) 35-6, 76
informal education 111, **232**
information, sharing 135-6, 204-5
informed consent **232**
integrated services **232**
integrated working: barriers to 205; and
being healthy 201-2; concept of 193-4,
196; core services 196; and *Every Child
Matters* (Helping Children Achieve
More) 201; historical context 198-200;
legislation 201; multi-agency panel
196; specialist services 195; and
staying safe 202; targeted services
195; universal services 195
integration **232**
inter-professional working **232**
intrinsic motivation **232**

Japan **211**, **213**, **218**, 220
Jasmine Beckford inquiry 198

Key Stage Two Framework for Languages
144, 145
key workers 128-9, **232**
kinaesthetic **232**

Lamb Inquiry (2009) 85
language learning *see* modern foreign
language learning
Layard, R. and Dunn, J. 182, 223
lead professionals 203-4, **232**
learning: academic reading 19-21; active and
passive learners 16-17, **16**, 39;
assignment writing 23-6; communities
of practice 39-40; critical thinking
21-3; learning needs, gifted and
talented children 75-6; motivation
14-15; pain barrier 12, **232**; stages of
12-13; stairway to critical thinking 22;
styles 15-16, **232**; surface and deep
learning 13-14; teaching approaches
38-9; time management 17-19, 35 *see
also* flexible work-based learning
learning pain barrier 12, **232**

Leeds Challenge 205

legislation: defined **232**; gifted and talented children 68, **69**; integrated working 201; modern foreign language teaching 143; partnerships, parents and community 178-80; for research 46-7; special educational need or disability (SEND) 86-9, **87, 88**; work-based learning 30-1 *see also individual subjects*

Lewis, J. 53

listening, active 125

literacy **232**

Lord Laming Report (2009) 1, 127, 131, 136, 199-201

Maccoby, E.E. and Martin, J.A. 181

Manchester City Council 93-4

Maria Colwell inquiry 198

Maslow, A. H. 129

McElwee, N. 108

MENSA 70

Menter, I. *et al* (2011) 49

mentoring 77-8, **232**

Mills, J. 189

minority ethnic groups 93-4

modern foreign language learning: aspects of 140-1; and cross-curricular links 153-4; curriculum 141-2; early years settings 145-6; frameworks 142-3; government initiatives 141; historical perspective 143; and improving literacy 152-3; and Intercultural or Cultural Understanding (IU) 150-1; Key Stage Two Framework for Languages 144, 145; legislation 143; National Centre for Languages 142-3; post 16 148-50; primary French 144-5; primary to secondary school transition 146-7; secondary school 147-8

Moon, J. 166

More Great Childcare (DfE, 2013) 30, 31

Morgan, C. Neil, P. 153

motivation 14-15, 54-5, **231**

multi-agency panel 196, **232**

multi-agency support hubs (MASH) 197

multi-agency support teams (MAST) 197

multi-agency team (MAT) 196-7, **232**

multi-agency working 126-8, 196-7, **232**

multi-element learning plan (MEP) 93

Multi-Element Plans (MEPs) 76

multi-sensory learning **232**

National Autistic Society (NAS) 83

National Centre for Languages 142-3

National Curriculum (England) 68, 143, 214, 217-18, **217**, 221-2

National Literacy Strategy (NLS) 153

National Occupational Standards (NOS) for Supporting Teachers and Learning 123-4

National Quality Standards in Gifted and Talented Education (2005) 70

National Standards for Head teachers (DfES, 2004) 123

New Zealand (*Te Whariki*) **211**, 216, **218**, 223

Next Steps 87-9

non-maleficence (research) 47-8, **232**

Norman, E. 106, 107

nuclear family **232**

OECD PISA (2009) 211, **211**, 214

OFSTED 145

Oliver, B. and Pitt, B. 126-7

online resources 5

oracy **233**

Organisation for Economic Cooperation and Development (OECD) 211, **211**, 214

Pachler, N. and Field, K. 152

parents/carers: access to SEND support systems 85; barriers to partnership 182-3; communicating with 85, 125, 130, 201-2; models of parenting 180-2; parenting style 129, **233**; promoting home-school collaboration 185-6; role of 179-80; term **233** *see also* partnerships, parents and community partnerships, with parents and the community: barriers to 182-3; communication 125-6, 134, 201-2; concept of 183-4; defined **233**; fostering 180; legislation 178-80; policies 178-80; promoting home-school collaboration 185-6; research 178-80; with the wider community 186-9, **188**

pedagogy 38-9, 125, **233**

PEET rule 25

Peiser G. and Jones, M. 150-1

Penn, H. 212, 214

Penn Green Centre 182

Peters, M. *et al* (2007) 182

physical health **233**

Piaget, Jean 129, 217

Plaza, C.M. *et al* (2007) 168

Plowden Report (1967) 178, 189, 216

policies: defined **233**; from integration to inclusion, SEND **88**; partnerships, parents and community 178-80; for research 46-7; work-based learning 30-1 *see also individual subjects*

Positive for Youth policy (DfE, 2011) 30, 31, 104

Potential Plus UK (previously NAGC) 67, 71, 80

practitioners: attitudes towards parents 182-4; care with use of definitions 100; front-line workers **231**; knowledge of integrated-working 198; lead professionals 203-4; promoting home-school collaboration 185-6; and responses to risk 107-8, 110-11; term 2, **233** *see also* partnerships, with parents and the community

Primary Literary Strategy 144

primary schools: curriculum 215-20; international comparisons **218**

Professional and National Occupational Standards for Youth Work (NYA) 123

professional standards: Higher Level Teaching Assistants (HLTA) 32;

National Occupational Standards (NOS) 32 *see also Common Core of Skills and Knowledge* (CWDC, 2010)

professionals, term 2

pseudonyms, research 53-4, **233**

Pupil Premium 68

Qualifications and Curriculum Authority (QCA) 70

Qualified Teacher Status standards 123

Raffaele, L.M. and Knoff, H.M. 185

readership, target 3-5, **3-4**

reference lists **233**

reflection *see* work-based reflection

reflective practices 38, 39, 158-60, **233**

Reiser, R. 86-7

research: legislation for 46-7; partnerships, parents and community 178-80; policies for 46-7; researcher protection 57; right to withdraw 56-7, **57**; work-based learning 30-1 *see also* ethics

resilience 101, 106-7, 110-11, **233**

risk: and control 103; defined **233**; and fear 106; management and development of risk framework 108, **109**, 110; managing self-exposure to 112-14, **113**; outcomes of 100-1; perceptions of 104-5; and positive attachments 110-11; professional responses to 110-11; professional responsibilities 101; and resilience 101, 106-7, 110-11, **233**; 'at risk,' term **230**; 'at risk' categories 104; risk factors and responses 107-8; risk-taking behaviour 104-5, 108; term 'at risk' 103-4; understanding 102

role models 125, **233**

role play 39, 165, **233**

Ruch, G. 161

safeguarding 131-3, **132**, **233**

Salamanca Statement and Framework of Acton 87, 89

scaffolding **233**

Schön, D. 160-1

school, starting ages (international) 212-15

SCoTENS 95

self-regulation **233**

2001 SEN Code of Practice 91-2

setting: collaboration with the community 186-9, *187*, **188**; safeguarding training 131; term 2, **233**

Shakespeare, P. 158

Sharp, J. 47

shower mapping 18, **233**

simulation **233**

skills mix 124, **233**

SMARTCE targets 18

Social and Emotional Aspects of Learning (SEAL) 201

social pedagogy 125, **233**

Social Research Association (SRA) 46

Socratic seminars 39, **233**

Spalding, N.J. 158

special educational need or disability (SEND): access to support systems 85; categories of SEND **92**; *Data Collection by Type of Special Educational Needs* 92; defining inclusive practice 89-91; gifted and talented children 68, 94-5; government initiatives 84-6; ICT applications 95; knowledge and understanding of 91-4; legislation 86-9, **87, 88**; medical model of disability and segregation 86-7, **87**; minority ethnic groups 93-4; multi-element learning plan (MEP) 93; multi-sensory learning 95; policy changes, integration to inclusion **88**; and professional support 83-4; 2001 SEN Code of Practice 91-2; social model of disability and inclusion 86-7, **87**; strategies to manage in educational settings 95-6; term **233**; terminology 85-6

specialist services 195, **233**

sports, research guidelines 49

Stakes (2003) 214

Steiner approach 214, 223

stress 14-15

study skills: academic reading 19-21; assessment methods, work-based learning *41*; assignment writing 23-6; critical thinking 21-3; defined 11; feedback, importance of 26; learning process 12-14; learning styles 15-16; motivation 14-15; skills audit 12; stairway to critical thinking *22*; study space 18-19; time management 17-19, 35

Support and Aspiration: A new approach to special education needs (Next Steps) 84, 87-9

support staff 30, 95, **233**

surface and deep learning **233**

Swarbrick, A. 143

Sweden 220

synaptic connection 13, **234**

talented: term 66-7, **234** *see also* gifted and talented children

targeted services 195, **234**

targeted support 2, **234**

Te Whariki (New Zealand) 216, 223

Teachers' Standards (Early Years) 32

team around the child (TAC) 197-8, **234**

technology 95, 222

terminology: grammatical 152; integrated working 194-5

Thomas RSA project (2012) 220

Thomsen, K. 107

Tickle, L. 158

Time for Standards: Reforming the school workforce (DfES, 2002) 30

time management 17-19, 35

Tooth, J. *et al* (2007) 47

trainee **234**

transitions 133-5, 146-7, **234**

Ungar, M. 106

United Kingdom 46, **211**

United Nations Convention on the Rights of the Child (UNCRC) 136
United States of America 46, **211**, **213**, **218**, 220
universal services 195, *234*

Valli, L. 161
Vos, H. and Cowen, J. 163
Vygotsky, Lev 129

Warnock Report: Special Educational Needs (1978) 86, 89, 178
Wenger, E. 39–40
Whalley, M. 185
Whitton, J.P. *et al* (2004) 168
work-based learning 30–1, *234*
work-based reflection: barriers to reflection 169; and continuing/initial professional development 157–8; Gibb's reflective cycle **163**; Greenaway's reflective cycle **162**; reflection, defined 158; reflection-in-action 160–1; reflection-on-action 160; reflective cycles 162–6, **164**; reflective diaries 166–7, **167**; reflective portfolios 168–9; reflective practices, defined 158–60; reflective tools 166; TASC wheel, case study 164–6
work-based research: beneficence 47–8, **230**; ethical guidelines 49–50; ethical issues 45–6; legislation 46–7; non-maleficence 47–8; reflection-for-action 161; types of reflection 160–2
workforce 122–3, *234*
writer's block 24, *234*

Youth Inclusion and Support Panel (YISP) 196
Youth Matters (DfES, 2005) 104
Youth Matters: Next Steps (DfES, 2006) 104
youth workers 150